# SIMPLY
# DELICIOUS

*Weight Watchers*

# SIMPLY DELICIOUS

*Winning Points*
*Cookbook*

## 245 No-Fuss Recipes—all 8 POINTS® or less

WEIGHT WATCHERS PUBLISHING GROUP

## A Word About Weight Watchers

Since 1963, Weight Watchers has grown from a handful of people to millions of members annually. Today, Weight Watchers is recognized as one of the leading names in safe and sensible weight control. Weight Watchers members form a diverse group, from youths to senior citizens, attending meetings around the globe.

Although weight-loss and weight-management results vary by individual, we recommend that you attend Weight Watchers meetings, follow the Weight Watchers food plan, and participate in regular physical activity. For the Weight Watchers meeting nearest you, call 1-800-651-6000. Visit our Web site at WeightWatchers.com.

WEIGHT WATCHERS PUBLISHING GROUP
Creative and Editorial Director: Nancy Gagliardi
Production Manager: Justin Torrento
Publishing Assistant: Jenny Laboy-Brace

Design Director: Nora Negron
Food Editor: Eileen Runyan
Recipe Developers: David Bonom, Maureen Luchejko, Susan McQuillan, Eileen Runyan
Photographer: Rita Maas
Food Stylist: William Smith
Prop Stylist: Bette Blau

Printed in the USA.
10  9  8  7  6  5  4  3

# CONTENTS

New Year's resolutions. For some people, they act as a road map to help navigate the year ahead. For others, they're nothing more than a nuisance and reminder of past—and present—missteps. Yet as the holiday hoopla winds down, before you start mulling the resolution issue, ask yourself this question: What can I do to make my life healthier in the coming year? Let's face it: Being healthy has a trickle-down effect on your life. If you're in good shape, you can do more and feel it less. Your state of mind also reaps a benefit or two—when everything is working smoothly, there's less for you to worry about, and that improves your overall quality of life.

We suggest that you start thinking seriously about taking on the number-one resolution of the majority of people in this country: losing weight. Our guess is that if you've picked up this cookbook, you're probably already on the weight-loss path; we're here to provide you with a little fuel so you can stay the course.

*Weight Watchers Simply Delicious* was created with you in mind. Based on *Weight Watchers Winning Points* program, we focused on recreating familiar recipes with deliciously different tastes and flavors. We even kept that popular resolution in mind: No recipe is more than *8 POINTS* per serving. We've also streamlined the ingredients and directions so you can whip up any one of the lunches, brunches, snacks, entrées, or sides whether you have a half an hour or half a day to get a meal on the table. We also think these recipes will become staples for your family because they taste simply delicious.

Good luck in staying the course and reaching all your healthy goals!

NANCY GAGLIARDI
Creative & Editorial Director

[20] In a rush? Recipes with this symbol take no more than 20 minutes from start to finish.

# appetizers

beef tenderloin & arugula toasts  korean steak on a stick
asian pork & scallion rolls
easy shu mai dumplings  stuffed portobello mushrooms
skinny pigs in blankets
mini crab cakes with dill mayonnaise
stuffed mussels
deviled eggs provençal  polenta & eggplant stacks
tomato & olive tart  beggar's purse mediterranean
onion & olive pizza squares  roasted vegetable crostini
creamy guacamole in endive

# beef tenderloin and arugula toasts [20]

**3 POINTS** PER SERVING | MAKES 12 SERVINGS

*Elegant and surprisingly easy, tenderloin of beef is wonderful for entertaining. Here, it makes a delicious first impression when paired with peppery, aromatic arugula, capers, and freshly shaved Parmesan cheese.*

2 (8-ounce) beef tenderloins, trimmed of all visible fat

1 teaspoon olive oil

½ teaspoon salt

¼ teaspoon freshly ground pepper

1 (20-inch) French baguette

1 cup arugula, cleaned

1 tablespoon capers, drained and coarsely chopped

2-ounce piece Parmesan cheese, shaved (½ cup)

2 tablespoons fresh lemon juice

1. **Preheat the oven** to 425°F.

2. **Heat a large nonstick skillet** over medium-high heat. Rub the tenderloins with the oil, salt, and pepper. Place in the skillet and cook until browned, about 5 minutes on each side. Transfer to a cutting board. Let stand 5 minutes, then thinly slice across the grain.

3. **Meanwhile, cut the baguette** diagonally into 24 slices. Arrange in a single layer on a large baking sheet. Bake until just beginning to brown, about 8 minutes. Let the toasts cool slightly.

4. **Place the arugula** on the toasts, then top with the beef slices, capers, and cheese. Sprinkle with the lemon juice.

**PER SERVING (2 TOASTS): 122 CALORIES**
5g total fat, 2g saturated fat, 25mg cholesterol, 304mg sodium, 7g total carbohydrate, 0g dietary fiber, 11g protein, 81mg calcium

COOK'S HINT COOK'S HINT **rinsing arugula** COOK'S HINT COOK'S HINT COOK'S HINT

Arugula must be rinsed thoroughly to remove any sand. To do this, place the arugula in a large bowl of cold water, drain and repeat until no sand remains. Dry the arugula between several layers of paper towels. Don't be tempted to use a salad spinner—it will bruise the delicate leaves. To get Parmesan cheese shavings, run a vegetable peeler firmly across a small wedge of cheese.

# korean steak on a stick

**4 POINTS** PER SERVING | MAKES 8 SERVINGS

*This flavorful Asian marinade goes well with just about anything—including chicken, pork, or grilled vegetables. When using bamboo skewers, make sure to soak them in cold water for at least 30 minutes before using to prevent them from burning.*

1. **Thread the steak** onto sixteen 12-inch bamboo skewers. Place the skewers in a large baking dish.

2. **Combine** the scallions, vinegar, soy sauce, honey, sugar, ginger, fish sauce, chili paste, and garlic in a small bowl; pour over the meat. Cover and refrigerate at least 2 hours.

3. **Spray the broiler rack** with nonstick spray; preheat the broiler. Drain the marinade into a saucepan; bring to a boil. Cook, stirring occasionally, over high heat, until the sauce is thickened and the consistency of syrup, about 15 minutes.

4. **Meanwhile, place the skewers** on the broiler rack and broil 4 inches from the heat, turning frequently, until the meat is browned on both sides, about 8 minutes. Arrange the skewers on a platter and drizzle with the sauce.

**PER SERVING (2 SKEWERS): 170 CALORIES**
5g total fat, 2g saturated fat, 40mg cholesterol, 400mg sodium, 15g total carbohydrate, 1g dietary fiber, 16g protein, 18mg calcium

1 (1¼-pound) flank steak, cut diagonally into thin strips

6 scallions, finely chopped

½ cup cider vinegar

¼ cup reduced-sodium soy sauce

¼ cup honey

2 tablespoons sugar

1 tablespoon grated peeled fresh ginger

2 teaspoons fish sauce (nam pla)

1 teaspoon chili paste

2 garlic cloves, minced

# asian pork and scallion rolls [20]

*1 POINT* PER SERVING | MAKES 10 SERVINGS

*Roasted, grilled whole, or cut into medallions as we've done in this recipe, versatile pork tenderloin is flavorful, satisfying, and tender. It is the leanest pork cut of all, comparable in fat content to skinless boneless chicken breasts.*

¾ pound pork tenderloin, cut diagonally into thin slices, (about 20 slices)

1 tablespoon reduced-sodium soy sauce

1 tablespoon rice vinegar

1 tablespoon oyster sauce

1 tablespoon honey

2 teaspoons Asian (dark) sesame oil

1 teaspoon grated peeled fresh ginger

1 garlic clove, minced

20 scallions, trimmed, cleaned, and cut into 3-inch lengths

1. **Place the pork slices** between two sheets of wax paper. With a meat mallet or rolling pin, gently tap each slice to flatten slightly. Combine the soy sauce, vinegar, oyster sauce, honey, sesame oil, ginger, and garlic in a bowl. Add the pork; toss to coat. Let stand 10 minutes.

2. **Preheat the broiler.** Line the broiler rack with foil.

3. **Wrap a slice of pork** around each scallion length. Arrange the rolls, seam-side down, on the broiler rack. Broil 4 inches from the heat until the meat is browned and the scallions are just tender, 4–6 minutes. Serve hot.

PER SERVING (2 ROLLS): 73 CALORIES
2g total fat, 1g saturated fat, 22mg cholesterol, 148mg sodium, 5g total carbohydrate, 1g dietary fiber, 8g protein, 25mg calcium

# easy shu mai dumplings

**2 POINTS** PER SERVING | MAKES 10 SERVINGS

*Since wonton wrappers are so readily available, these dumplings are easy
and fun to make with impressive results. They are available in the refrigerator
case of most supermarkets and Asian stores.*

1. **To prepare the dipping sauce**, combine the ¼ cup soy sauce, the vinegar,
1 of the scallions, 2 teaspoons of the sesame oil, 1 teaspoon of the ginger,
and the crushed red pepper in a bowl.

2. **To prepare the filling**, purée the ground turkey, water chestnuts, the remaining
3 scallions, remaining 1 teaspoon ginger, the garlic, egg white, remaining
1 teaspoon soy sauce, remaining 1 teaspoon sesame oil, and the salt in a food
processor. Transfer to a bowl.

3. **Place the wonton wrappers** on a dry work surface. Drop 1 teaspoon
of the filling into the center of each wonton wrapper. Brush the edges with
water, and then fold into half-circles. Press the filling to release any
trapped air; press the edges to seal. Repeat with the remaining filling
and wontons.

4. **Arrange the dumplings**, in batches, in a steamer basket; set in a saucepan
over 1 inch of boiling water. Cover tightly and steam the dumplings
until cooked through, about 7 minutes. Serve hot with the dipping sauce.

**PER SERVING (3 DUMPLINGS WITH 1 TABLESPOON SAUCE): 118 CALORIES**
3g total fat, 1g saturated fat, 26mg cholesterol, 411mg sodium, 15g total carbohydrate,
1g dietary fiber, 8g protein, 15mg calcium

¼ cup + 1 teaspoon
reduced-sodium
soy sauce

¼ cup seasoned
rice vinegar

4 scallions, chopped

3 teaspoons Asian
(dark) sesame oil

2 teaspoons grated
peeled fresh ginger

¼ teaspoon crushed
red pepper

½ pound ground skinless
turkey breast

¼ cup water chestnuts,
chopped

1 garlic clove, chopped

1 egg white

½ teaspoon salt

30 (3-inch round)
wonton wrappers

# stuffed portobello mushrooms

*2 POINTS* PER SERVING | MAKES 8 SERVINGS

*Portobello mushrooms vary in size, but for this recipe, you'll need them about 4 inches in diameter.*

1 teaspoon canola oil

½ pound sweet turkey sausage, casings removed

4 ounces nonfat cream cheese

1 small tomato, seeded and chopped

½ cup shredded reduced-fat cheddar cheese

2 tablespoons chopped parsley

4 drops hot pepper sauce

4 large portobello mushrooms (about 1 pound), stems removed and wiped clean

1. **Preheat the oven** to 425°F. Spray a baking sheet with nonstick spray.

2. **Heat the oil** in a nonstick skillet. Crumble the sausage into the skillet and cook, breaking apart with a wooden spoon, until the sausage is browned and no pink remains, about 10 minutes. Transfer to a medium bowl. Stir in the cream cheese, tomato, cheddar cheese, parsley, and hot pepper sauce until blended.

3. **Place the mushrooms** on the baking sheet. Fill the cavity of each mushroom with the sausage mixture, mounding it slightly. Bake until the mushrooms are tender and the filling is hot, about 25 minutes. Cut each mushroom into four wedges. Serve hot.

PER SERVING (2 WEDGES): 86 CALORIES
4g total fat, 1g saturated fat, 16mg cholesterol, 276mg sodium, 4g total carbohydrate, 1g dietary fiber, 9g protein, 75mg calcium

# skinny pigs in blankets [20]

**3 POINTS** PER SERVING | MAKES 16 SERVINGS

*We've updated this retro appetizer, giving it a healthy, 21st-century edge.*
*Serve these little dogs with spicy, no-POINTS mustard.*

1. **Preheat the oven** to 450°F. Spray a baking sheet with nonstick spray.

2. **Combine** the baking mix and milk in a bowl until a soft dough forms. Turn onto a surface lightly sprinkled with baking mix. Knead 10 times.

3. **Roll the dough** into an 8 x 12-inch rectangle. Cut the dough into 8 squares. Cut each square in half to form 2 triangles. Starting from the narrow end, wrap each triangle around a hot dog half. Place on the baking sheet.

4. **Bake until golden** and browned, about 10 minutes. Serve hot.

**PER SERVING (1 APPETIZER): 126 CALORIES**
5g total fat, 2g saturated fat, 24mg cholesterol, 463mg sodium, 13g total carbohydrate, 0g dietary fiber, 5g protein, 54mg calcium

2½ cups reduced-fat all-purpose baking mix

¾ cup low-fat (1%) milk

8 reduced-fat chicken or turkey hot dogs, cut in half

COOK'S HINT COOK'S HINT **storing leftovers** COOK'S HINT COOK'S HINT COOK'S HINT COOK'S HINT

Wrap and freeze any leftovers. To reheat, unwrap and heat on a tray in a preheated 450°F oven until hot, about 12 minutes.

# mini crab cakes
# with dill mayonnaise

*2 POINTS* PER SERVING | MAKES 14 SERVINGS

*These crab cakes, lightly dipped in cornflake crumbs, have a deliciously crunchy coating. If jumbo lump crabmeat isn't in your budget, you can use imitation crab or surimi, which is made from Alaska pollock, a fish with lean firm flesh that has a delicate, slightly sweet flavor.*

1 pound cooked
jumbo lump crabmeat,
picked over

¼ cup plain dry
bread crumbs

½ cup reduced-calorie
mayonnaise

¼ cup grated onion

4 teaspoons
Dijon mustard

1 egg white

4 drops hot pepper sauce

½ cup cornflake crumbs

¼ cup sweet pickle relish

2 tablespoons
chopped dill

1 tablespoon
canola oil

1. **Combine** the crabmeat, bread crumbs, ¼ cup of the mayonnaise, the onion, 3 teaspoons of the mustard, the egg white, and hot pepper sauce in a bowl. Form into 14 patties.

2. **Place the cornflake crumbs** on wax paper. Dredge the patties in crumbs, then transfer to a plate. Refrigerate, covered, about 30 minutes.

3. **Meanwhile,** combine the remaining ¼ cup mayonnaise, the relish, dill, and the remaining 1 teaspoon mustard in a small bowl.

4. **Heat the oil** in a large nonstick skillet or griddle until a drop of water sizzles. Add the patties a few at a time; cook until crisp and golden, about 3 minutes. Turn over and cook 2–3 minutes longer. Serve with the mayonnaise mixture.

PER SERVING (1 CRAB CAKE AND 2 TEASPOONS MAYONNAISE): 94 CALORIES
5g total fat, 1g saturated fat, 35mg cholesterol, 252mg sodium, 6g total carbohydrate,
0g dietary fiber, 7g protein, 41mg calcium

# stuffed mussels

*2 POINTS* PER SERVING | MAKES 8 SERVINGS

*When purchasing mussels, look for unbroken, tightly closed shells or shells that close when lightly tapped. Rinse them well under running cold water to remove any sand. Discard any shells that remain open.*

1. **Combine** the bread crumbs, shallot, oil, cheese, oregano, and garlic in a small bowl.

2. **Preheat** the oven to 425°F.

3. **Place the mussels** in a large pot with a small amount of boiling water. Simmer, covered, until all the shells open, about 5 minutes; drain. When cool enough to handle, remove the upper shell and discard. Discard any mussels that do not open.

4. **Arrange the mussels** on a baking sheet. Spoon 1 teaspoon filling onto the mussels; spray lightly with nonstick spray. Bake until the top is golden and the filling is hot, about 10 minutes.

PER SERVING (3 MUSSELS): 87 CALORIES
3g total fat, 1g saturated fat, 17mg cholesterol, 210mg sodium, 7g total carbohydrate, 0g dietary fiber, 7g protein, 53mg calcium

½ cup plain dry bread crumbs

1 large shallot, minced

4 teaspoons extra-virgin olive oil

1 tablespoon grated Parmesan cheese

1 tablespoon chopped oregano

1 garlic clove, minced

24 mussels, scrubbed and debearded

COOK'S HINT COOK'S HINT **debearding mussels** COOK'S HINT COOK'S HINT COOK'S HINT

The hairy filaments that protrude from a mussel are known as a "beard." To remove, pinch the filaments between thumb and forefinger and pull firmly. Wait to debeard mussels until as close to cooking time as possible. Scrub mussels thoroughly under running water before cooking.

# deviled eggs provençal [20]

**2 POINTS** PER SERVING | MAKES 12 SERVINGS

*Since only half of the egg yolks are used in this recipe, use the remaining yolks in salads and sandwiches for the kids.*

12 hard-cooked eggs, shelled

6 tablespoons reduced-calorie mayonnaise

3 tablespoons finely minced red onion

4 kalamata olives, pitted and chopped

2 teaspoons chopped capers

2 teaspoons mustard powder

¼ teaspoon cayenne

**Halve the eggs lengthwise.** Remove the yolks. Press 6 of the yolks through a sieve into a small bowl. Reserve the remaining yolks for another use. Stir in the mayonnaise, onion, olives, capers, mustard, and cayenne until blended. Spoon or pipe (using a large plain tip) into the egg white halves. Place the eggs on a plate, cover loosely with plastic wrap, and chill until ready to serve.

**PER SERVING (2 DEVILED EGGS): 74 CALORIES**
5g total fat, 1g saturated fat, 109mg cholesterol, 141mg sodium, 1g total carbohydrate, 0g dietary fiber, 5g protein, 16mg calcium

COOK'S HINT COOK'S HINT **make ahead** COOK'S HINT COOK'S HINT COOK'S HINT COOK'S HINT

You can make the filling, leaving out the onion, a day ahead. When ready to use, chop and add the onion just before filling the egg white halves.

# polenta and eggplant stacks

*2 POINTS* PER SERVING | MAKES 12 SERVINGS

*Layers of eggplant, polenta, and creamy ricotta topped with fresh*
*marinara sauce make an elegant first course or buffet dish.*

1. Heat the oil in a large skillet, then add the garlic. Sauté until golden, about 1 minute. Add the tomatoes, salt, sugar, and red pepper; bring to a boil. Simmer, uncovered, until the sauce thickens slightly, about 15 minutes. Remove from the heat and stir in the basil.

2. Spray the broiler rack with nonstick spray; preheat the broiler. Place the eggplant on the broiler rack and broil 4 inches from the heat until lightly browned, about 3 minutes on each side. Let cool. Preheat the oven to 375°F.

3. Spoon about 1 cup sauce on the bottom of a nonstick 9 x 13-inch baking pan. Place 12 of the eggplant slices in the pan, then top each with a polenta slice, a tablespoon of ricotta cheese, and the remaining eggplant. Spoon the remaining sauce over all.

4. Bake, covered loosely with foil, until heated through and the sauce is bubbly, about 25 minutes. Top each stack with about 2 teaspoons mozzarella cheese. Bake, uncovered, until the cheese melts, about 10 minutes. Sprinkle with the cheese. Serve hot or at room temperature.

PER SERVING (1 APPETIZER): 107 CALORIES
5g total fat, 2g saturated fat, 8mg cholesterol, 356mg sodium, 12g total carbohydrate, 3g dietary fiber, 5g protein, 109mg calcium

2 tablespoons olive oil

2 garlic cloves, chopped

1 (28-ounce) can Italian peeled tomatoes, broken up

¼ teaspoon salt

½ teaspoon sugar

¼ teaspoon crushed red pepper

½ cup chopped basil

1 (1½-pound) eggplant, cut into 24 (¼-inch) slices

1 (16-ounce) tube refrigerated polenta, cut into 12 (½-inch) slices

¾ cup part-skim ricotta cheese

½ cup shredded part-skim mozzarella cheese

1 tablespoon grated Parmesan cheese

COOK'S HINT COOK'S HINT **polenta** COOK'S HINT COOK'S HINT COOK'S HINT COOK'S HINT

Pre-packaged polenta is available in a 16-ounce tube in the refrigerator section of your supermarket. Be sure to select a variety labeled fat-free.

# tomato and olive tart

*2 POINTS* PER SERVING | MAKES 12 SERVINGS

*One bite of this French tart and you'll feel like you're in Provence. All the flavors of the Mediterranean—tomatoes, shallots, olives, fennel, thyme, and garlic—top sheets of flaky phyllo dough. We use plum tomatoes instead of regular tomatoes, because they are firm, meaty, and hold up well in cooking.*

5 plum tomatoes, thinly sliced

15 small oil-cured black olives, pitted and chopped

1 large shallot, minced

1 tablespoon minced fresh thyme, or 1 teaspoon dried

1 tablespoon finely crushed fennel seeds

1 teaspoon olive oil

8 (12 x 17-inch) sheets phyllo dough, at room temperature

½ cup shredded Havarti cheese

¼ cup chopped basil

1. **Place the tomato slices** on 2 or 3 layers of paper towels; cover with more paper towels and blot gently. Let stand 10 minutes. Combine the olives, shallot, thyme, fennel, and oil in a small bowl.

2. **Preheat the oven** to 400°F. Spray a baking sheet with nonstick spray. Cover the sheets of phyllo with plastic wrap to keep them from drying out. Lay one sheet of phyllo across the baking sheet; lightly spray with nonstick spray. Repeat layering the remaining phyllo and spraying each sheet lightly with nonstick spray. Roll the edges of the phyllo in to make a rimmed edge.

3. **Arrange the tomatoes** across the phyllo. Sprinkle the olive mixture on top of the tomatoes; spread the mixture evenly with a fork. Bake until the edges of the phyllo are golden brown and the tomatoes are softened, about 20 minutes. Sprinkle the tart with the cheese. Bake until the cheese melts, about 5 minutes. Sprinkle with the basil. Cut the tart into 12 pieces, then cut each piece diagonally in half. Serve hot.

PER SERVING (1 APPETIZER): 77 CALORIES
3g total fat, 1g saturated fat, 5mg cholesterol, 115mg sodium, 11g total carbohydrate, 1g dietary fiber, 3g protein, 38mg calcium

COOK'S HINT COOK'S HINT **fennel seeds** COOK'S HINT COOK'S HINT COOK'S HINT COOK'S HINT

To crush the fennel seeds, mound them in a small pile on a chopping board and drizzle with a dash of olive oil. Using a large chef's knife, crush the seeds with a rocking, back and forth motion. If using a spice grinder, pulse several times until the seeds are finely crushed.

# beggar's purse mediterranean

**2 POINTS** PER SERVING | MAKES 8 SERVINGS

*Pretty enough for any buffet table, these tender pockets are filled with spinach, olives, herbs, and cheese, then tied with a scallion top to resemble a tiny purse.*

1. **Preheat the oven** to 375°F. Lightly spray a baking sheet with nonstick spray.

2. **Cut the green tops off the scallions.** Cook the tops in boiling water 2 minutes. Drain and plunge into ice water. Drain; set aside. Finely chop the remaining white part of the scallions. Combine the chopped scallions, spinach, goat cheese, olives, and dill in a bowl.

3. **Cover the sheets of phyllo** with plastic wrap to keep them from drying out. Place 1 phyllo sheet on a clean, dry work surface; lightly spray with nonstick spray. Top with a second phyllo sheet; cut into 4 rectangles. Spoon ⅛ of the filling in the center of each square. Gather the 4 corners of phyllo, and crimp to seal, forming a purse. Tie one scallion strip around the top of each purse. Repeat with the remaining phyllo, filling, and scallions strips.

4. **Place the purses** on the baking sheet. Bake until golden brown and heated through, about 12 minutes.

**PER SERVING (1 PURSE): 86 CALORIES**
4g total fat, 2g saturated fat, 13mg cholesterol, 124mg sodium, 9g total carbohydrate, 1g dietary fiber, 4g protein, 113mg calcium

4 scallions

1 (10-ounce) package frozen chopped spinach, thawed and squeezed dry

4 ounces reduced-fat goat cheese

4 kalamata olives, pitted and chopped

2 tablespoons chopped dill

4 (12 x 17-inch) sheets phyllo dough, at room temperature

COOK'S HINT **draining spinach** COOK'S HINT COOK'S HINT COOK'S HINT COOK'S HINT

Make sure to thoroughly squeeze the spinach so it is completely dry. The most effective way to do this is by draining it through a sieve and using both hands to squeeze out all the excess liquid.

# onion and olive pizza squares

***3 POINTS*** PER SERVING | MAKES 12 SERVINGS

*To make the pizza dough easier to work with, allow it to stand covered at room temperature for 15 minutes (it will be easier to stretch the dough into the pan). If you can't find refrigerated pizza dough, frozen bread dough, thawed, will work just as well.*

1 teaspoon olive oil

3 red onions, thinly sliced

1 teaspoon sugar

¼ teaspoon salt

10 small oil-cured black olives, pitted and chopped

1 tablespoon chopped fresh oregano, or 1 teaspoon dried

1 (16-ounce) package refrigerated pizza dough, at room temperature

4 ounces goat cheese, crumbled

¼ cup chopped basil

1. **Heat the oil** in a large nonstick skillet over low heat, then add the onions, sugar, and salt. Cook covered, stirring occasionally, until the onions are well softened, about 20 minutes. Remove from the heat, stir in the olives and oregano; let cool slightly.

2. **Preheat the oven** to 450°F. Spray a 10½ x 15½-inch jelly-roll pan with nonstick spray.

3. **With floured hands,** stretch and press the pizza dough onto the bottom of the pan. Spread the onion mixture onto the dough. Sprinkle with the goat cheese.

4. **Bake** on the bottom rack of the oven until the crust is browned and the cheese is slightly melted, about 20 minutes. Sprinkle with the basil. Cut the pizza into 12 squares.

**PER SERVING (1 SQUARE): 149 CALORIES**
4g total fat, 2g saturated fat, 9mg cholesterol, 288mg sodium, 23g total carbohydrate, 1g dietary fiber, 5g protein, 59mg calcium

COOK'S HINT COOK'S HINT **onions** COOK'S HINT COOK'S HINT COOK'S HINT COOK'S HINT

When cooking onions in a small amount of oil, add a little water, a few tablespoons at a time, to the skillet if they seem too dry. This will not only keep the onions moist without adding fat, but will hasten their cooking time.

# roasted vegetable crostini

*2 POINTS* PER SERVING | MAKES 12 SERVINGS

*Crostini, originally from Tuscany, are small, thin slices of toasted bread
with a variety of chopped toppings.*

1. **Preheat the oven** to 425°F.

2. **Combine** the eggplant, bell peppers, zucchini, squash, onion, oil, thyme,
oregano, and salt in a large bowl; toss to coat. Spread the vegetables
in a large, shallow roasting pan. Roast, stirring occasionally, until the
vegetables are tender and browned, about 45 minutes. Stir in the basil.

3. **Spoon the vegetable mixture** onto the toasts. Sprinkle with the cheese.
Serve at once.

PER SERVING (2 CROSTINI): 113 CALORIES
3g total fat, 1g saturated fat, 1mg cholesterol, 329mg sodium, 19g total carbohydrate,
3g dietary fiber, 4g protein, 50mg calcium

---

1 (1-pound) eggplant,
cut into ½-inch pieces

2 red bell peppers,
seeded and finely
chopped

1 medium zucchini,
finely chopped

1 medium yellow squash,
finely chopped

1 red onion,
cut into 8 wedges

1 tablespoon
extra-virgin olive oil

2 teaspoons
dried thyme

1 teaspoon
dried oregano

¾ teaspoon salt

½ cup chopped basil

1 French baguette,
cut into 24 slices, toasted

2 tablespoons grated
Romano cheese

---

COOK'S HINT COOK'S HINT **make ahead** COOK'S HINT COOK'S HINT COOK'S HINT COOK'S HINT

The vegetables and toasts can be made ahead separately. Refrigerate
the vegetables for up to 2 days and bring them to room temperature before
serving. Keep the toasts in an airtight container for up to 2 days.

# creamy guacamole in endive [20]

*1 POINT* PER SERVING | MAKES 16 SERVINGS

*Haas avocados are particularly rich and creamy. You can recognize them by their dark, rough-textured skin. To ripen hard avocados, place them in a paper bag for about 3 days.*

2 ripe avocados, peeled, pit removed and chopped

2 tablespoons reduced-calorie mayonnaise

1 small tomato, seeded and chopped

1 small jalapeño pepper, seeded and minced (wear gloves to prevent irritation)

½ small red onion, chopped

½ cup chopped cilantro

2 tablespoons cider vinegar

2 teaspoons grated lemon zest

½ teaspoon salt

2 large heads Belgian endive, leaves separated

**Pulse the avocados,** mayonnaise, tomato, jalapeño, onion, cilantro, vinegar, lemon zest, and salt in a food processor, until smooth and creamy. Mound or pipe 1 heaping teaspoon of the mixture onto each endive leaf. Serve at once.

**PER SERVING (2 LEAVES): 55 CALORIES**
4g total fat, 1g saturated fat, 1mg cholesterol, 104mg sodium, 5g total carbohydrate, 3g dietary fiber, 1g protein, 38mg calcium

COOK'S HINT COOK'S HINT **avocados** COOK'S HINT COOK'S HINT COOK'S HINT COOK'S HINT

Once avocado flesh is exposed to the air it discolors rapidly, so it is best to serve any dishes containing avocado promptly. The addition of lemon or lime juice helps prevent discoloration.

spicy garlic shrimp savory potato and ham chunks

ham and cheese quesadilla

hogazas with sausage and peppers

chunky balsamic mushrooms

beef and asparagus rolls indonesian-style mini meatballs

turkey and red pepper panini

chinese steamed dumplings asian sesame noodles

artichoke hearts au gratin

baked apples with cheddar and walnuts

roasted chickpeas with feta on pita toast

pizza nachos garlicky parmesan pita chips

multigrain soft pretzels sweet snacking sandwich

maple-glazed popcorn snack mix

creamy mango slush

# tapas & light bites

# spicy garlic shrimp [20]

*1 POINT* PER SERVING | MAKES 8 SERVINGS

*Seafood is a common ingredient in traditional Spanish tapas. Serve this quick and simple shrimp dish hot or at room temperature. You can make it a few hours ahead and refrigerate it until ready to serve. Remove from the refrigerator and bring to room temperature 30 minutes before serving.*

1 tablespoon olive oil

4 garlic cloves, minced

1 pound (24) large shrimp, peeled and deveined

¾ teaspoon dried oregano

⅛ teaspoon crushed red pepper

**Heat a very large nonstick skillet** over medium heat. Swirl in the oil, then add the garlic. Sauté until softened, about 1 minute. Increase the heat to medium-high and add the shrimp, oregano, and crushed pepper; sauté, stirring constantly, until the shrimp are just opaque, about 2 minutes.

**PER SERVING (3 SHRIMP): 45 CALORIES**
2g total fat, 0g saturated fat, 53mg cholesterol, 62mg sodium, 1g total carbohydrate, 0g dietary fiber, 6g protein, 15mg calcium

COOK'S HINT COOK'S HINT **deveining shrimp** COOK'S HINT COOK'S HINT COOK'S HINT

To devein shrimp, cut a shallow slit down the back of the peeled shrimp with a small sharp knife and pull out the dark vein. Rinse the shrimp briefly under cold running water and pat dry with paper towels before cooking.

# savory potato and ham chunks

**4 POINTS** PER SERVING | MAKES 4 SERVINGS

*The combination of paprika, tomato paste, and vinegar in this sweet-and-tangy dish is a typical sauce used in many classic Spanish tapas recipes. Crunchy carrot spears provide a nice contrast to this savory mix.*

**1. Spray a very large nonstick skillet** with nonstick spray and set over medium heat. Add the ham and cook, stirring often, until lightly browned, 2–3 minutes. Transfer the ham to a large bowl.

**2. Heat the same skillet.** Swirl in 2 teaspoons of the oil, then add the potatoes and cook, stirring often, until golden, 2–3 minutes. Add 1 cup of the broth and simmer, covered, until the potatoes are just tender, about 15 minutes. Uncover and cook until any remaining liquid evaporates. Transfer the potatoes to the bowl with the ham.

**3. Swirl the remaining 1 teaspoon oil** in the same skillet, then add the flour and paprika and cook, stirring constantly, 1 minute. Gradually add the remaining 1 cup chicken broth, and the vinegar, stirring to keep the mixture smooth. Add the tomato paste and cayenne. Simmer, stirring occasionally, until the sauce is smooth and thickened, 6–8 minutes.

**4. Return the ham** and potatoes to the skillet and stir gently until evenly coated with sauce. Serve hot.

**PER SERVING (1 CUP): 241 CALORIES**
5g total fat, 1g saturated fat, 15mg cholesterol, 413mg sodium, 37g total carbohydrate, 4g dietary fiber, 11g protein, 24mg calcium

4 ounces thickly-sliced lean ham, chopped

1 tablespoon olive oil

1½ pounds potatoes, scrubbed and cut into 1-inch chunks

2 cups fat-free, low-sodium chicken broth

2 teaspoons all-purpose flour

½ teaspoon paprika

1 tablespoon white wine vinegar

1 tablespoon tomato paste

⅛ teaspoon cayenne

COOK'S HINT COOK'S HINT **paprika** COOK'S HINT COOK'S HINT COOK'S HINT COOK'S HINT

Paprika is a powdered blend of sweet red peppers that can range in flavor from mild to hot. Most varieties sold in supermarkets that are simply labeled "paprika" are mildly spicy. If you can find it, use smoked paprika for extra flavor. Or, to bring out the flavor of a mild paprika, roast it in a dry skillet over medium heat, stirring constantly, 1 to 2 minutes, then cool before using.

# ham and cheese quesadilla [20]

*2 POINTS* PER SERVING | MAKES 4 SERVINGS

*Shredded green cabbage adds crunch, fiber, and flavor to this Tex-Mex classic. An equal amount of shredded carrot or three or four thin slices of tomato, would make good alternative fillings, if you prefer.*

2 (1¼-ounce) slices reduced-fat, reduced-sodium Swiss cheese

2 (8-inch) whole-wheat flour tortillas

½ cup finely shredded green cabbage or coleslaw mix

2 ounces (6 thin slices) 97% fat-free smoked ham

1. **Heat a large nonstick skillet** over medium heat. Fit one slice of the cheese on one of the tortillas to come within 1 inch of the edge. Sprinkle evenly with the cabbage and top with overlapping slices of ham. Top with the remaining cheese, then the remaining tortilla. Transfer the quesadilla to the skillet.

2. **Cook the quesadilla**, occasionally pressing down gently with a spatula, until the bottom tortilla is toasted crisp, about 1½ minutes. Carefully turn the quesadilla over and cook until crisp and the cheese melts, 1½ minutes longer. Transfer to a plate and cut into four wedges. Serve warm.

**PER SERVING (1 WEDGE):** 97 CALORIES
3g total fat, 1g saturated fat, 16mg cholesterol, 413mg sodium, 9g total carbohydrate, 1g dietary fiber, 8g protein, 133mg calcium

COOK'S HINT COOK'S HINT **tortillas** COOK'S HINT COOK'S HINT COOK'S HINT COOK'S HINT

Use leftover tortillas to make your own baked tortilla chips. Stack 2 to 3 tortillas and cut them into 8 triangles. Arrange in a single layer on a nonstick baking sheet and bake in a preheated 350°F oven until crisp, 5–7 minutes. Store the chips in a tightly covered container for up to 3 days.

# hogazas with sausage and peppers [20]

*2 POINTS* PER SERVING | MAKES 4 SERVINGS

*Hogazas are the Spanish version of Italian bruschetta or crostini or, put simply, toasted bread with a topping. This is a great way to get a taste of authentic Spanish sausage without using an excessive number of POINTS. When it comes to flavor, in fact, a little bit of smoky chorizo goes a long way.*

1. **Peel the papery casing** from the chorizo and pierce the sausage all over with a fork. Place in a nonstick skillet with enough water to cover and simmer for 15 minutes. Transfer the sausage to a cutting board. Finely chop the sausage and the roasted pepper and combine them in a small bowl.

2. **Toast the bread slices** until golden. Spoon the chopped sausage and pepper mixture on the toasts. Sprinkle with the cilantro.

**PER SERVING (2 HOGAZAS): 92 CALORIES**
3g total fat, 1g saturated fat, 6mg cholesterol, 205mg sodium, 11g total carbohydrate, 1g dietary fiber, 4g protein, 18mg calcium

2 ounces chorizo sausage

1 red bell pepper, roasted

8 (2-inch) slices Italian bread

1 tablespoon minced cilantro or parsley

COOK'S HINT COOK'S HINT **roasting peppers** COOK'S HINT COOK'S HINT COOK'S HINT

To roast bell peppers, preheat the broiler and line a baking sheet with foil. Cut the peppers lengthwise in half and remove the seeds. Place the pepper halves on the baking sheet. Broil 5 inches from the heat, turning frequently with tongs, until lightly charred, 6–8 minutes. Fold up the foil to cover the peppers and let steam 10 minutes. When cool enough to handle, peel off and discard the skin.

# chunky balsamic mushrooms

*1 POINT* PER SERVING | MAKES 4 SERVINGS

*Tapas bars throughout Spain often include a small plate of simple, sautéed mushrooms on the menu. While traditional recipes are often swimming in oil, this version gets a flavor boost from balsamic vinegar and thyme.*

2 teaspoons
extra-virgin olive oil

1 pound cremini or white mushrooms, cleaned, stems discarded, and caps halved

2 garlic cloves, minced

¼ teaspoon dried thyme

¼ teaspoon salt

1 tablespoon
balsamic vinegar

1. **Heat a very large nonstick skillet** over medium-high heat. Swirl in the oil, then add the mushrooms. Sauté, stirring frequently, 1 minute. Add the garlic, thyme, and salt; sauté until fragrant, stirring frequently, 1 minute.

2. **Add the vinegar** and cook, stirring often, until all the liquid evaporates and the mushrooms are golden, about 2 minutes. Serve warm or at room temperature.

**PER SERVING** (½ CUP): 50 CALORIES
3g total fat, 0g saturated fat, 0mg cholesterol, 150mg sodium, 6g total carbohydrate, 1g dietary fiber, 2g protein, 9mg calcium

COOK'S HINT COOK'S HINT COOK'S HINT olive oil COOK'S HINT COOK'S HINT COOK'S HINT COOK'S HINT

Whenever oil is used for flavoring, as well as cooking a food, choose a rich, flavorful variety, such as extra-virgin olive oil. For these Spanish tapas, you might want to try a Spanish extra-virgin olive oil.

# beef and asparagus rolls ✦[20]

*3 POINTS* PER SERVING | MAKES 4 SERVINGS

*Keep this quick, versatile snack in the refrigerator to have on hand as an
informal midday munch; or serve it as a formal finger food at your next party.
You can substitute steamed scallions or green beans for the asparagus, or
make it no-cook and use raw cucumber sticks.*

1. Cook the asparagus in a large pan of salted boiling water until crisp-tender,
3–5 minutes. Using tongs, transfer the asparagus to a large bowl of ice water.
Cool the asparagus for 1 minute, then drain on layers of paper towels.

2. Meanwhile, combine the mayonnaise and horseradish in a small bowl.
Spread a thin layer over each slice of roast beef. Place an asparagus stalk
at one end of each beef slice and roll tightly. Serve at once, or cover tightly
and refrigerate to serve within 1 day. Bring to room temperature for
30 minutes before serving.

**PER SERVING (4 ROLLS): 138 CALORIES**
5g total fat, 1g saturated fat, 50mg cholesterol, 179mg sodium, 3g total carbohydrate,
1g dietary fiber, 19g protein, 15mg calcium

**16 asparagus spears**
(½ pound), trimmed and
fibrous stalks peeled

**2 tablespoons**
low-fat mayonnaise

**2 teaspoons prepared**
horseradish

**½ pound very thinly**
sliced lean roast beef

COOK'S HINT COOK'S HINT **asparagus** COOK'S HINT COOK'S HINT COOK'S HINT COOK'S HINT

Choose asparagus stalks that are close in size and thickness so they'll
cook evenly. If your asparagus is somewhat tough and thick-skinned, peel
the skin from the stems with a vegetable peeler before cooking.

# indonesian-style mini meatballs

**2 POINTS** PER SERVING | MAKES 8 SERVINGS

*You can prepare these snack-size meatballs ahead of time and bake them just before serving but it's best to make the peanut-yogurt sauce at the last minute. If you buy from the butcher, it's sometimes easier to get lean ground meat combinations than it is by shopping from the meat case in the supermarket. Round out this "light bite" with crisp cucumber and carrot sticks.*

1 pound lean ground meat mixture (10% or less fat) for meatloaf (beef, pork, and veal)

2 scallions, minced

2 tablespoons oat bran or instant wheat cereal

2 tablespoons minced cilantro

1 teaspoon ground cumin

¼ teaspoon salt

¼ teaspoon ground allspice

⅛ teaspoon freshly ground pepper

¾ cup plain nonfat yogurt

1 egg white

¼ cup water

1 tablespoon smooth peanut butter

1 teaspoon reduced-sodium soy sauce

1. **Preheat the oven** to 400°F. Spray a baking sheet with nonstick spray. Combine the ground meat mixture, scallions, oat bran, 1 tablespoon of the cilantro, the cumin, salt, allspice, pepper, ¼ cup of the yogurt, and the egg white in a medium bowl. Form into 24 one-inch meatballs.

2. **Place the meatballs** on the baking sheet and bake until no longer pink in the center, about 10 minutes.

3. **Meanwhile, to prepare the sauce,** heat the water and peanut butter in a small saucepan over medium-high heat, whisking constantly, until blended. Remove from the heat and stir in the remaining ½ cup yogurt and the soy sauce. Heat through but do not boil. Stir in the remaining 1 tablespoon cilantro. Serve the sauce warm with the hot meatballs.

**PER SERVING (3 MEATBALLS AND 1½ TABLESPOONS SAUCE): 108 CALORIES**
4g total fat, 1g saturated fat, 40mg cholesterol, 164mg sodium, 4g total carbohydrate, 1g dietary fiber, 14g protein, 61mg calcium

COOK'S HINT COOK'S HINT **microwave** COOK'S HINT COOK'S HINT COOK'S HINT COOK'S HINT

You can cook both the meatballs and the sauce in the microwave oven. Arrange the meatballs in 6 rows on a microwavable roasting rack. Microwave on High 2 minutes. Rearrange the meatballs so the center rows are on the outside and the outer rows are now in the center. Microwave 1 minute or until the meatballs are no longer pink in the center. Set aside, covered to keep warm. Combine the water and peanut butter in a 2-cup glass measure. Microwave on High 1 minute. Stir well to blend; stir in the yogurt and soy sauce. Microwave 15–20 seconds until warm (do not boil). Stir in the cilantro.

# turkey and red pepper panini [20]

*3 POINTS* PER SERVING | MAKES 2 SERVINGS

*Italian panini are simply "small breads" made into sandwiches with thin layers of filling. Our version is pressed and lightly toasted in a skillet for a grilled effect. Substitute ham for the turkey, and Swiss cheese for the mozzarella, if you prefer.*

1. **Slice the bread** lengthwise almost all the way through. Layer with the red pepper on the bottom half. Drizzle with the olive oil; top with the basil, turkey, and cheese. Gently flatten the sandwich with the palm of your hand.

2. **Lightly spray** a small nonstick skillet with nonstick spray and set over medium-high heat. Add the sandwich and top with a heavy weight, such as a small cast-iron pan. Cook until the bread is crisp, about 2 minutes. With a spatula, turn the sandwich, weigh it down, and cook until the other side is crisp, about 2 minutes. Cut the sandwich in half.

**PER SERVING (½ SANDWICH): 148 CALORIES**
4g total fat, 2g saturated fat, 19mg cholesterol, 251mg sodium, 16g total carbohydrate, 1g dietary fiber, 11g protein, 131mg calcium

2-ounce (4-inch) piece semolina or French bread

⅓ cup sliced jarred roasted red bell peppers

¼ teaspoon extra-virgin olive oil

1 large basil leaf or ⅛ teaspoon dried basil

3 very thin slices (1 ounce) fat-free turkey, folded in half

¼ cup shredded part-skim mozzarella cheese

COOK'S HINT COOK'S HINT **bread** COOK'S HINT COOK'S HINT COOK'S HINT COOK'S HINT COOK'S HINT

Try to use semolina rather than ordinary French bread for this recipe. You'll find the texture far superior, thanks to the coarsely ground semolina wheat flour that is used to make the bread.

# chinese steamed dumplings

**3 POINTS** PER SERVING | MAKES 4 SERVINGS

*These tender morsels are similar to dumplings you'll find in Chinese restaurants. They are juicy and flavorful enough that you won't need a dipping sauce, other than some low-sodium, no-POINTS soy sauce to pass on the side.*

1 large egg

½ teaspoon Asian (dark) sesame oil

½ cup minced cabbage

1 scallion, minced

2 tablespoons water

1 tablespoon reduced-sodium soy sauce

½ teaspoon minced peeled fresh ginger

Pinch Chinese five-spice powder

12 dumpling wrappers

**1. Spray a small nonstick skillet** with nonstick spray and set over medium heat. Lightly beat the egg and oil in a small bowl, then pour into the skillet. Cook, without stirring, until set like a small omelet. Transfer the egg to a cutting board and finely chop.

**2. Combine** the cooked egg, cabbage, scallion, water, soy sauce, ginger, and five-spice powder in a small bowl. Spoon evenly into the center of each dumpling wrapper. Bring the edges of the wrappers up and over the top of the filling; pinch together in the center to seal the dumplings.

**3. Put the dumplings** in a steamer basket; set in a saucepan over 1 inch of boiling water. Cover tightly and steam until tender, about 20 minutes. Serve hot.

**PER SERVING (3 DUMPLINGS): 145 CALORIES**
2g total fat, 1g saturated fat, 53mg cholesterol, 169mg sodium, 25g total carbohydrate, 1g dietary fiber, 5g protein, 21mg calcium

COOK'S HINT COOK'S HINT **dumpling wrappers** COOK'S HINT COOK'S HINT COOK'S

You can find dumpling wrappers in Asian markets. Or it's easy to make your own: Stir together 1 cup all-purpose flour and 3 tablespoons cold water in a small bowl. (You may need to add up to 1 teaspoon more water to make a workable dough.) Knead the dough into a small ball in the bowl, cover and set aside for 30 minutes. Divide the dough in half then divide each half into six equal pieces. Roll each piece out into a 3½-inch round. Fill and steam as directed above, using wet fingers to pinch and seal each dumpling.

# asian sesame noodles

**3 POINTS** PER SERVING | MAKES 6 SERVINGS

*Unlike the fatty noodles you find in restaurants, our high-fiber noodles are served in a light, nutty sauce. This dish is delicious hot, at room temperature, or chilled. Try it with a crisp green salad for a more substantial meal.*

1. **Combine** the chicken broth, soy sauce, peanut butter, and garlic in a small saucepan; bring to a boil. Reduce the heat and simmer 15 minutes. Remove the sauce from the heat and stir in the scallion, lemon juice, and sesame oil.

2. **Meanwhile, cook the spaghetti** according to package directions. Drain; rinse under warm running water and drain again.

3. **Combine** the spaghetti, the sauce, carrot, and sesame seeds in a large bowl. Toss gently to mix. Serve warm or cover and refrigerate for up to 2 days. Bring to room temperature 30 minutes before serving.

PER SERVING ($^2/_3$ CUP): 174 CALORIES
4g total fat, 1g saturated fat, 0mg cholesterol, 239mg sodium, 29g total carbohydrate, 5g dietary fiber, 8g protein, 27mg calcium

2 cups fat-free, low-sodium chicken broth

2 tablespoons reduced-sodium soy sauce

1 tablespoon smooth peanut butter

1 garlic clove, finely chopped

1 scallion, thinly sliced

1 tablespoon fresh lemon or lime juice

2 teaspoons Asian (dark) sesame oil

8 ounces whole-wheat spaghetti or linguine, or thin buckwheat noodles

1 small carrot, finely shredded

1 tablespoon toasted sesame seeds

COOK'S HINT COOK'S HINT **sesame seeds** COOK'S HINT COOK'S HINT COOK'S HINT COOK'S HINT

To toast sesame seeds, place them in a small dry skillet over medium-low heat. Cook, stirring constantly, until lightly browned and fragrant, 2–3 minutes. Watch them carefully when toasting; seeds can burn quickly.

# artichoke hearts au gratin [20]

***2 POINTS*** PER SERVING | MAKES 4 SERVINGS

*For a simple lunch, two people could share this yummy vegetable dish, along with a few slices of lean ham and some breadsticks. It also makes a tasty side dish for an egg-based brunch or a pasta supper.*

1 (9-ounce) box frozen artichoke hearts, thawed

½ cup cherry tomatoes, cut in half

½ teaspoon dried thyme

½ cup shredded reduced-fat Swiss cheese

1 slice whole-wheat bread, made into crumbs

2 tablespoons grated Parmesan cheese

**1. Preheat the broiler.** Cook the artichoke hearts according to package directions. Drain well and combine with the tomatoes in a large au gratin dish or other shallow, flameproof dish. Sprinkle with the thyme, then the Swiss cheese.

**2. Broil** 4 inches from the heat until the cheese starts to melt, about 1 minute. Combine the bread crumbs and Parmesan cheese and sprinkle evenly over the cheese. Broil until the bread crumbs are browned, about 1 minute.

PER SERVING (GENEROUS ½ CUP): 104 CALORIES
3g total fat, 2g saturated fat, 7mg cholesterol, 122mg sodium, 12g total carbohydrate, 4g dietary fiber, 9g protein, 255mg calcium

# baked apples with cheddar and walnuts

***3 POINTS*** PER SERVING | MAKES 4 SERVINGS

*You can easily halve this recipe to make just 2 servings. Just about any other apple variety would work here, but be sure the apples are baked until tender before you fill them with the cheese and nut mixture.*

1. **Preheat the oven** to 350°F. Place the nuts on a baking sheet and bake until golden and fragrant, 4–5 minutes. Transfer the nuts to a plate to cool.

2. **Pare the skin** from the top third of the apples. Core the apples, leaving a ½-inch base intact at the bottom and a 1½-inch wide opening at the top. Place the apples in a small baking pan, cover loosely with foil, and bake until tender, about 15 minutes.

3. **Combine** the walnuts, cheese, and cereal in a bowl. Stuff the apples with the cheese mixture. Cover loosely with the foil and return to the oven. Bake until the cheese melts and the apples are tender, about 5 minutes. Let cool 10-15 minutes before serving.

**PER SERVING (1 STUFFED APPLE): 154 CALORIES**
5g total fat, 2g saturated fat, 8mg cholesterol, 75mg sodium, 24g total carbohydrate, 4g dietary fiber, 5g protein, 117mg calcium

2 tablespoons chopped walnuts

4 McIntosh apples

½ cup shredded reduced-fat cheddar cheese

¼ cup spoon-size shredded wheat cereal, crushed

COOK'S HINT COOK'S HINT **leftovers** COOK'S HINT COOK'S HINT COOK'S HINT COOK'S HINT

You can store leftover baked apples in the refrigerator for a day or two and reheat them in a microwave oven at 50% power for 1-2 minutes.

# roasted chickpeas
# with feta on pita toast

***3 POINTS*** PER SERVING | MAKES 6 SERVINGS

*You can serve this savory snack like a small pizza, or as a chunky dip.*
*For the latter, just break up the toasted pita rounds and use them to scoop up*
*the creamy chickpea mixture.*

1 (15-ounce) can
chickpeas, drained
and rinsed

3 garlic cloves, minced

1 teaspoon olive oil

½ teaspoon ground cumin

1 ripe tomato, chopped

6 large ripe olives,
finely chopped

½ teaspoon dried
oregano

¼ teaspoon salt

⅛ teaspoon freshly
ground pepper

1 ounce feta cheese,
crumbled

1 tablespoon minced
flat-leaf parsley

3 whole-wheat pita
breads, split into 6 rounds

1. **Preheat the oven** to 400°F. Combine the chickpeas, garlic, oil, and cumin in an 8-inch square baking pan. Toss gently until well mixed. Roast, stirring occasionally, 15 minutes.

2. **Remove the pan** from the oven and stir in the tomato, olives, oregano, salt, and pepper. Sprinkle evenly with the feta cheese. Return the pan to the oven and bake until the cheese melts slightly and the mixture is heated through, 6–8 minutes. Remove the pan from the oven, sprinkle with parsley, and let cool slightly.

3. **Meanwhile, place the pita rounds,** split-side up, on a large baking sheet. Bake until crisp and lightly toasted, 5 minutes. Spoon the chickpea mixture onto the toasted pita rounds and serve warm.

**PER SERVING (WITH ½ PITA BREAD AND ½ CUP CHICKPEA MIXTURE):**
171 CALORIES
4g total fat, 1g saturated fat, 4mg cholesterol, 428mg sodium, 28g total carbohydrate,
5g dietary fiber, 8g protein, 62mg calcium

COOK'S HINT COOK'S HINT **parsley** COOK'S HINT COOK'S HINT COOK'S HINT COOK'S HINT

Flat-leaf parsley and curly-leaf parsley can be used interchangeably,
but the flat-leaf variety has a more refreshingly intense flavor.

# pizza nachos [20]

*2 POINTS* PER SERVING | MAKES 4 SERVINGS

*This recipe takes care of a pizza or nacho craving in one fell swoop.
It's also easily doubled, or even tripled, for a party.*

**Preheat the broiler.** Arrange the tortilla chips in a single layer on a pizza
pan or small jelly-roll pan. Drizzle with the tomato sauce and sprinkle with
the oregano. Top with the mozzarella and Parmesan cheeses. Broil until
the chips just start to brown and the cheese starts to melt, about 1 minute.

**PER SERVING (¼ OF THE NACHOS):** 107 CALORIES
3g total fat, 2g saturated fat, 8mg cholesterol, 317mg sodium, 14g total carbohydrate,
1g dietary fiber, 6g protein, 124mg calcium

2 ounces (26) baked
tortilla chips

½ cup prepared tomato
or marinara sauce

½ teaspoon dried
oregano

½ cup shredded
part-skim
mozzarella cheese

2 teaspoons grated
Parmesan cheese

# garlicky parmesan pita chips

**2 POINTS** PER SERVING | MAKES 8 SERVINGS

*It's best to make these chips within an hour or two of serving. They make for a flavorful snack, but can also be teamed with a yogurt or bean dip, or be served in lieu of bread with a main meal.*

4 (6-inch) whole-wheat or oat-bran pita rounds

2 egg whites

1 tablespoon olive oil

3 garlic cloves, minced

¼ teaspoon salt

¼ teaspoon dried basil

¼ teaspoon dried oregano

2 tablespoons grated Parmesan cheese

**1. Preheat the oven** to 300°F. Cut each pita into 4 triangles; split each triangle into two.

**2. Combine** the egg whites, oil, garlic, salt, basil, and oregano in a small bowl. Brush over each of the pita wedges. Sprinkle with the cheese. Place the triangles on two baking sheets.

**3. Bake** until the edges of the pita triangles are browned and the topping is set, 15–17 minutes. Transfer the chips to racks to cool completely.

PER SERVING (4 CHIPS): 101 CALORIES
3g total fat, 1g saturated fat, 1mg cholesterol, 261mg sodium, 16g total carbohydrate, 2g dietary fiber, 4g protein, 29mg calcium

# multigrain soft pretzels

*3 POINTS* PER SERVING | MAKES 16 SERVINGS

*You can prepare the dough for these pretzels up to 24 hours in advance, then shape and bake them the next day. Baked soft pretzels should be served warm, but you can store the baked pretzels for up to a week in a tightly covered container then reheat them in a preheated 300°F oven for a minute or two.*

1. **Combine** the water and sugar in a large bowl. Sprinkle in the yeast and let stand until foamy, about 5 minutes. Add the oil, egg, and salt.

2. **Combine** the all-purpose flour, whole wheat flour, cornmeal, and oat bran in another bowl. Stir half the flour mixture into the yeast mixture until smooth. Gradually work in the remaining flour mixture until a stiff dough forms. Spray a large bowl with nonstick spray; put the dough in the bowl. Cover lightly with plastic wrap and refrigerate for at least 2 hours or up to 24 hours.

3. **Spray 2 baking sheets** with nonstick spray. Turn the dough out onto a lightly floured board and divide into 16 pieces. With your hands, gently roll each piece into a 20-inch long rope. Shape into pretzel twists. Brush the pretzels lightly with the egg white-water mixture and sprinkle with the seeds. Place on the baking sheets. Cover lightly with plastic wrap and let rise in a warm spot until double in size, about 45 minutes.

4. **Meanwhile, preheat** the oven to 400°F. Bake the pretzels until golden, about 15 minutes. Transfer to racks to cool slightly.

PER SERVING (1 PRETZEL): 143 CALORIES
3g total fat, 0g saturated fat, 13mg cholesterol, 227mg sodium, 25g total carbohydrate, 2g dietary fiber, 4g protein, 9mg calcium

1 cup warm
(105–115°F) water

¼ cup sugar

1 package active
dry yeast

2 tablespoons olive oil

1 large egg

1½ teaspoons salt

2½ cups all-purpose flour

½ cup whole-wheat flour

½ cup cornmeal

¼ cup oat bran

1 egg white mixed with
2 tablespoons water

2 tablespoons sesame
seeds or poppy seeds

# sweet snacking sandwich [20]

**3 POINTS** PER SERVING | MAKES 4 SERVINGS

*Here's a quick way to satisfy those late afternoon or evening cravings—with minimal **POINTS**. You can substitute sliced peach, mango, pineapple, or kiwi fruit for the strawberries and use toasted cinnamon-raisin bread in place of the English muffins.*

1 banana

¼ cup part-skim ricotta cheese

1 ounce nonfat cream cheese

2 cinnamon-raisin English muffins, split and toasted

4 ripe strawberries, thinly sliced

**1. Combine** ½ the banana, the ricotta, and the cream cheese in a blender. Whirl just until smooth. Thinly slice the remaining banana half.

**2. Spread** the banana mixture evenly over the toasted muffins. Top with overlapping slices of banana and strawberries.

**PER SERVING (1 OPEN SANDWICH): 142 CALORIES**
2g total fat, 1g saturated fat, 5mg cholesterol, 187mg sodium, 26g total carbohydrate, 2g dietary fiber, 6g protein, 106mg calcium

COOK'S HINT COOK'S HINT COOK'S HINT **leftovers** COOK'S HINT COOK'S HINT COOK'S HINT COOK'S HINT

If you have leftover banana-cheese mixture, store it in the refrigerator, with plastic wrap directly on the surface of the mixture to prevent it from turning brown. It will keep for a day or two.

# maple-glazed popcorn snack mix

*3 POINTS* PER SERVING | MAKES 8 SERVINGS

*This sweet and crunchy snack will last up to two weeks in a tightly covered container.*

1. **Preheat the oven** to 350°F. Toast the almonds in a single layer on a small baking sheet until just golden and fragrant, 4–5 minutes. Transfer the almonds to a plate to cool. Reduce the oven temperature to 250°F.

2. **Spray** a large baking sheet and a glass baking dish or bowl with nonstick spray. Combine the popcorn and cereal in the baking dish. Place in the oven to warm.

3. **Combine** the brown sugar, maple syrup, and cinnamon in a small nonstick saucepan. Bring to a boil over medium heat. Cook until the mixture reaches 250°F on a candy thermometer (hard ball stage). Stir in the butter and cook until the mixture reaches 280°F (hard crack stage).

4. **Remove the popcorn mixture** from the oven. Quickly and carefully pour half the glaze over the mix, tossing with a metal spoon. Sprinkle the nuts over the mix and pour on the remaining glaze, tossing to coat evenly. Spoon the mixture onto the sprayed baking sheet, spreading out and breaking into small clumps. Cool completely, then store in an airtight container.

**PER SERVING (1 CUP): 163 CALORIES**
5g total fat, 1g saturated fat, 4mg cholesterol, 17mg sodium, 30g total carbohydrate, 2g dietary fiber, 2g protein, 35mg calcium

1½ ounces almonds, coarsely chopped

6 cups air-popped popcorn

2 cups puffed seven-whole-grain and sesame cereal (kashi)

½ cup packed light brown sugar

¼ cup maple syrup

¼ teaspoon cinnamon

1 tablespoon butter

COOK'S HINT COOK'S HINT **maple glaze** COOK'S HINT COOK'S HINT COOK'S HINT COOK'S HINT

Just as in candy making, the success of this maple glaze depends on the accurate temperature of the syrup during cooking. Use a candy thermometer to determine the stage of hardness—don't use guesswork or rely on "cold water tests" you might find in older cookbooks. Candy thermometers are sold in the housewares department of most department stores. If you have an old candy thermometer, check its accuracy by placing it in boiling water for three minutes. If the thermometer reads 212°F it is still fine to use.

# creamy mango slush [20]

**2 POINTS** PER SERVING | MAKES 2 SERVINGS

*Banana adds creaminess to this icy refresher without adding fat. You can easily double the recipe, however, be sure to make it in two batches to avoid over filling the blender.*

1 cup pineapple juice

½ cup mango cubes

½ ripe banana

1 tablespoon fresh lime juice

1 cup crushed ice

1 teaspoon chopped fresh mint, or ⅛ teaspoon dried

**Combine** the juice, mango, banana, and lime juice in a blender. Whirl until smooth, 30 seconds. Add the ice; pulse until the mixture is slushy. Pour into two glasses and sprinkle with the mint. Serve cold.

PER SERVING (1 CUP): 125 CALORIES
0g total fat, 0g saturated fat, 0mg cholesterol, 5mg sodium, 31g total carbohydrate, 2g dietary fiber, 1g protein, 31mg calcium

COOK'S HINT COOK'S HINT mangos COOK'S HINT COOK'S HINT COOK'S HINT COOK'S HINT

To cube a mango, peel off the skin and halve the fruit lengthwise, cutting around the large center pit. Cut the slices into cubes. Or, leaving the skin on, halve the mango lengthwise, then score a crosshatch pattern on the fruit, leaving the skin intact. Push from the skin side to turn the mango inside out and cut off the cubes of fruit.

# salads & soups

mixed greens with pear and toasted almonds

spinach and pink grapefruit salad

stacked boston lettuce with fennel, blue cheese, and toasted walnuts

sunflower caesar salad

asparagus and grape tomatoes with dill dressing

picnic pasta salad

red and green bean salad with sage-lemon dressing

oven-roasted salade niçoise

chicken and sugar-snap pea salad with mint-lemon dressing

exotic winter fruit salad

simple chicken soup cabbage soup with kielbasa

cod chowder

white bean soup with fresh tomatoes and basil

curried red lentil soup creamy mushroom soup

tomato egg-drop soup chinese velvet corn soup

green gazpacho

# mixed greens with pear and toasted almonds [20]

*2 POINTS* PER SERVING | MAKES 4 SERVINGS

*Sweet pear, orange vinaigrette, and the freshest of greens sprinkled with crunchy toasted almonds make this a tantalizing salad. When choosing salad greens, fresh is the key word. Buy the bagged prewashed greens only if they look crisp (with no brown edges) and you want to save time. Or use loose mesclun.*

1 teaspoon grated orange zest

2 tablespoons fresh orange juice

2 tablespoons balsamic vinegar

1 tablespoon olive oil

1 teaspoon minced fresh marjoram, or ¼ teaspoon dried

¼ teaspoon salt

¼ teaspoon freshly ground pepper

1 (5-ounce) bag red leafy mix salad greens

½ red bell pepper, seeded and thinly sliced

2 ripe pears

2 tablespoons sliced almonds, toasted

1. **To make the dressing,** combine the orange zest, juice, vinegar, oil, marjoram, salt, and ground pepper in a medium bowl. Place the greens and bell pepper in a salad bowl.

2. **Core and slice** the pears and toss immediately with the dressing to prevent the pears from turning brown. Add the pears and dressing to the salad and toss gently. Sprinkle with the almonds and serve at once.

**PER SERVING: 111 CALORIES**
5g total fat, 1g saturated fat, 0mg cholesterol, 151mg sodium, 16g total carbohydrate, 3g dietary fiber, 2g protein, 41mg calcium

COOK'S HINT COOK'S HINT **almonds** COOK'S HINT COOK'S HINT COOK'S HINT COOK'S HINT

To toast the almonds, place them in a small dry skillet over medium-low heat. Toast, shaking the pan and stirring constantly, until lightly browned and fragrant, 3–4 minutes. Watch them carefully when toasting; almonds can burn quickly. Transfer the nuts to a plate to cool.

# spinach and pink grapefruit salad [20]

*2 POINTS* PER SERVING | MAKES 4 SERVINGS

*Nutty black sesame seeds and tart grapefruit make for an intriguing spinach salad. You can find black sesame seeds in Asian markets and some supermarkets.*

1. **To make the dressing,** combine the juice, vinegar, oil, soy sauce, sherry, and pepper in a small bowl.

2. **Place the spinach** in a large salad bowl. Add the dressing and toss gently. Top with the grapefruit and sprinkle with the sesame seeds. Serve at once.

**PER SERVING:** 90 CALORIES
5g total fat, 1g saturated fat, 0mg cholesterol, 158mg sodium, 9g total carbohydrate, 3g dietary fiber, 4g protein, 86mg calcium

2 tablespoons fresh grapefruit juice

1 tablespoon rice vinegar

2 teaspoons Asian (dark) sesame oil

2 teaspoons reduced-sodium soy sauce

1 teaspoon cream sherry

¼ teaspoon freshly ground pepper

1 (10-ounce) bag baby spinach

1 pink or white grapefruit, cut into sections

2 tablespoons black sesame seeds

COOK'S HINT COOK'S HINT **sesame seeds** COOK'S HINT COOK'S HINT COOK'S HINT COOK'S HINT COOK'S HINT

As with ivory-colored sesame seeds, the oil in the black seeds easily turns rancid. So store sesame seeds in the freezer for up to 1 year, in the refrigerator for up to 6 months, or on the pantry shelf for up to 3 months. If you prefer, substitute regular sesame seeds for the black and toast them to bring out their fullest flavor.

# stacked boston lettuce with fennel, blue cheese, and toasted walnuts [20]

*2 POINTS* PER SERVING | MAKES 4 SERVINGS

*Boston and Bibb lettuces are sometimes called butterhead or butter lettuce because of their soft, buttery-textured leaves. Handle their tender leaves gently to avoid bruising.*

1 teaspoon grated lemon zest

2 tablespoons fresh lemon juice

2 tablespoons low-sodium chicken or vegetable broth

2 teaspoons walnut or canola oil

1 teaspoon honey

¼ teaspoon freshly ground pepper

2 heads Boston or Bibb lettuce

½ fennel bulb, trimmed and very thinly sliced

2 tablespoons walnut pieces, toasted

¼ cup finely chopped red onion

1-ounce piece blue cheese, frozen

1. **To make the dressing,** combine the lemon zest, juice, broth, oil, honey, and pepper in a small bowl.

2. **Clean and separate** the lettuce leaves; cut out and discard a V-shape from the white part of each stem end. Gently press the leaves to flatten slightly and stack about 5 lettuce leaves on each of 4 plates. Top with the fennel, walnuts, and red onion.

3. **Spoon the dressing** over the salads and grate the blue cheese on top. (Crumble the last bits of ungrated blue cheese over the salads). Serve at once.

**PER SERVING:** 97 CALORIES
6g total fat, 2g saturated fat, 5mg cholesterol, 126mg sodium, 8g total carbohydrate, 2g dietary fiber, 3g protein, 74mg calcium

COOK'S HINT COOK'S HINT **blue cheese** COOK'S HINT COOK'S HINT COOK'S HINT COOK'S HINT COOK'S HINT

To create an appealing presentation, sprinkle the salad and plate with a blanket of cheese "snow": Place the 1-ounce piece of blue cheese in the freezer until frozen, at least 1 hour. Then grate the cheese directly onto the salad using the medium-sized grate on a four-sided grater.

# sunflower caesar salad [20]

**2 POINTS** PER SERVING | MAKES 6 SERVINGS

*Typically, a dressing for a Caesar salad to serve six would contain upwards of a half-cup of olive oil. Here, we've substituted tangy buttermilk and yogurt, spiked with lemon, garlic, and balsamic vinegar to create a creamy and flavorful dressing. Sunflower seeds add crunch and their natural oil gives extra flavor.*

**1. Place** the egg, buttermilk, yogurt, lemon juice, vinegar, garlic, salt, and pepper in a blender or food processor and pulse until smooth, about 1 minute.

**2. Place the lettuce** in a large serving bowl. Pour the dressing over the lettuce and toss well. Sprinkle the salad with the croutons, cheese, and sunflower seeds. Serve at once.

**PER SERVING: 82 CALORIES**
4g total fat, 1g saturated fat, 39mg cholesterol, 236mg sodium, 6g total carbohydrate, 2g dietary fiber, 6g protein, 129mg calcium

1 soft-cooked egg

3 tablespoons low-fat buttermilk

3 tablespoons nonfat plain yogurt

1 tablespoon fresh lemon juice

1 tablespoon balsamic vinegar

1 small garlic clove, minced

¼ teaspoon salt

¼ teaspoon freshly ground pepper

1 large head romaine lettuce, cleaned and torn (about 12 cups)

1 cup reduced-fat croutons

¼ cup grated Parmesan cheese

2 tablespoons dry-roasted, unsalted shelled sunflower seeds

COOK'S HINT COOK'S HINT **croutons** COOK'S HINT COOK'S HINT COOK'S HINT COOK'S HINT

To make your own croutons, cut a French baguette into 1-inch cubes. Spray a baking sheet with nonstick spray. Arrange the croutons in a single layer on the sheet. Mist lightly with nonstick spray; sprinkle with 1 teaspoon herbes de Provence (found in the spice section of most supermarkets) and 2 tablespoons finely grated Parmesan cheese and bake in a preheated 375°F oven until lightly browned, about 8 minutes. Store in an airtight container at room temperature for up to 2 days, or in a zip-close plastic bag in the freezer for up to 2 weeks.

# asparagus and grape tomatoes with dill dressing [20]

*1 POINT* PER SERVING | MAKES 4 SERVINGS

*Turn this refreshing side-salad into a complete lunch by sprinkling with reduced-fat goat cheese and serving with a crusty French baguette.*

1 pound asparagus, trimmed and fibrous stalks peeled

1 tablespoon fresh lemon juice

1 tablespoon extra-virgin olive oil

1 teaspoon white balsamic or white wine vinegar

½ teaspoon mustard powder

½ teaspoon sugar

¼ teaspoon salt

¼ teaspoon freshly ground pepper

2 tablespoons minced dill

½ pint grape or cherry tomatoes, halved

2 tablespoons finely chopped red onion

1. **Blanch the asparagus** in a large pan of salted boiling water until crisp-tender, 3–5 minutes. Using tongs, transfer the asparagus to a large bowl of ice water. Cool the asparagus for 1 minute, then drain on layers of paper towels.

2. **To make the dressing,** combine the juice, oil, vinegar, mustard, sugar, salt, and pepper in a small bowl; stir in the dill.

3. **Arrange the asparagus** on a serving platter, top with the tomatoes, drizzle with the dressing, and sprinkle with the red onion.

PER SERVING: 62 CALORIES
4g total fat, 1g saturated fat, 0mg cholesterol, 153mg sodium, 6g total carbohydrate, 2g dietary fiber, 2g protein, 19mg calcium

COOK'S HINT COOK'S HINT **vegetables** COOK'S HINT COOK'S HINT COOK'S HINT COOK'S HINT

Blanching vegetables is a good cooking technique for vegetables such as asparagus, broccoli, green beans, sugar snap peas, and snow peas which need to be cooked lightly, then cooled quickly before serving. Blanching heightens their color and preserves their flavor.

# picnic pasta salad

*3 POINTS* PER SERVING | MAKES 8 SERVINGS

*You'll find this pasta salad as creamy as your favorite recipe, but rest assured:*
*It has little fat and loads of crunchy, great-tasting, and healthful vegetables.*

1. **Cook the pasta** according to package directions; drain. Rinse under cold
running water for 1 minute; drain again. Place the pasta in a large bowl.

2. **Add** the carrots, broccoli, fennel, bell pepper, red onion, and parsley
to the pasta.

3. **Combine** the mayonnaise, yogurt, sour cream, lemon juice, salt, and ground
pepper in a medium bowl; stir into the pasta and vegetable mixture. Stir in the
tomatoes and serve at once, or cover and refrigerate for up to 2 days.

PER SERVING (GENEROUS 1 CUP): 191 CALORIES
5g total fat, 1g saturated fat, 6mg cholesterol, 262mg sodium, 32g total carbohydrate,
4g dietary fiber, 6g protein, 64mg calcium

½ pound macaroni or
other small pasta

3 carrots, shredded

2 cups chopped fresh broccoli

½ fennel bulb or
2 celery stalks, chopped

1 red bell pepper, seeded
and finely chopped

½ cup finely chopped
red onion

¼ cup minced flat-leaf
parsley

⅓ cup reduced-fat
mayonnaise

¼ cup nonfat plain yogurt

¼ cup light sour cream

4 teaspoons fresh
lemon juice

½ teaspoon salt

½ teaspoon freshly
ground pepper

½ pint grape or cherry
tomatoes, halved

COOK'S HINT COOK'S HINT **pasta salads** COOK'S HINT COOK'S HINT COOK'S HINT

If you're not going to serve this salad right away, refrigerate it covered
without the tomatoes. Cold damages the texture and flavor of tomatoes,
so stir them in at the last minute.

# red and green bean salad [20]
# with sage-lemon dressing

**2 POINTS** PER SERVING | MAKES 6 SERVINGS

*If snow peas or sugar-snap peas are in season you could substitute them for the green beans (be sure to steam them for 2 minutes). For extra flair and fiber, serve the salad on a bed of green or red leaf lettuce.*

1 pound fresh green beans, trimmed and cut into 1-inch pieces

2 tablespoons minced fresh sage, or 2 teaspoons dried

2 tablespoons dry red wine

2 tablespoons balsamic vinegar

1½ tablespoons extra-virgin olive oil

1 large garlic clove, minced

1 teaspoon grated lemon zest

½ teaspoon salt

¼ teaspoon freshly ground pepper

1 (19-ounce) can red kidney beans, rinsed and drained

1 yellow bell pepper, seeded and finely chopped

½ cup finely chopped red onion

½ pint grape or cherry tomatoes, halved

**1. Place the green beans** in a steamer basket; set in a saucepan over 1-inch of boiling water. Cover tightly and steam the beans, until crisp-tender, 3–4 minutes. Drain and transfer the beans to a large bowl of ice water. Cool the beans for 1 minute and then drain on layers of paper towels.

**2. Meanwhile, combine** the sage, wine, vinegar, oil, garlic, lemon zest, salt, and ground pepper in a large bowl. Add the green beans, kidney beans, bell pepper, onion, and tomatoes; toss well to coat. Serve at once.

**PER SERVING (GENEROUS 1 CUP): 123 CALORIES**
4g total fat, 1g saturated fat, 0mg cholesterol, 414mg sodium, 18g total carbohydrate, 6g dietary fiber, 5g protein, 53mg calcium

COOK'S HINT COOK'S HINT **an option** COOK'S HINT COOK'S HINT COOK'S HINT COOK'S HINT

For an elegant appetizer, spoon 1 to 2 tablespoons of the bean mixture into Belgian endive leaves and sprinkle with a few shreds of Parmesan cheese.

# oven-roasted salade niçoise

***7 POINTS*** PER SERVING | MAKES 2 SERVINGS

*Roasting fresh tuna and vegetables makes this traditional favorite from the south of France more flavorful—and fun to eat—than the original. If you don't want to turn on the oven, use canned water-packed tuna, boil the potatoes, and steam the green beans.*

1. **Preheat the oven** to 450°F. Spray two baking sheets with nonstick spray. Place the potatoes on one sheet and bake 15 minutes. Add the green beans and bake until the potatoes and green beans are lightly browned and tender, about 10 minutes.

2. **Place the tuna** on the second sheet and roast until the tuna is slightly browned on the outside, but pink on the inside, 7–8 minutes.

3. **Combine** the vinegar, broth, oil, garlic, and pepper in a small bowl. Place the lettuce on a large platter. Arrange mounds of potatoes, green beans, tuna, tomatoes, olives, and eggs on the lettuce. Drizzle all with the dressing, sprinkle with the capers, and garnish with the parsley. Serve at once.

**PER SERVING:** 373 CALORIES
9g total fat, 2g saturated fat, 169mg cholesterol, 272mg sodium, 44g total carbohydrate, 7g dietary fiber, 31g protein, 96mg calcium

---

1½ pounds red potatoes, scrubbed and quartered

½ pound green beans, trimmed

1 pound yellow fin tuna, cut into 1½-inch chunks

2 tablespoons balsamic vinegar

2 tablespoons low-sodium vegetable or chicken broth

1 tablespoon extra-virgin olive oil

1 garlic clove, minced

½ teaspoon freshly ground pepper

2 large heads Boston or Bibb lettuce, leaves separated and rinsed

16 red and yellow cherry tomatoes

8 small Niçoise olives

2 hard-cooked eggs, peeled and halved

1 tablespoon tiny capers, rinsed and drained

Parsley sprigs for garnish

---

COOK'S HINT COOK'S HINT **olives** COOK'S HINT COOK'S HINT COOK'S HINT

Niçoise olives, only available in gourmet or specialty stores, are worth hunting down; their delicate flavor is incomparable. If you can't find them, substitute any other oil-cured black olive.

# chicken and sugar-snap pea salad with mint-lemon dressing [20]

**4 POINTS** PER SERVING | MAKES 4 SERVINGS

*Aside from their crunchy texture and great flavor, sugar-snap peas and snow peas are terrific because they are easy to prepare. No peeling or scraping is necessary; just rinse them, pinch off their stem ends, and eat raw or cook the whole pea, pod and all.*

1 pound skinless boneless chicken breasts, cut into chunks

½ teaspoon salt

¼ teaspoon freshly ground pepper

1 pound fresh sugar-snap peas

¼ cup plain low-fat yogurt

2 tablespoons light sour cream

1 tablespoon minced mint

1 teaspoon grated lemon zest

2 teaspoons fresh lemon juice

1 head green-leaf lettuce, cleaned and separated into leaves

1 (7-ounce) jar roasted red peppers, drained

**1. Spray a large nonstick skillet** with nonstick spray and set over medium-high heat. Add the chicken; sprinkle with the salt and pepper and sauté until the chicken is just cooked through, but still moist, about 8 minutes.

**2. Place the sugar-snap peas** in a steamer basket; set in a saucepan over 1-inch of boiling water. Cover tightly and steam the peas until crisp-tender, 2–3 minutes. Drain and transfer the peas to a large bowl of ice water. Cool the peas for 1 minute and then drain on layers of paper towels.

**3. Combine** the yogurt, sour cream, mint, lemon zest, and lemon juice in a small bowl. Arrange the lettuce on a large serving platter. Top with the chicken, snap peas, and the roasted red peppers. Drizzle with the dressing.

**PER SERVING: 215 CALORIES**
4g total fat, 1g saturated fat, 65mg cholesterol, 477mg sodium, 13g total carbohydrate, 5g dietary fiber, 30g protein, 118mg calcium

COOK'S HINT COOK'S HINT **spring vegetables** COOK'S HINT COOK'S HINT COOK'S HINT

If you can't find fresh sugar-snap peas, try using another fresh, no-**POINTS** spring vegetable, such as snow peas or asparagus (trimmed and cut into 2-inch lengths). Or, use 2 (9-ounce) packages frozen sugar-snap peas.

# exotic winter fruit salad ⟨20

**4 POINTS** PER SERVING | MAKES 4 SERVINGS

*Unusual fruits from the southern hemisphere or southern United States are available in our supermarkets in winter time. Passion fruit, native to Brazil, has a dark purple skin and golden flesh, studded with edible black seeds. To use, simply cut the fruit in half, scoop out the flesh and seeds, and stir them into the salad. If you can't find all of the fruits listed in this recipe, be adventurous and try something else that's available.*

1. **Cut the pomegranate** into quarters. Peel back the skin and carefully scrape the seeds into a large bowl, leaving the yellow pith and skin behind.

2. **Toss the pomegranate seeds** with the oranges, kiwi fruit, grapes, mango, persimmon, and passion fruit. Sprinkle with the Grand Marnier and orange juice; toss well.

3. **Transfer the fruit salad** to a clear glass bowl and garnish with the mint.

**PER SERVING (1½ CUPS): 237 CALORIES**
1g total fat, 0g saturated fat, 0mg cholesterol, 7mg sodium, 56g total carbohydrate, 8g dietary fiber, 3g protein, 58mg calcium

1 pomegranate

2 navel oranges, cut into sections

2 kiwi fruit, peeled and sliced

2 cups seedless red or green grapes

1 mango, peeled and cubed

1 persimmon, peeled and cubed

1 passion fruit, halved, flesh and seeds scooped out

3 tablespoons Grand Marnier or 1 tablespoon vanilla extract

2 tablespoons fresh orange juice

Mint sprigs, to garnish

COOK'S HINT COOK'S HINT **pomegranates** COOK'S HINT COOK'S HINT COOK'S HINT

Look for pomegranates from October through December; their tart-sweet flavor and festive red color add sparkle to any dish.

# simple chicken soup [20]

**5 POINTS** PER SERVING | MAKES 4 SERVINGS

*Nostalgia in a bowl! All you need is a crusty bread for dipping and a crisp salad on the side. By all means, use this basic recipe as a guide for making your own version of chicken soup. You can add any variety of leftover rice, and substitute other favorite vegetables such as mushrooms, peas, spinach, bell pepper, or zucchini for the carrot and tomatoes.*

4 cups reduced-sodium chicken broth

2 scallions, trimmed and thinly sliced

1 garlic clove, finely chopped

¼ teaspoon salt

⅛ teaspoon freshly ground pepper

¾ pound skinless boneless chicken breasts, cut into bite-size pieces

1 carrot, thinly sliced

2 ripe plum tomatoes, seeded and finely chopped

2 cups cooked brown basmati rice

**1. Combine** the broth, scallions, garlic, salt, and pepper in a large saucepan; bring to a boil.

**2. Add the chicken** and carrot. Reduce the heat and simmer until the chicken is just cooked through, about 5 minutes. Add the tomatoes and rice. Simmer just until heated through, about 2 minutes.

**PER SERVING (1½ CUPS): 262 CALORIES**
5g total fat, 1g saturated fat, 47mg cholesterol, 685mg sodium, 27g total carbohydrate, 3g dietary fiber, 26g protein, 43mg calcium

COOK'S HINT COOK'S HINT **variations** COOK'S HINT COOK'S HINT COOK'S HINT COOK'S HINT

For a Tex-Mex touch, add 1 teaspoon chile powder and ½ teaspoon ground cumin with the broth, substitute corn kernels for the rice, and sprinkle the soup with cilantro. For Italian flavor, add 2 tablespoons minced basil along with the tomatoes and rice. To give the soup an Asian edge, add 2 teaspoons soy sauce (omit the salt), ¼ teaspoon Asian (dark) sesame oil, and a pinch of Chinese five-spice powder to the broth along with the scallions and garlic.

# cabbage soup with kielbasa

*2 POINTS* PER SERVING | MAKES 6 SERVINGS

*Satisfy a hearty appetite with a bowl of this warm, comforting main-dish soup, served with slices of sourdough or rye bread on the side.*

1. **Heat the oil** in a very large saucepan, then add the onion. Sauté until translucent, 3–5 minutes. Add the kielbasa and garlic; sauté until fragrant, about 2 minutes. Add the water, bay leaf, salt, thyme, marjoram, and pepper; bring to a boil. Reduce the heat and simmer, partially covered, about 15 minutes.

2. **Stir in** the cabbage, potato, carrot, and vinegar; return to a boil. Reduce the heat and simmer, partially covered, until all of the vegetables are very tender, about 30 minutes. Discard the bay leaf.

PER SERVING (GENEROUS 1 CUP): 125 CALORIES
3g total fat, 1g saturated fat, 11mg cholesterol, 659mg sodium, 20g total carbohydrate, 4g dietary fiber, 7g protein, 81mg calcium

2 teaspoons olive oil

1 onion, finely chopped

6 ounces low-fat kielbasa, thinly sliced

3 garlic cloves, minced

8 cups water

1 bay leaf

1 teaspoon salt

¼ teaspoon dried thyme

¼ teaspoon dried marjoram

⅛ teaspoon freshly ground pepper

1 small head cabbage, shredded (8 cups)

1 (8-ounce) all-purpose potato, peeled and coarsely shredded

1 large carrot, coarsely shredded

1 tablespoon cider vinegar

COOK'S HINT COOK'S HINT COOK'S HINT **sodium** COOK'S HINT COOK'S HINT COOK'S HINT COOK'S HINT

If you're watching your sodium intake, and if you have time, let the soup sit for about 20 minutes before serving. You'll probably find you don't need as much salt after all the flavors have fully developed. Then reheat and serve.

# cod chowder [20]

*5 POINTS* PER SERVING | MAKES 4 SERVINGS

*If you're in a time crunch, you can make the base for this soup ahead of time. Prepare the recipe through step 1, then cover and refrigerate for up to 2 days. When you are ready, bring the soup to a boil, then proceed with step 2. You can substitute any firm, white-fleshed fish such as scrod, haddock, snapper, tilefish, monkfish, grouper, sea bass, or tilapia for the cod.*

2 teaspoons olive oil

1 onion, finely chopped

1 pound all-purpose potatoes, peeled and chopped

2 cups reduced-sodium chicken broth

1 (6-ounce) bottle clam juice

½ teaspoon dried thyme

½ teaspoon fennel seeds, crushed

1 (14½-ounce) can diced tomatoes in juice

1 pound cod fillet or other firm white fish, cut into 1-inch pieces

1. Heat the oil in a large saucepan, then add the onion. Sauté until translucent, 3–5 minutes. Add the potatoes, broth, clam juice, thyme, and fennel; bring to a boil. Reduce the heat and simmer, partially covered, until the potatoes are just tender, 8–10 minutes.

2. Add the tomatoes and cod to the saucepan. Simmer, stirring occasionally, until the fish is just opaque in the center, 3–5 minutes.

**PER SERVING (1½ CUPS): 263 CALORIES**
5g total fat, 1g saturated fat, 62mg cholesterol, 604mg sodium, 28g total carbohydrate, 3g dietary fiber, 27g protein, 70mg calcium

# white bean soup with fresh tomatoes and basil [20]

*4 POINTS* PER SERVING | MAKES 4 SERVINGS

*If dinner on the table in 10 minutes sounds appealing to you, try this easy bean soup. It's quick and full of fresh flavors. Serve chunks of semolina bread and cut-up vegetables, such as carrots and celery, to round out the meal.*

**1. Heat a medium saucepan.** Swirl in the oil, then add the garlic and sauté until fragrant, about 30 seconds. Add the beans and broth. Transfer 1 cup of the mixture to a blender or food processor and purée until smooth.

**2. Return the purée** to the saucepan and bring the mixture to a boil. Reduce the heat and simmer, 4–5 minutes. Add the tomatoes and basil; simmer until heated through, 3–4 minutes. Serve with the cheese.

**PER SERVING (1 CUP): 196 CALORIES**
5g total fat, 2g saturated fat, 5mg cholesterol, 369mg sodium, 27g total carbohydrate, 8g dietary fiber, 12g protein, 144mg calcium

2 teaspoons olive oil

2 garlic cloves, minced

1 (19-ounce) can cannellini (white kidney) beans, rinsed and drained

2 cups low-sodium chicken broth

2 ripe plum tomatoes, seeded and chopped

¼ cup basil leaves, shredded, or 1 teaspoon dried

¼ cup grated Parmesan cheese

COOK'S HINT COOK'S HINT **SOUPS** COOK'S HINT COOK'S HINT COOK'S HINT

Puréeing some of the soup, as we have here, gives a creamy base, while keeping an interesting texture from the unpuréed ingredients. Try this trick to thicken any favorite soup, such as black bean or minestrone.

# curried red lentil soup

*3 POINTS* PER SERVING | MAKES 6 SERVINGS

*Red lentils, also known as Egyptian lentils, turn yellow when cooked and are quicker cooking than brown or green lentils. When cooked a little longer, they take on the consistency of split pea soup. You can use other types of lentils in this soup, but you'll need to allow additional cooking time. Top this hearty chill-chaser with a dollop of plain nonfat yogurt before serving, if you like.*

1 tablespoon olive oil

1 onion, finely chopped

1 carrot, finely chopped

1 garlic clove, minced

1 tablespoon curry powder

2 teaspoons minced peeled fresh ginger

⅛ teaspoon cayenne

4 cups reduced-sodium chicken broth

1 cup red lentils, picked over, rinsed, and drained

1 (14½-ounce) can diced tomatoes in juice

1 sweet or tart apple, finely chopped

1. Heat the oil in a large nonstick saucepan, then add the onion. Sauté until translucent, about 3 minutes. Add the carrot and sauté until softened, 3–5 minutes. Add the garlic, curry powder, ginger, and cayenne; sauté until fragrant, about 1 minute.

2. Stir in the broth, lentils, tomatoes, and apple; bring to a boil. Reduce the heat and simmer, until the lentils are very tender, about 20 minutes.

PER SERVING (1 CUP): 197 CALORIES
4g total fat, 1g saturated fat, 0mg cholesterol, 440mg sodium, 30g total carbohydrate, 10g dietary fiber, 13g protein, 56mg calcium

# creamy mushroom soup

**2 POINTS** PER SERVING | MAKES 6 SERVINGS

*This recipe makes a smooth and tasty soup from mushrooms, but you could easily substitute 2 to 3 cups of just about any chopped vegetable, such as broccoli, cauliflower, carrots, asparagus, celery, beets, green peas, winter squash, red bell pepper, or even more potatoes. Simply adjust the cooking time to be sure the vegetables are tender before you purée them.*

1. **Heat a large nonstick saucepan** over low-medium heat. Swirl in the butter. Add the onion and sauté until softened, 3–5 minutes. Add the mushrooms and garlic and sauté, stirring often, until the mushrooms start to wilt, about 5 minutes. Add the potato and broth; bring to a boil. Reduce the heat and simmer, partially covered, until the potatoes are very tender, 8–10 minutes.

2. **With a slotted spoon,** transfer the solids to a food processor or blender. Add about ½ cup of the broth and purée, scraping down the side of the container as needed. Stir the purée back into the saucepan. Add the milk and simmer until heated through, about 3 minutes.

**PER SERVING (1 CUP): 105 CALORIES**
3g total fat, 2g saturated fat, 7mg cholesterol, 358mg sodium, 13g total carbohydrate, 1g dietary fiber, 6g protein, 66mg calcium

1 tablespoon butter

1 onion, finely chopped

½ pound mushrooms, chopped

1 garlic clove, minced

1 (8-ounce) all-purpose potato, peeled and chopped

4 cups reduced-sodium chicken broth

1 cup low-fat (1%) milk

COOK'S HINT COOK'S HINT **variations** COOK'S HINT COOK'S HINT COOK'S HINT COOK'S HINT

Onion and garlic are a perfect seasoning base for most vegetable soups, but you can always add herbs and spices for additional flavor and variety. Try basil with peas, yellow summer squash, or zucchini; cilantro with carrots or red bell pepper; dill with beets, carrots, peas, or potatoes; rosemary with peas, spinach, or zucchini; or thyme with mushrooms.

# tomato egg-drop soup [20]

**2 POINTS** PER SERVING | MAKES 6 SERVINGS

*This quick, Cuban-style soup with built-in croutons is for garlic lovers only!*

2 teaspoons
extra-virgin olive oil

8 garlic cloves, minced

4 cups reduced-sodium
chicken broth

2 cups drained, chopped
canned tomatoes

1 bay leaf, broken in half

2 large eggs, lightly
beaten

6 (2-inch) slices Italian
bread, toasted

1 tablespoon
minced parsley

1. **Heat a large nonstick saucepan.** Swirl in the oil, then add the garlic and sauté, until golden, about 1 minute. Add the broth, tomatoes, and bay leaf; bring to a boil. Reduce the heat and simmer 20 minutes. Remove the bay leaf.

2. **With a fork,** slowly whisk in the eggs until they form fine shreds. Place a slice of toast in each soup bowl. Pour the soup gently over the bread and sprinkle with the parsley.

**PER SERVING (1 CUP): 109 CALORIES**
5g total fat, 1g saturated fat, 71mg cholesterol, 524mg sodium, 10g total carbohydrate, 1g dietary fiber, 7g protein, 50mg calcium

COOK'S HINT COOK'S HINT **egg-drop know-how** COOK'S HINT COOK'S HINT COOK'S HINT

Whether you're making a Cuban-style or Chinese-style egg-drop soup, the trick to getting fine pieces of egg throughout the soup is to slowly pour the eggs into the simmering broth, while stirring constantly with a fork.

# chinese velvet corn soup [20]

***3 POINTS*** PER SERVING | MAKES 4 SERVINGS

*For a heartier soup to serve as a main dish, add ¾ pound of lean ground pork, chicken, or turkey to the broth in step 1. Then add an additional teaspoon soy sauce and ¼ teaspoon Asian (dark) sesame oil to the broth with the meat.*

**1. Combine** the broth, soy sauce, and sesame oil in a medium saucepan; bring just to a boil.

**2. Slowly pour in the eggs,** stirring constantly with a fork to form shreds of egg. Stir in the corn and the spinach. Simmer until heated through, 3–5 minutes.

PER SERVING (1 CUP): 149 CALORIES
5g total fat, 1g saturated fat, 106mg cholesterol, 677mg sodium, 21g total carbohydrate, 3g dietary fiber, 9g protein, 50mg calcium

2 cups reduced-sodium chicken broth

1 teaspoon reduced-sodium soy sauce

¼ teaspoon Asian (dark) sesame oil

2 large eggs, lightly beaten

1 (14½-ounce) can cream-style corn

2 cups torn fresh spinach leaves or ½ (10-ounce) box frozen chopped spinach, thawed and squeezed dry

# green gazpacho

**2 POINTS** PER SERVING | MAKES 8 SERVINGS

*Like traditional red gazpacho, cool green gazpacho is a refreshing blend of fresh vegetables and herbs. You can substitute white balsamic or sherry vinegar for the white-wine vinegar, if you like, and add a dash or two of hot pepper sauce if you want more spice.*

2 slices oatmeal bread

2 cucumbers, peeled, seeded and coarsely chopped

2 cups watercress leaves

½ cup cilantro sprigs

¼ cup flat-leaf parsley sprigs

1 small garlic clove, chopped

1 yellow bell pepper, seeded and cut into chunks

3 scallions, trimmed and coarsely chopped

1 celery stalk, peeled, and cut into chunks

1 jalapeño pepper, seeded and minced (wear gloves to prevent irritation)

4 cups low-sodium vegetable broth

2 tablespoons olive oil

¼ cup white wine vinegar

½ teaspoon salt

¼ teaspoon freshly ground pepper

1. Soak the bread in enough cold water to cover in a medium bowl, for 5 minutes. Squeeze out and discard the excess water. Combine the soaked bread, cucumbers, watercress, cilantro, parsley, and garlic in a food processor; pulse until almost puréed. Spoon into a large bowl.

2. Combine the bell pepper, scallions, celery, and jalapeño pepper in the same food processor. Pulse until coarsely chopped. Add to the cucumber mixture. Stir in the broth, oil, vinegar, salt, and pepper. Refrigerate for at least several hours or overnight and serve chilled.

PER SERVING (1 CUP): 72 CALORIES
4g total fat, 1g saturated fat, 0mg cholesterol, 186mg sodium, 9g total carbohydrate, 1g dietary fiber, 2g protein, 36mg calcium

COOK'S HINT COOK'S HINT **vegetables** COOK'S HINT COOK'S HINT COOK'S HINT

To seed a cucumber, peel it first, then cut it in half lengthwise and scoop out the seeds with a teaspoon. To peel a celery stalk, snap back the wide end and gently pull down to remove the strings and tough outer skin. Use a small sharp knife to peel off any skin and strings that remain.

Beef Tenderloin and Arugula Toasts, Mini Crab Cakes with Dill Mayonnaise, Creamy Guacamole in Endive, Beggar's Purse Mediterranean

Tomato and Olive Tart. Opposite: Asian Sesame Noodles.

Stacked Boston Lettuce with Fennel, Blue Cheese, and Toasted Walnuts.
Opposite: Baked Apples with Cheddar and Walnuts.

Oven-Roasted Salade Niçoise. Opposite: Green Gazpacho.

Exotic Winter Fruit Salad

# brunch & lunch

tostada brunch  potato, pepper, and egg scramble

bacon, tomato, and cheese strata

banana-raisin bread pudding  baked orange french toast

cinnamon-peach and almond pancakes

berry parfait with ricotta cream

salmon cakes with dill tartar sauce

grilled salmon with roasted corn salad  pan bagna

chinese chicken and cabbage slaw

asian noodles with vegetables and shredded pork

orzo salad with ham and peas

grilled lamb kebabs and red lentil salad

roasted vegetable wraps

# tostada brunch [20]

**4 POINTS** PER SERVING | MAKES 4 SERVINGS

*A Mexican classic made healthy, this recipe is perfect for a crowd or a casual weekend brunch or supper. To save time, use 2 cups frozen, cubed potatoes, thawed, instead of the baking potato.*

2 plum tomatoes, chopped

3 tablespoons finely chopped red onion

2 tablespoons chopped cilantro

1 tablespoon red wine vinegar

1 teaspoon extra-virgin olive oil

½ teaspoon salt

⅛ teaspoon freshly ground pepper

1 large baking potato, peeled, diced, cooked

2 ounces lean ham, chopped

2 cups fat-free egg substitute

4 (6-inch) fat-free flour tortillas, warmed

Cilantro sprigs, to garnish

1. **Combine** the tomatoes, onion, chopped cilantro, vinegar, oil, ¼ teaspoon of the salt, and the pepper in a bowl.

2. **Spray a nonstick skillet** with nonstick spray and set over medium heat. Add the potato and ham; cook, shaking the pan often, until the potatoes and ham are browned, about 5 minutes. Transfer to a bowl and keep warm.

3. **Wipe the skillet clean,** spray with nonstick spray, and set over medium heat. Add the egg substitute and the remaining ¼ teaspoon salt. Cook, stirring constantly, until the eggs are set, about 4 minutes.

4. **Top the tortillas** with the eggs, then the potato mixture, then the tomato mixture. Garnish with the cilantro sprigs.

**PER SERVING: 202 CALORIES**
2g total fat, 0g saturated fat, 8mg cholesterol, 756mg sodium, 29g total carbohydrate, 3g dietary fiber, 16g protein, 83mg calcium

COOK'S HINT COOK'S HINT **tortillas** COOK'S HINT COOK'S HINT COOK'S HINT COOK'S HINT

To warm tortillas, stack them on a microwavable plate; cover with damp paper towels and microwave on High for about 30 seconds.

# potato, pepper, and egg scramble [20]

*2 POINTS* PER SERVING | MAKES 4 SERVINGS

*This simple scramble is a one-skillet, meal-in-minutes that's easy on POINTS and your budget. Green frying peppers, also known as cubanelle peppers, are long, pale green, and banana-shaped with a mild, sweet flavor. If green or red bell peppers are more readily available, by all means, use them as a substitute.*

**1. Heat the oil** in a large nonstick skillet, then add the frying peppers and onion. Sauté until softened, about 8 minutes. Stir in the potato. Cook, until the flavors are blended, about 5 minutes. Transfer to a bowl; wipe the skillet clean.

**2. Spray the same skillet** with nonstick spray and set over medium heat. Add the egg substitute, parsley, salt, and ground pepper; cook until almost set, stirring often, about 3 minutes. Stir in the frying pepper mixture; heat through.

PER SERVING: 134 CALORIES
2g total fat, 0g saturated fat, 0mg cholesterol, 452mg sodium, 17g total carbohydrate, 3g dietary fiber, 11g protein, 54mg calcium

2 teaspoons olive oil

3 green frying peppers (¾ pound), seeded and chopped

1 small onion, thinly sliced

1 large baking potato, peeled, cubed, cooked

2 cups fat-free egg substitute

1 tablespoon chopped parsley

½ teaspoon salt

¼ teaspoon freshly ground pepper

# bacon, tomato, and cheese strata

**5 POINTS** PER SERVING | MAKES 8 SERVINGS

*A strata is a savory bread pudding that boasts rich layers of bread, cheese, and any variety of vegetables; meat can also make an appearance. Be as creative as you like, substituting ingredients that strike your fancy or choosing whatever looks freshest at your market.*

1 teaspoon canola oil

2 onions, thinly sliced

8 slices turkey bacon, chopped

1 large tomato, chopped

2 cups fat-free milk

3 large eggs

3 egg whites

½ teaspoon salt

½ teaspoon dried thyme

16 slices reduced-calorie stone-ground wheat bread, cut into ½-inch cubes

6 ounces reduced-fat Jarlsberg cheese, shredded

1. Spray a 9 x 13-inch baking dish with nonstick spray.

2. Heat the oil in a large nonstick skillet, then add the onions and bacon. Sauté until the onions are softened, about 8 minutes. Remove from the heat; stir in the tomato.

3. Whisk together the milk, eggs, egg whites, salt, and thyme in a bowl until blended. Arrange half the bread cubes in the baking dish; top with half the onion mixture and half the cheese. Pour half the milk mixture over the cheese. Repeat with the remaining bread, onion mixture, cheese, and milk mixture. Cover and chill at least 1 hour or overnight.

4. Preheat the oven to 350°F.

5. Bake, uncovered, until puffed and golden, and a knife inserted in the center comes out clean, about 1 hour. Let stand 5 minutes before serving.

**PER SERVING:** 250 CALORIES
9g total fat, 4g saturated fat, 104mg cholesterol, 747mg sodium, 27g total carbohydrate, 6g dietary fiber, 19g protein, 285mg calcium

COOK'S HINT COOK'S HINT **chill out** COOK'S HINT COOK'S HINT COOK'S HINT COOK'S HINT

We recommend chilling the uncooked strata at least 1 hour or overnight. Letting the strata stand overnight in the refrigerator blends the flavors and allows time for the bread to absorb the liquid. You can apply this trick to any sweet or savory bread pudding.

# banana-raisin bread pudding

*7 POINTS* PER SERVING | MAKES 6 SERVINGS

*While bread puddings are typically served as a dessert, we think this sweet recipe makes a lovely weekend breakfast. Serve it warm with a refreshing bowl of fresh, sliced strawberries, orange wedges, or thick slices of cantaloupe or honeydew melon.*

**1. Preheat the oven** to 350°F. Spray a 9 x 13-inch baking dish with nonstick spray.

**2. Whisk together** the milk, half-and-half, eggs, egg whites, vanilla, cinnamon, and nutmeg in a large bowl until blended. Stir in the bread and banana; let soak 15 minutes, stirring occasionally.

**3. Spoon the bread mixture** into the baking dish. Bake until a knife inserted in the center comes out clean and the top is lightly browned, about 1 hour. Sprinkle with confectioners' sugar. Serve at once.

PER SERVING: 336 CALORIES
7g total fat, 2g saturated fat, 110mg cholesterol, 426mg sodium, 52g total carbohydrate, 4g dietary fiber, 13g protein, 222mg calcium

2 cups low-fat (1%) milk

1 cup fat-free half-and-half

3 large eggs

2 egg whites

1 teaspoon vanilla extract

1 teaspoon cinnamon

⅛ teaspoon nutmeg

1 (16-ounce) loaf raisin bread, cut into 1-inch chunks

1 medium banana, sliced

1 tablespoon confectioners' sugar

# baked orange french toast

**7 POINTS** PER SERVING | MAKES 6 SERVINGS

*Challah bread, a traditional Jewish yeast bread with a light, airy texture, transforms deliciously into superb French toast. Look for it in your local bakery, Jewish deli, or supermarket.*

1¾ cups low-fat (1%) milk

¼ cup orange juice

3 large eggs

2 egg whites

2 tablespoons sugar

1 tablespoon cinnamon

1 tablespoon grated orange zest

1 teaspoon vanilla extract

1 pound loaf Challah bread, cut into twelve slices

1 orange, sectioned

1 cup raspberries

1 cup blueberries

1 cup strawberries, sliced

2 tablespoons maple syrup

**1. Preheat the oven** to 425°F. Spray 2 jelly-roll pans with nonstick spray.

**2. Whisk together** the milk, orange juice, eggs, egg whites, sugar, cinnamon, orange zest, and vanilla in a large bowl. Add the bread, two pieces at a time, and soak, turning, until saturated, about 1 minute. Place the soaked bread on the pans. Bake until slightly puffed and browned, about 12 minutes on each side.

**3. Meanwhile, combine** the orange, raspberries, blueberries, strawberries, and maple syrup in a bowl. Serve with the French toast.

PER SERVING (2 PIECES FRENCH TOAST AND ½ CUP FRUIT): 79 CALORIES 8g total fat, 2g saturated fat, 142mg cholesterol, 223mg sodium, 63g total carbohydrate, 5g dietary fiber, 14g protein, 179mg calcium

COOK'S HINT COOK'S HINT **oranges** COOK'S HINT COOK'S HINT COOK'S HINT COOK'S HINT

To section an orange, use a sharp paring knife and slice away the top and bottom ends of the orange. Position the orange upright on a chopping board and carefully slice away the rind, removing all of the pith. Working over a large bowl to catch the juices, cut the orange sections out from between the membranes, letting each one fall into the bowl, as you cut it free. Discard seeds.

# cinnamon-peach and almond pancakes

**7 POINTS** PER SERVING | MAKES 4 SERVINGS

*Canned peaches, pears, or apricots, drained well and coarsely chopped to make 1 cup are a convenient substitute for the fresh peaches called for in this kid-pleasing recipe. Fresh ripe nectarines, pears, apricots, or apples also work.*

1. **Melt the butter** in a nonstick skillet, then add the peaches, 1 teaspoon sugar, and the cinnamon. Sauté until the peaches are tender, about 4 minutes.

2. **Meanwhile, combine** the baking mix, almonds, milk, egg, vanilla, and the remaining 2 tablespoons sugar in a bowl. Stir just until blended.

3. **Spray a large nonstick skillet** or griddle with nonstick spray and heat until a drop of water sizzles. Pour the batter, by ¼ cup measures into the skillet. Place a tablespoon of the peach mixture in the center of each pancake. Cook just until bubbles begin to appear at the edges of the pancakes, 2–3 minutes. Flip and cook 2 minutes longer. Repeat with the remaining batter, making a total of 12 pancakes.

**PER SERVING (3 PANCAKES):** 342 CALORIES
9g total fat, 3g saturated fat, 61mg cholesterol, 723mg sodium, 53g total carbohydrate, 2g dietary fiber, 9g protein, 160mg calcium

2 teaspoons butter

2 small ripe peaches, peeled and chopped

2 tablespoons plus 1 teaspoon sugar

½ teaspoon cinnamon

2 cups reduced-fat all-purpose baking mix

1 tablespoon sliced almonds

1¼ cups low-fat (1%) milk

1 large egg, lightly beaten

1 teaspoon vanilla extract

# berry parfait with ricotta cream [20]

**5 *POINTS*** PER SERVING | MAKES 6 SERVINGS

*The sweet, creamy ricotta mixture—reminiscent of the filling typically used in the Italian pastry cannoli—is layered with fresh, maple-glazed berries for this sophisticated treat. For those who insist on a touch of sweet chocolate, a few mini-chocolate chips can be folded into the cream or sprinkled on top. Or, for a more authentic Italian touch, add a few teaspoons of chopped candied citron.*

1 cup raspberries

1 cup blueberries

2 tablespoons maple syrup

1 tablespoon chopped mint

1 (15-ounce) container part-skim ricotta cheese

3 tablespoons confectioners' sugar

1 teaspoon grated lemon zest

½ teaspoon cinnamon

⅛ teaspoon nutmeg

6 frozen cinnamon waffles, thawed, toasted and cut into strips

**1. Combine** the raspberries, blueberries, maple syrup, and mint in a bowl. Let stand 5 minutes.

**2. Purée** the ricotta cheese, confectioners' sugar, lemon zest, cinnamon, and nutmeg in a food processor. Alternately layer the berry mixture with the ricotta cream, ending with the berries, in six 6-ounce parfait glasses. Serve with the waffle strips.

**PER SERVING: 213 CALORIES**
8g total fat, 4g saturated fat, 28mg cholesterol, 265mg sodium, 27g total carbohydrate, 2g dietary fiber, 10g protein, 225mg calcium

COOK'S HINT COOK'S HINT **seasonal fruit** COOK'S HINT COOK'S HINT COOK'S HINT

Substitute 2 cups of any fresh fruit that's in season for the raspberries and blueberries.

# salmon cakes
# with dill tartar sauce

*6 POINTS* PER SERVING | MAKES 4 SERVINGS

*Not only are the cakes elegant and delicious, they also tout the nutritional powerhouse, canned salmon. When you eat the bones (which are soft and edible), a serving of canned salmon has more calcium than a glass of milk. Simply mash the bones along with the salmon and other ingredients.*

1. **To prepare the sauce,** combine the ¼ cup mayonnaise, the relish, 2 teaspoons dill, the lemon zest, lemon juice, and hot sauce in a small bowl. Cover and chill under ready to serve.

2. **To prepare the salmon cakes,** mash the salmon and the bones with a fork in a bowl. Add the 6 tablespoons mayonnaise, the celery, 3 tablespoons bread crumbs, the onion, and 3 tablespoons dill. Shape into 4 patties. Cover and refrigerate 1 hour.

3. **Place the remaining ¼ cup** bread crumbs on a sheet of wax paper. Dredge the patties in the crumbs. Heat the oil in a nonstick skillet, then add the patties. Cook until crisp and golden, about 5 minutes on each side. Serve with the tartar sauce.

PER SERVING (1 SALMON CAKE AND GENEROUS 1 TABLESPOON SAUCE):
248 CALORIES
9g total fat, 2g saturated fat, 57mg cholesterol, 984mg sodium, 18g total carbohydrate,
1g dietary fiber, 22g protein, 257mg calcium

¼ cup + 6 tablespoons
nonfat mayonnaise

1 tablespoon
sweet pickle relish

2 teaspoons + 3
tablespoons chopped dill

1 teaspoon grated
lemon zest

1 teaspoon fresh
lemon juice

Dash hot pepper sauce

1 (14¾-ounce) can
salmon, drained

1 celery stalk,
finely chopped

3 tablespoons + ¼ cup
plain dry bread crumbs

3 tablespoons
grated onion

2 teaspoons canola oil

# grilled salmon with roasted corn salad

**7 POINTS** PER SERVING | MAKES 4 SERVINGS

*Roasting corn brings its flavor to a deliciously intense, sweet level. For an extra kick, just before roasting, toss the corn with a little chili powder and cumin. For a spectacular presentation, serve the salmon on top of the corn salad.*

3 cups fresh corn kernels or 2 (10-ounce) packages frozen corn, thawed and drained

1 red bell pepper, seeded and finely chopped

4 scallions, thinly sliced

½ cup chopped cilantro

1 jalapeño pepper, seeded, deveined, and minced (wear gloves to prevent irritation)

3 tablespoons cider vinegar

1 tablespoon honey

1 tablespoon olive oil

1 teaspoon Dijon mustard

¾ teaspoon salt

4 (5-ounce) salmon fillets

1. **Preheat the oven** to 425°F. Spray a baking sheet with nonstick spray. Spread the corn on the baking sheet. Roast, stirring occasionally, until lightly browned, about 20 minutes; cool completely.

2. **Meanwhile, combine** the bell pepper, scallions, cilantro, jalapeño pepper, vinegar, honey, 2 teaspoons of the oil, the mustard, and ¼ teaspoon of the salt in a large bowl. Stir in the corn. Cover and chill until ready to serve.

3. **Rub the salmon steaks** with the remaining 1 teaspoon oil and remaining ½ teaspoon salt. Heat a nonstick ridged grill pan or skillet over medium-high heat. Cook the salmon until browned on the outside and just opaque in the center, about 4 minutes on each side.

PER SERVING (1 CUP SALAD): 363 CALORIES
12g total fat, 3g saturated fat, 93mg cholesterol, 547mg sodium, 33g total carbohydrate, 4g dietary fiber, 34g protein, 40mg calcium

COOK'S HINT COOK'S HINT COOK'S HINT **fresh corn** COOK'S HINT COOK'S HINT COOK'S HINT COOK'S HINT COOK'S HINT

Fresh corn kernels cut from the cob are delicious. Buy fresh corn locally in the summer months, or look for it in supermarkets from May right on through summer (it's usually shipped from Florida and sold at a very reasonable price). To remove the kernels from the cobs, stand the cobs upright on a cutting board and with a sharp knife, working from top to bottom, scrape away the kernels. One ear of fresh corn yields about ½ cup kernels. For this recipe you will need about 6 ears.

# pan bagna [20]

**7 POINTS** PER SERVING | MAKES 4 SERVINGS

*Pan Bagna, traditionally made with canned tuna, is a French version of the American submarine sandwich. Here, we've transformed it from a lowly tuna sub into a far more elegant salmon sandwich. Sliced grilled chicken breast also works deliciously in place of the tuna.*

**1. Mash the salmon,** including its bones, the vinegar, capers, parsley, olives, and lemon juice in a bowl until blended.

**2. Slice the baguette** lengthwise almost all the way through; spread open. Layer with the lettuce, tomato, and onion, then top with salmon mixture. Close the bread, then cut into 4 sandwiches.

**PER SERVING (1 SANDWICH): 347 CALORIES**
10g total fat, 2g saturated fat, 57mg cholesterol, 1140mg sodium, 38g total carbohydrate, 6g dietary fiber, 28g protein, 294mg calcium

1 (14¾-ounce) can salmon, drained

¼ cup red wine vinegar

2 tablespoons capers, drained and chopped

2 tablespoons chopped parsley

8 kalamata olives, pitted and chopped

1 tablespoon fresh lemon juice

1 (10-ounce) whole-wheat baguette

4 green leaf lettuce leaves

1 tomato, cut into 8 slices

½ red onion, thinly sliced

COOK'S HINT COOK'S HINT **storing** COOK'S HINT COOK'S HINT COOK'S HINT COOK'S HINT

If you'd like to take this sandwich to a picnic, do not cut it. Rather, wrap the whole filled baguette securely with plastic wrap and store in your refrigerator. Bring it as is to the picnic, then slice just before serving.

# chinese chicken and cabbage slaw [20]

**5 POINTS** PER SERVING | MAKES 4 SERVINGS

*Light, refreshing, and so easy to prepare, napa or Chinese cabbage adds crisp texture and delicate flavor to stir-fries and salads. If you like, substitute turkey breast, pork cutlets, or a beef flank steak for the chicken.*

½ teaspoon canola oil

4 (¼-pound) skinless boneless chicken breasts

2 tablespoons seasoned rice vinegar

1 tablespoon reduced-sodium soy sauce

1 tablespoon honey

1 tablespoon Asian (dark) sesame oil

1 teaspoon grated peeled fresh ginger

1 small head napa cabbage, finely shredded

1 small head radicchio, finely shredded

1 cup shredded carrots

3 scallions, thinly sliced diagonally

1. **Heat the oil** in a nonstick skillet, then add the chicken. Sauté until browned and cooked through, about 4 minutes on each side. Transfer to a plate; let rest 5 minutes, then thinly slice on the diagonal.

2. **Meanwhile, whisk together** the vinegar, soy sauce, honey, sesame oil, and ginger in a large bowl until blended. Add the cabbage, radicchio, carrots, scallions and the chicken; toss to coat.

**PER SERVING (1¼ CUPS): 216 CALORIES**
7g total fat, 1g saturated fat, 62mg cholesterol, 257mg sodium, 11g total carbohydrate, 2g dietary fiber, 26g protein, 90mg calcium

COOK'S HINT COOK'S HINT **time saver** COOK'S HINT COOK'S HINT COOK'S HINT COOK'S HINT

If you're in a time crunch, use 3 cups of pre-packaged coleslaw mix instead of the napa cabbage, and 1 cup pre-shredded carrots that are sold in 10-ounce bags in the produce section of your market.

# asian noodles with vegetables and shredded pork

**5 POINTS** PER SERVING | MAKES 4 SERVINGS

*Long, thin, translucent rice noodles are easy to prepare because they require no boiling; you simply soak them in hot water for a few minutes then drain. Look for them in the Asian section of your supermarket or in Asian markets. Angel-hair pasta or vermicelli make fine substitutes, but they require a bit more cooking.*

1. **Whisk together** the broth, cornstarch, soy sauce, sugar, and sesame oil in a small bowl.

2. **Heat 1 teaspoon** of the canola oil in a large nonstick skillet over high heat, then add the pork. Sauté until browned, about 5 minutes. Stir in the ginger and garlic. Sauté, stirring occasionally, until fragrant, about 1 minute; transfer to a bowl. Wipe the skillet clean.

3. **Meanwhile, plunge the noodles** in the hot water. Let stand 10 minutes; drain.

4. **Heat the remaining 1 teaspoon** canola oil in the skillet, then add the cabbage, mushrooms, and carrots. Cook until the cabbage begins to wilt and the vegetables are tender, about 6 minutes. Stir in the pork mixture and the broth mixture; bring to a boil, stirring constantly. Reduce the heat and simmer, uncovered, until the sauce begins to thicken, about 2 minutes. Stir in the noodles.

**PER SERVING (1¼ CUPS): 232 CALORIES**
6g total fat, 1g saturated fat, 36mg cholesterol, 358mg sodium, 28g total carbohydrate, 3g dietary fiber, 16g protein, 51mg calcium

½ cup low-sodium chicken broth

2 tablespoons cornstarch

2 tablespoons reduced-sodium soy sauce

1 teaspoon sugar

1 teaspoon Asian (dark) sesame oil

2 teaspoons canola oil

½ pound pork tenderloin, sliced crosswise and cut into thin strips

2 teaspoons grated peeled fresh ginger

1 garlic clove, minced

3½ ounces thin rice noodles (½ of a 7-ounce package)

8 cups hot water

1 (½-pound) head savoy cabbage, thinly sliced

6 ounces white mushrooms, sliced

2 carrots, finely chopped

# orzo salad with ham and peas ◀ [20]

**4 POINTS** PER SERVING | MAKES 6 SERVINGS

*This springtime dish calls for grape tomatoes, tiny juicy gems that are smaller and much sweeter than the standard cherry tomatoes. If you like, add yellow pear tomatoes for a delightful contrast and presentation.*

1 cup orzo

2 cups fresh sugar snap peas

½ pound lean ham in one piece, cut into ½-inch chunks

1 cup grape tomatoes, cut in half

½ red onion, thinly sliced

3 tablespoons chopped parsley

3 tablespoons grated Parmesan cheese

3 tablespoons white wine vinegar

1 tablespoon extra-virgin olive oil

½ teaspoon salt

6 Boston lettuce leaves

**1. Cook the orzo** according to package directions. During the last 5 minutes of cooking, add the sugar snap peas. Drain; transfer to a large bowl.

**2. Add the ham,** tomatoes, onion, parsley, cheese, vinegar, oil, and salt; toss to coat. Spoon the mixture onto the lettuce leaves.

PER SERVING: 204 CALORIES
6g total fat, 2g saturated fat, 22mg cholesterol, 714mg sodium, 24g total carbohydrate, 3g dietary fiber, 14g protein, 78mg calcium

# grilled lamb kebabs and red lentil salad

*8 POINTS* PER SERVING | MAKES 4 SERVINGS

*This delectable recipe highlights several key ingredients frequently used in Middle Eastern cuisine. Red lentils add color and cook quicker than brown lentils. If watercress is unavailable, consider using chopped fresh arugula.*

1. **Bring the water,** lentils, carrots, onion, and garlic to a boil in a large saucepan. Reduce the heat and simmer, covered, until the lentils are tender, about 15 minutes. Drain.

2. **Meanwhile, whisk together** the vinegar, 2 teaspoons of the oil, the mustard, and ½ teaspoon of the salt in a large bowl until blended. Add the lentil mixture and watercress; toss to coat.

3. **Spray the broiler rack** with nonstick spray; preheat the broiler.

4. **Mix the lamb,** oregano, remaining 1 teaspoon olive oil, and remaining ½ teaspoon salt in a bowl until well coated. Thread the lamb onto 4 metal skewers. Broil 5 inches from the heat until the lamb is just cooked through, about 4 minutes on each side. Spoon the lentil mixture onto a platter and top with the kebabs.

**PER SERVING (1 KEBAB AND ¾ CUP LENTIL SALAD): 390 CALORIES**
12g total fat, 3g saturated fat, 75mg cholesterol, 681mg sodium, 35g total carbohydrate, 13g dietary fiber, 37g protein, 81mg calcium

4 cups water

1 cup red lentils, picked over, rinsed, and drained

2 carrots, chopped

1 onion, chopped

2 garlic cloves, chopped

2 tablespoons balsamic vinegar

1 tablespoon extra-virgin olive oil

1 teaspoon Dijon mustard

1 teaspoon salt

1 bunch watercress, cleaned and coarsely chopped (2 cups)

1 pound boneless lean lamb, trimmed of all visible fat, and cut into 1½-inch chunks

1 teaspoon dried oregano

# roasted vegetable wraps

***5 POINTS*** PER SERVING | MAKES 4 SERVINGS

*Wraps were all the rage towards the end of the last century—and we're still fans, thanks to their quick-meal appeal. These wraps will keep nicely for up to 1 hour at room temperature if you lay damp paper towels on top, then cover them with plastic wrap to prevent them from drying out.*

1 (1-pound) eggplant, cut into ¾-inch chunks

1 zucchini, cut into ¾-inch chunks

2 red bell peppers, seeded and cut into ¾-inch chunks

1 tablespoon extra-virgin olive oil

½ teaspoon salt

1 bunch arugula, cleaned and coarsely chopped

1 tomato, finely chopped

1 tablespoon red wine vinegar

2 ounces goat cheese, at room temperature

4 (8-inch) fat-free flour tortillas, warmed

1. Preheat the oven to 450°F. Spray a large roasting pan with nonstick spray.

2. Toss the eggplant, zucchini, bell peppers, 2 teaspoons of the oil, and the salt in a large bowl. Spread the vegetables in the pan. Roast, stirring occasionally, until the vegetables are tender and browned, about 40 minutes.

3. Meanwhile, combine the arugula, tomato, vinegar, and the remaining 1 teaspoon oil in a bowl.

4. Spread the goat cheese on the warmed tortillas. Divide the roasted vegetables and arugula mixture among the tortillas. Roll up, then cut diagonally in half.

PER SERVING (1 WRAP): 237 CALORIES
7g total fat, 3g saturated fat, 13mg cholesterol, 556mg sodium, 38g total carbohydrate, 6g dietary fiber, 8g protein, 176mg calcium

mediterranean roast chicken citrus broiled chicken
unfried chicken rosemary-garlic baked chicken
chicken and dumplings
lemon-crumb chicken grilled herbed chicken
goat cheese and herb-stuffed chicken breasts
chicken with fresh tomato sauce chicken parmesan
grapefruit chicken grilled chicken with diced beets and yellow pepper
curried chicken with apples and mango chutney
thai chicken with ginger sauce
thai coconut chicken
braised chicken with mushrooms chicken and broccoli pizza
chili chicken kebabs with yogurt sauce
barbecued chicken tostadas chinese chicken legs
turkey-stuffed cabbage rolls baked turkey and ziti casserole
turkey and cheddar burgers turkey chili verde
warm grilled turkey sausage and roasted potato salad

poultry

# mediterranean roast chicken

**6 POINTS** PER SERVING | MAKES 6 SERVINGS

*The roasting technique used for the chicken in this recipe is healthy—and flavorful. The potatoes and olives are cooked in a separate baking pan instead of alongside the chicken. Otherwise, the chicken fat would drip on to the potatoes creating calorie chaos! Add a salad and the meal is complete.*

1 tablespoon chopped thyme

1 teaspoon dried oregano

1 teaspoon olive oil

1 garlic clove, minced

½ teaspoon salt

1 (3½-pound) roasting chicken

1 lemon, quartered

1½ pounds large red potatoes, cut into wedges

8 kalamata olives, pitted

Thyme sprigs, to garnish

1. **Preheat the oven** to 400°F. Spray the rack of a roasting pan with nonstick spray and place in the pan. Spray a nonstick baking pan with nonstick spray.

2. **Combine** the chopped thyme, oregano, oil, garlic, and salt in a small bowl. Gently loosen the skin from the breast of the chicken. Spread the herb mixture evenly under the skin. Place the lemon inside the cavity of the chicken. Tuck the wings behind the chicken and tie the legs together with kitchen twine. Place the chicken, breast-side up, on the rack, in the roasting pan. Place the potatoes and olives in the baking pan.

3. **Roast the chicken** until an instant-read thermometer inserted in the thigh registers 180°F, about 1 hour and 10 minutes. During the last 45 minutes of roasting, place the potatoes and olives in the oven. Stir occasionally, until the potatoes are tender and browned.

4. **Let the chicken stand** 10 minutes. Discard the lemon, twine, and skin, then carve. Serve with the potatoes and olives. Garnish with the thyme sprigs.

**PER SERVING:** 280 CALORIES
7g total fat, 2g saturated fat, 77mg cholesterol, 320mg sodium, 23g total carbohydrate, 2g dietary fiber, 29g protein, 38mg calcium

COOK'S HINT COOK'S HINT **healthy roasting** COOK'S HINT COOK'S HINT COOK'S HINT

Leaving the skin on—while rubbing the herbs underneath it—traps in the flavor and keeps the chicken moist. Just before carving, remove the skin. Try any herb mixture you like—oregano, basil, or sage all work well.

# citrus broiled chicken

*6 POINTS* PER SERVING | MAKES 6 SERVINGS

*Try this zesty marinade of oranges, lemons, and honey for skinless boneless
chicken breast cubes or pork cubes to make into kebabs. Serve on a bed of
couscous mixed with a little chopped mint.*

1. Place the chicken, orange zest, orange juice, lemon juice, honey, mustard,
sugar, salt, and pepper in a large zip-close plastic bag. Squeeze out the
air and seal the bag; turn to coat the chicken. Refrigerate, turning the bag
occasionally, at least 1 hour or overnight.

2. Spray the broiler rack with nonstick spray. Preheat the broiler.

3. Remove the chicken from the marinade. Pat the chicken dry with paper
towels. Reserve the marinade.

4. Arrange the chicken on the broiler rack. Broil 7 inches from the heat,
turning frequently, until the chicken is browned and cooked though,
about 25 minutes.

5. Meanwhile, pour the marinade into a small saucepan; bring to a boil.
Boil, stirring occasionally, until the sauce thickens slightly, about 10 minutes.
Stir in the currants. Spoon the sauce over the chicken and sprinkle with the
mint. Serve with the orange and lemon wedges, if using.

PER SERVING: 262 CALORIES
7g total fat, 2g saturated fat, 86mg cholesterol, 312mg sodium, 19g total carbohydrate,
1g dietary fiber, 31g protein, 38mg calcium

1 (3½-pound) chicken,
cut in eighths, skin
removed

1 tablespoon grated
orange zest

¾ cup orange juice

3 tablespoons
fresh lemon juice

1 tablespoon honey

1 tablespoon
Dijon mustard

1 tablespoon packed
dark brown sugar

½ teaspoon salt

¼ teaspoon freshly
ground pepper

½ cup currants

¼ cup chopped mint

1 orange, cut into
wedges, optional

1 lemon, cut into wedges,
optional

# unfried chicken

*6 POINTS* PER SERVING | MAKES 6 SERVINGS

*This is the best "unfried" chicken you will ever have. The coating also works well on skinless boneless chicken tenders to make into chicken fingers for the kids. You might want to serve this with "unfried" fries: Slice two or three baking potatoes into ½-inch-thick strips, sprinkle them with a little salt and pepper, and bake on a greased baking sheet alongside the chicken.*

¼ cup reduced-calorie mayonnaise

1 teaspoon Dijon mustard

2 teaspoons grated lemon zest

½ teaspoon salt

4 drops hot pepper sauce

1 (3½-pound) chicken, cut in eighths, skin removed

¾ cup cornflake crumbs

1. **Preheat the oven** to 375°F. Spray a large, shallow baking pan with nonstick spray.

2. **Whisk together** the mayonnaise, mustard, lemon zest, salt, and pepper sauce in a large bowl. Add the chicken; toss to coat.

3. **Place the cornflake crumbs** in a large zip-close plastic bag. Add the chicken, one piece at a time, and shake to coat.

4. **Place the chicken** in the baking pan. Spray the top of the chicken lightly with nonstick spray. Bake until golden brown and cooked through (do not turn), about 45 minutes.

PER SERVING: 249 CALORIES
11g total fat, 3g saturated fat, 89mg cholesterol, 424mg sodium, 6g total carbohydrate, 0g dietary fiber, 30g protein, 23mg calcium

COOK'S HINT COOK'S HINT **cornflake crumbs** COOK'S HINT COOK'S HINT COOK'S HINT

If you can't find cornflake crumbs, simply make your own by placing regular cornflakes in a zip-close plastic bag; finely crush with a rolling pin. You'll need about 1¼ cups of the flakes to make ¾ cup crumbs.

# rosemary-garlic baked chicken

*5 POINTS* PER SERVING | MAKES 6 SERVINGS

*This tangy dish couldn't be simpler. Serve it with roasted potatoes and a green salad.*

1. **Preheat the oven** to 400°F. Spray a 9 x 13-inch baking pan with nonstick spray.

2. **Combine** the onion, vinegar, oil, mustard, rosemary, garlic, and salt in a small bowl.

3. **Place the chicken** in the baking pan. Spoon the onion mixture on top of the chicken. Bake until the chicken is browned and cooked through (do not turn), about 45 minutes.

**PER SERVING:** 217 CALORIES
9g total fat, 2g saturated fat, 86mg cholesterol, 309mg sodium, 2g total carbohydrate, 0g dietary fiber, 30g protein, 30mg calcium

1 small onion, chopped

¼ cup red wine vinegar

1 tablespoon olive oil

1 tablespoon Dijon mustard

1 tablespoon chopped fresh rosemary, or 1 teaspoon dried, chopped

2 garlic cloves, cut into thin slivers

½ teaspoon salt

1 (3½-pound) chicken, cut in eighths, skin removed

COOK'S HINT COOK'S HINT **rosemary** COOK'S HINT COOK'S HINT COOK'S HINT COOK'S HINT

If you're using dried rosemary, make sure to chop it well before adding it to the chicken. Spray the rosemary with a little nonstick spray before you begin chopping—this helps keep the herb on the cutting board.

# chicken and dumplings

**7 POINTS** PER SERVING | MAKES 6 SERVINGS

*Here, our rendition of an all-time favorite, hearty, one-pot, meal that is sure to please everyone.*

2 teaspoons canola oil

1 (3½-pound) chicken, cut in eighths, skin removed

½ teaspoon salt

1 onion, chopped

2 small carrots, chopped

2 small celery stalks, chopped

3 cups low-sodium chicken broth

1 cup frozen peas, thawed

1⅔ cups reduced-fat all-purpose baking mix

⅔ cup fat-free milk

1 tablespoon chopped parsley

1. **Heat the oil** in a nonstick Dutch oven, then add the chicken. Sprinkle with the salt and sauté until browned, about 6 minutes. Add the onion, carrots, and celery. Sauté, until the vegetables begin to soften and brown slightly, about 6 minutes. Add the broth; bring to a boil. Reduce the heat and simmer, covered, until the chicken is cooked through, about 35 minutes. Stir in the peas.

2. **Meanwhile, to prepare** the dumplings, combine the baking mix, milk, and parsley in a bowl until a soft dough forms.

3. **Drop the dough,** by rounded tablespoonfuls, onto the simmering stew. Simmer, uncovered, 10 minutes. Cover and cook until the dumplings have doubled in size and cooked through, about 10 minutes longer.

**PER SERVING** (1½ PIECES OF CHICKEN AND 1½ DUMPLINGS): 353 CALORIES 10g total fat, 2g saturated fat, 74mg cholesterol, 701mg sodium, 30g total carbohydrate, 3g dietary fiber, 32g protein, 102mg calcium

COOK'S HINT COOK'S HINT **chicken** COOK'S HINT COOK'S HINT COOK'S HINT COOK'S HINT

To make skinning chicken easier, use a paper towel to get a better grip to pull off the skin.

# lemon-crumb chicken

*4 POINTS* PER SERVING | MAKES 4 SERVINGS

*Lemon zest adds a refreshing flavor to this crunchy coating. To grate the zest from lemons, use the medium grate of a four-sided grater. Make sure you grate only the outer yellow skin of the lemon, as the white part, also known as the pith, is bitter. This fresh bread crumb coating is also good on turkey cutlets or fish fillets, such as flounder or sole.*

1. **Preheat the oven** to 425°F. Spray a nonstick baking pan with nonstick spray. Combine the bread crumbs, cheese, parsley, and lemon zest in a medium bowl; transfer to a sheet of wax paper.

2. **Sprinkle the chicken** with the salt and pepper; spread both sides with the mayonnaise. Coat the chicken on both sides with the crumb mixture. Arrange the chicken on the baking pan; spray the tops lightly with nonstick spray. Bake until the crust is golden and the chicken is cooked through, 20–25 minutes (do not turn).

PER SERVING: 193 CALORIES
6g total fat, 2g saturated fat, 66mg cholesterol, 518mg sodium, 8g total carbohydrate, 1g dietary fiber, 27g protein, 49mg calcium

2 slices firm whole-wheat sandwich bread, made into crumbs (1 cup)

1 tablespoon grated Parmesan cheese

1 tablespoon minced parsley

1 tablespoon grated lemon zest

4 (¼-pound) skinless boneless chicken breasts, lightly pounded

½ teaspoon salt

½ teaspoon freshly ground pepper

2 tablespoons reduced-calorie mayonnaise

COOK'S HINT COOK'S HINT **prepping chicken** COOK'S HINT COOK'S HINT COOK'S HINT

Lightly pounding the chicken breasts will ensure even cooking throughout. Place the chicken breasts between two sheets of wax paper. Using a rolling pin or meat mallet, lightly tap the breasts to an even thickness. Avoid pounding too hard as this will break the delicate fibers of the meat.

# grilled herbed chicken [20]

**4 POINTS** PER SERVING | MAKES 4 SERVINGS

*This quick and delicious recipe makes good use of the fresh herbs from your garden. If you don't have fresh herbs on hand, substitute one teaspoon dried for one tablespoon fresh herbs. Serve this dish with grilled asparagus or zucchini, rice, and a salad.*

2 tablespoons chopped oregano

1 tablespoon chopped thyme

1 tablespoon chopped rosemary

2 teaspoons olive oil

½ teaspoon salt

4 (¼-pound) skinless boneless chicken breasts

**1. Combine** the oregano, thyme, rosemary, oil, and salt in a small bowl. Rub the herb mixture on both sides of each chicken breast.

**2. Heat a nonstick ridged grill pan** over medium-high heat. Add the chicken and cook until browned and cooked through, about 4 minutes on each side. Transfer the chicken to a cutting board; let stand 5 minutes before slicing on the diagonal.

**PER SERVING:** 155 CALORIES
5g total fat, 1g saturated fat, 62mg cholesterol, 348mg sodium, 1g total carbohydrate, 0g dietary fiber, 25g protein, 25mg calcium

COOK'S HINT COOK'S HINT **carving** COOK'S HINT COOK'S HINT COOK'S HINT COOK'S HINT

Allowing the chicken to rest for 5 minutes, after removing from the oven and just before slicing, will keep it tender and juicy. If you slice it before it has had a few minutes to rest, the juices will run out, making the chicken dry.

# goat cheese and herb-stuffed chicken breasts

***6 POINTS*** PER SERVING | MAKES 4 SERVINGS

*Brushing the chicken lightly with a little reduced-calorie mayonnaise rather than dipping in flour and egg before dredging in bread crumbs saves time, cuts calories, and tastes terrific. The herbs called for in this recipe are fresh, but if you don't have fresh basil, omit it. Rather, increase the scallion to two.*

**1. Preheat the oven** to 425°F. Spray a nonstick baking pan with nonstick spray.

**2. Combine** the cheese, tomatoes, scallion, basil, and thyme in a bowl, mashing with a fork, until blended. Place the bread crumbs in another small bowl.

**3. Cut a pocket** into the side of each chicken breast about 2½-inches long. Place one-quarter of the goat cheese mixture inside each slit. Lightly press the pocket closed with a fork. Brush the top side of each breast with the mayonnaise. Dip the chicken, one piece at a time, coated-side down into the bread crumbs. Transfer coated-side up to the baking pan.

**4. Spray the tops** of the chicken lightly with nonstick spray. Bake until the chicken is cooked through and the crust is golden, about 25 minutes.

**5. Meanwhile, place the spinach** in a large steamer basket set in a saucepan over 1 inch of boiling water. Cover tightly and steam until the spinach just wilts, about 3 minutes. Transfer the spinach to a platter, then top with the chicken.

**PER SERVING:** 284 CALORIES
12g total fat, 5g saturated fat, 80mg cholesterol, 356mg sodium, 12g total carbohydrate, 5g dietary fiber, 34g protein, 284mg calcium

2 ounces goat cheese

2 oil-packed sun-dried tomatoes, rinsed under water, patted dry, and finely chopped

1 scallion, chopped

1 tablespoon chopped basil

2 teaspoons chopped thyme

¼ cup plain dry bread crumbs

4 (¼-pound) skinless boneless chicken breasts

4 teaspoons reduced-calorie mayonnaise

1½ pounds baby spinach, rinsed

# chicken with fresh tomato sauce

**4 POINTS** PER SERVING | MAKES 4 SERVINGS

*This dish highlights what Italian cooking is all about: using fresh ingredients to create a simple, yet delicious, dish.*

1 teaspoon olive oil

4 (¼-pound) skinless boneless chicken breasts

2 teaspoons chopped rosemary

½ teaspoon salt

1 large shallot, minced

1 garlic clove, minced

3 tablespoons balsamic vinegar

6 plum tomatoes, diced

¼ cup low-sodium chicken broth

¼ cup chopped basil

**1. Heat the oil** in a nonstick skillet. Sprinkle both sides of the chicken with the rosemary and salt, then add to the skillet. Sauté the chicken until browned and cooked through, 3–4 minutes on each side. Transfer the chicken to a platter. Let stand 5 minutes.

**2. Meanwhile, add the shallot** and garlic to the same skillet. Cook until softened, about 2 minutes. Add the vinegar, stirring to scrape up the browned bits and cook until the vinegar is almost evaporated. Stir in the tomatoes and chicken broth; bring to a boil. Reduce the heat and simmer, uncovered, until the tomatoes just begin to soften, about 3 minutes. Stir in the basil. Spoon the sauce over the chicken.

**PER SERVING:** 167 CALORIES
5g total fat, 1g saturated fat, 62mg cholesterol, 360mg sodium, 5g total carbohydrate, 1g dietary fiber, 26g protein, 31mg calcium

# chicken parmesan [20]

*7 POINTS* PER SERVING | MAKES 4 SERVINGS

*This version is refreshingly different from the sauce and cheese-laden Italian classic. The lightly breaded cutlets are topped with sliced fresh tomatoes, basil leaves, and a sprinkling of mozzarella cheese, then quickly baked.*

1. **Preheat the oven** to 425°F. Spray a baking sheet with nonstick spray.

2. **Sprinkle the chicken** with the salt, then brush both sides with the mayonnaise. Place the bread crumbs in a large zip-close plastic bag. Add the chicken, one piece at a time and shake to coat.

3. **Place the chicken** on the baking sheet. Top each with tomato slices; sprinkle with the oil, basil, and mozzarella cheese. Bake until the chicken is cooked through and the cheese is melted and bubbly, about 12 minutes. Sprinkle with the Parmesan.

PER SERVING: 297 CALORIES
13g total fat, 4g saturated fat, 73mg cholesterol, 629mg sodium, 13g total carbohydrate, 1g dietary fiber, 31g protein, 174mg calcium

4 (¼-pound) skinless boneless chicken breasts

½ teaspoon salt

2 tablespoons reduced-calorie mayonnaise

½ cup plain dry bread crumbs

1 large tomato, cut into 8 slices

1 tablespoon olive oil

8 basil leaves

½ cup shredded part-skim mozzarella cheese

1 tablespoon grated Parmesan cheese

# grapefruit chicken [20]

*4 POINTS* PER SERVING | MAKES 4 SERVINGS

*For a pretty presentation, we suggest using one pink and one white grapefruit for contrast.*

2 grapefruits
(about 1¾ pounds)

4 (¼-pound) skinless
boneless chicken breasts

1 tablespoon
chopped thyme

½ teaspoon salt

1 tablespoon apple jelly

1 teaspoon butter

Mint sprigs, to garnish

1. **Peel and section** the grapefruits, reserving ½ cup juice. Set sections and juice aside.

2. **Spray a nonstick skillet** with nonstick spray and set over medium-high heat. Sprinkle both sides of the chicken with the thyme and salt. Sauté the chicken until browned and cooked through, 3–4 minutes on each side. Transfer to a platter.

3. **Add the reserved** ½ cup grapefruit juice, the jelly, and butter to the skillet; bring to a boil. Cook, stirring constantly, until the sauce thickens slightly, about 2 minutes. Spoon the sauce and reserved grapefruit sections over the chicken. Garnish with the mint.

PER SERVING: 194 CALORIES
4g total fat, 2g saturated fat, 65mg cholesterol, 356mg sodium, 14g total carbohydrate, 2g dietary fiber, 25g protein, 34mg calcium

# grilled chicken with diced beets and yellow pepper [20]

**6 POINTS** PER SERVING | MAKES 4 SERVINGS

*This recipe makes good use of summer's bounty. Although we suggest using canned beets for convenience, you may want to substitute cooked fresh beets—their taste is far superior.*

1. **To make the dressing,** whisk together the orange juice, vinegar, honey, oil, ¼ teaspoon of the salt, and the ground pepper; set aside.

2. **Combine** the apple jelly and mustard in a small bowl. Sprinkle the cutlets with the remaining ½ teaspoon salt; brush both sides with the apple jelly mixture.

3. **Heat a nonstick ridged grill pan** over medium-high heat. Add the cutlets and cook until browned, about 4 minutes on each side; transfer the cutlets to a cutting board. Let rest 5 minutes. Cut each cutlet diagonally into thirds.

4. **Arrange the greens on a platter.** Sprinkle with the beets and yellow pepper. Top with the chicken and drizzle with the dressing.

**PER SERVING: 294 CALORIES**
7g total fat, 1g saturated fat, 62mg cholesterol, 653mg sodium, 32g total carbohydrate, 4g dietary fiber, 27g protein, 75mg calcium

¾ cup orange juice

2 tablespoons
cider vinegar

1 tablespoon honey

1 tablespoon
extra-virgin olive oil

¾ teaspoon salt

¼ teaspoon freshly
ground pepper

¼ cup apple jelly

1 teaspoon
Dijon mustard

4 (¼-pound) chicken
or turkey cutlets

6 cups mixed
salad greens

2 (8¼-ounce) cans
whole baby beets,
drained and halved

2 yellow bell peppers,
seeded and diced

COOK'S HINT COOK'S HINT **essentials** COOK'S HINT COOK'S HINT COOK'S HINT COOK'S HINT

Creating delicious summer salads for main dish meals is easy when you have a well-stocked pantry: chicken broth, dry white wine, various vinegars (including raspberry, balsamic, rice wine, and herbed variations), good-quality oils, Dijon mustard, olives, jarred roasted peppers and artichokes in water, capers, and an array of herbs and spices all can add small touches of powerful flavor.

# curried chicken with apples and mango chutney [20]

**7 POINTS** PER SERVING | MAKES 6 SERVINGS

*If you've never tried curry, this dish is a delectable initiation. When shopping for curry powder, read the labels—there are numerous types that pack varying degrees of heat.*

2 teaspoons canola oil

1½ pounds skinless boneless chicken breasts, cut into 2-inch pieces

½ teaspoon salt

¼ teaspoon freshly ground pepper

1 Granny Smith apple, unpeeled, cored, and chopped

1 onion, chopped

1 teaspoon grated peeled fresh ginger

1 garlic clove, minced

1 tablespoon curry powder

½ cup mango chutney

¼ cup currants

¼ cup low-sodium chicken broth

¼ cup fat-free half-and-half

1 tablespoon chopped parsley

2 tablespoons slivered almonds, toasted

3 cups cooked white rice

1. **Heat the oil** in a large nonstick skillet, then add the chicken and sprinkle with the salt and pepper. Sauté until browned, about 6 minutes. Transfer to a plate.

2. **Add the apple**, onion, ginger, and garlic to the skillet. Cook until the apple and onion are tender, about 6 minutes. Stir in the curry powder; cook 1 minute. Add the chicken, chutney, currants, broth, half-and-half, and parsley; bring to a boil. Simmer, uncovered, until the flavors are blended and the sauce thickens slightly, about 3 minutes. Sprinkle with the almonds. Serve over rice.

**PER SERVING (1 CUP CHICKEN MIXTURE AND ½ CUP RICE): 342 CALORIES**
6g total fat, 1g saturated fat, 62mg cholesterol, 279mg sodium, 42g total carbohydrate, 2g dietary fiber, 28g protein, 58mg calcium

COOK'S HINT COOK'S HINT **leftovers** COOK'S HINT COOK'S HINT COOK'S HINT

Leftovers? Spoon the cold chicken mixture onto crisp lettuce leaves for a cool and tasty chicken salad lunch.

# thai chicken with ginger sauce

**7 POINTS** PER SERVING | MAKES 4 SERVINGS

*Fish sauce, also called nam pla, is strong-flavored and salty, so only a tiny amount is needed. It can be found in the ethnic section of most supermarkets or in Asian markets. Dried wood ear mushrooms are a type of mushroom commonly used in Asian cuisine. But don't let their little package fool you— when reconstituted they increase almost 6 times in size.*

1. **Bring the water to a boil** in a small saucepan. Add the dried mushrooms; remove from the heat and let stand 20 minutes. Drain the mushrooms; coarsely chop and set aside.

2. **Meanwhile, whisk together** the broth, soy sauce, vinegar, cornstarch, and fish sauce in a small bowl; set aside.

3. **Heat the oil** over high heat in a large nonstick skillet, then add the chicken. Sauté until lightly browned, about 3 minutes. Transfer to a plate.

4. **Return the skillet to the heat,** then add the scallions, ginger, and garlic. Sauté until fragrant and the scallions have softened slightly, about 1 minute. Add the mushrooms, chicken, snap peas, and broth mixture; bring to a boil, stirring constantly. Reduce the heat and simmer, stirring constantly, until heated through and slightly thickened, about 2 minutes. Stir in the cilantro. Serve with the rice.

**PER SERVING (1¼ CUPS CHICKEN MIXTURE AND ½ CUP RICE): 353 CALORIES**
8g total fat, 2g saturated fat, 77mg cholesterol, 456mg sodium, 33g total carbohydrate, 4g dietary fiber, 37g protein, 78mg calcium

1 cup water

1 (½-ounce) package dried wood ear mushrooms

1 cup low-sodium chicken broth

2 tablespoons reduced-sodium soy sauce

1 tablespoon rice vinegar

1 tablespoon cornstarch

1 teaspoon Asian fish sauce (nam pla)

2 teaspoons canola oil

1¼ pounds skinless boneless chicken breasts, cut into ¾-inch pieces

8 scallions, cut diagonally into 2-inch pieces

2 teaspoons minced peeled fresh ginger

1 garlic clove, chopped

½ pound sugar snap peas

¼ cup chopped cilantro

2 cups cooked brown rice

COOK'S HINT COOK'S HINT **chicken** COOK'S HINT COOK'S HINT COOK'S HINT

When browning chicken in a skillet, make sure the heat is high and add the pieces in one layer without touching each other. Also, don't "stir" the chicken—use tongs to turn the pieces. Low heat, overcrowding the pan, and stirring all will cause the chicken to steam instead of brown.

# thai coconut chicken

**8 POINTS** PER SERVING | MAKES 4 SERVINGS

*Coconut milk and curry are two ingredients commonly used in Thai cooking. Here we use red curry paste. It's hot, so a little goes a long way. Look for it in the ethnic section of your supermarket. The coconut milk is unsweetened, and not to be confused with "cream of coconut" which is used mainly in mixed drinks and desserts. Purple basil is also a popular ingredient in Thai dishes.*

2 teaspoons canola oil

1 pound skinless boneless chicken breasts, cut into ½-inch strips

¼ teaspoon salt

1 onion, thinly sliced

2 garlic cloves, minced

1 teaspoon grated peeled fresh ginger

1 tablespoon packed light brown sugar

2 teaspoons Thai red curry paste

½ teaspoon ground cumin

½ pound asparagus, cut diagonally into 2-inch pieces

½ cup unsweetened coconut milk

1 tablespoon fish sauce (nam pla)

¼ cup fresh purple or green basil, chopped

2 cups cooked brown rice

1. Heat 1 teaspoon of the oil in a large nonstick skillet, then add the chicken and sprinkle with the salt. Sauté until browned and cooked through, about 5 minutes. Transfer the chicken to a plate.

2. Heat the remaining 1 teaspoon oil in the same skillet over low heat, then add the onion, garlic, and ginger. Sauté until fragrant and the onions are softened, about 6 minutes. Stir in the sugar, curry paste, and cumin; cook 1 minute, stirring constantly. Add the asparagus, coconut milk, and fish sauce; bring to a boil. Reduce the heat and simmer, covered, until the asparagus is crisp-tender, about 3 minutes.

3. Add the chicken and basil; heat through. Serve with the rice.

PER SERVING (1 CUP CHICKEN MIXTURE AND ½ CUP RICE): 372 CALORIES
13g total fat, 7g saturated fat, 62mg cholesterol, 389mg sodium, 34g total carbohydrate, 4g dietary fiber, 30g protein, 64mg calcium

COOK'S HINT COOK'S HINT coconut milk COOK'S HINT COOK'S HINT

In this recipe, don't be tempted to substitute "lite" coconut milk for regular coconut milk. The flavor of the regular is far superior and worth the extra **POINTS**.

Banana-Raisin Bread Pudding

Cinnamon-Peach and Almond Pancakes. Opposite: Grilled Salmon with Roasted Corn Salad.

Mediterranean Roast Chicken. Opposite: Grilled Lamb Kebabs and Red Lentil Salad.

Goat Cheese and Herb-Stuffed Chicken Breasts. Opposite: Braised Chicken with Mushrooms.

Chicken and Broccoli Pizza

# braised chicken with mushrooms

**6 POINTS** PER SERVING | MAKES 6 SERVINGS

*The term "braise" is a cooking method in which food is browned first, then cooked in a small amount of liquid. This stew is done in 30 minutes or less using chunks of boneless chicken thighs.*

1. **Cook the noodles** according to package directions; drain.

2. **Meanwhile, heat the oil** in a large nonstick skillet, then add the chicken. Sprinkle with the thyme, salt, and pepper; sauté until browned, about 6 minutes. Stir in the mushrooms, onion, and water. Cook, uncovered, stirring occasionally, until the onion is tender, about 8 minutes.

3. **Add the tomatoes,** broth, wine, and garlic; bring to a boil. Reduce the heat and simmer, covered, 10 minutes to blend the flavors. Stir in the noodles, spinach, half-and-half, and cheese. Simmer, uncovered, until the spinach just begins to wilt.

**PER SERVING (SCANT 1½ CUPS): 321 CALORIES**
9g total fat, 3g saturated fat, 86mg cholesterol, 284mg sodium, 34g total carbohydrate, 4g dietary fiber, 26g protein, 153mg calcium

1 (8-ounce) package no-yolk wide egg noodles

1 teaspoon olive oil

1 pound skinless boneless chicken thighs, trimmed of all fat and cut into 2-inch pieces

½ teaspoon dried thyme

¼ teaspoon salt

¼ teaspoon freshly ground pepper

½ pound shiitake mushrooms, stemmed and sliced

1 red onion, thinly sliced

¼ cup water

¾ pound plum tomatoes, seeded and chopped

1 cup low-sodium chicken broth

½ cup dry white wine

2 garlic cloves, minced

1 bunch spinach, cleaned and coarsely chopped

¼ cup fat-free half-and-half

3 tablespoons grated Parmesan cheese

COOK'S HINT COOK'S HINT **shiitake** COOK'S HINT COOK'S HINT COOK'S HINT

Unlike many other mushrooms, the stems of shiitake mushrooms are inedible and should be removed and discarded.

# chicken and broccoli pizza

**6 POINTS** PER SERVING | MAKES 6 SERVINGS

*A sure-fire way to get the kids to eat their broccoli—and actually love it!*
*Breaded chicken fingers top this pizza to make it extra kid-friendly.*

1 tablespoon reduced-calorie mayonnaise

1 teaspoon low-fat (1%) milk

½ pound skinless boneless chicken breasts, cut into ½-inch strips

½ cup cornflake crumbs

¾ cup part-skim ricotta cheese

1 (10-ounce) package thin crust pizza crust

1 (10-ounce) package frozen chopped broccoli, thawed and patted dry

3 tablespoons grated Parmesan cheese

½ cup shredded part-skim mozzarella cheese

1. Preheat the oven to 450°F. Spray a small baking pan with nonstick spray.

2. Combine the mayonnaise and milk in a medium bowl. Add the chicken; toss to coat.

3. Place the cornflake crumbs in a large zip-close plastic bag. Add the chicken and shake until coated. Place the chicken in the baking pan in one layer. Bake until the chicken is cooked through and browned, turning once, about 10 minutes.

4. Meanwhile, spoon the ricotta cheese evenly onto the pizza crust. Top with the broccoli, Parmesan cheese, chicken, and mozzarella.

5. Bake until hot and the cheese is melted and bubbly, about 15 minutes. Serve at once.

PER SERVING: 295 CALORIES
10g total fat, 4g saturated fat, 39mg cholesterol, 453mg sodium, 31g total carbohydrate, 2g dietary fiber, 20g protein, 230mg calcium

# chili chicken kebabs with yogurt sauce

**7 POINTS** PER SERVING | MAKES 6 SERVINGS

*Spicy kebabs are perfectly counterbalanced by a refreshing, cool yogurt sauce.*
*You can make the sauce up to a day ahead and store in the refrigerator.*
*Serve with basmati or jasmine rice.*

1. **Combine** the chicken, orange juice, honey, 2 tablespoons of the vinegar, the oil, chili powder, cumin, ginger, and garlic in a large zip-close plastic bag. Squeeze out the air and seal the bag; turn to coat the chicken. Refrigerate, turning the bag occasionally, at least 1 hour or overnight.

2. **To make the sauce,** combine the yogurt, red onion, cilantro, the remaining 1 tablespoon vinegar, the lime zest, lime juice, and salt in a small bowl until blended. Cover and refrigerate until ready to use.

3. **Spray the broiler rack** with nonstick spray; preheat the broiler. Thread the chicken and cherry tomatoes onto six 18-inch metal skewers. Discard the marinade. Place the kebabs on the broiler rack and broil 5 inches from the heat until the chicken is browned and cooked through, about 6 minutes on each side. Serve the kebabs with the sauce.

**PER SERVING:** 310 CALORIES
12g total fat, 3g saturated fat, 105mg cholesterol, 334mg sodium, 15g total carbohydrate, 1g dietary fiber, 35g protein, 107mg calcium

2 pounds skinless boneless chicken thighs, trimmed of all fat and cut into 2½-inch pieces

½ cup orange juice

¼ cup honey

3 tablespoons cider vinegar

1 tablespoon canola oil

2 teaspoons chili powder

1 teaspoon ground cumin

1 teaspoon grated peeled fresh ginger

1 garlic clove, minced

1 (8-ounce) container low-fat plain yogurt

2 tablespoons minced red onion

2 tablespoons chopped cilantro

2 teaspoons lime zest

1 tablespoon lime juice

½ teaspoon salt

1½ pints cherry tomatoes

COOK'S HINT COOK'S HINT **skewers** COOK'S HINT COOK'S HINT COOK'S HINT

You can use bamboo skewers instead of metal skewers, just make sure to soak them in cold water for at least 30 minutes before using, to prevent them from burning.

# barbecued chicken tostadas

**8 POINTS** PER SERVING | MAKES 7 SERVINGS

*For an easy dinner or a summer pool party, everyone will love these tostadas—especially the cook since they're so easy to prepare.*

2 pounds skinless boneless chicken thighs, trimmed of all fat and cut into strips

1 cup prepared barbecue sauce

1 (4½-ounce) can chopped mild green chiles, drained

2 tomatoes, seeded and diced

½ small red onion, minced

¼ cup chopped cilantro

1 garlic clove, minced

1 tablespoon red wine vinegar

2 teaspoons olive oil

¼ teaspoon salt

8 (6-inch) fat-free flour tortillas

1 cup canned fat-free refried beans

8 scallions, finely chopped

1 cup shredded reduced-fat Monterey Jack cheese

¼ cup light sour cream

Cilantro sprigs, to garnish

1. **Combine** the chicken, barbecue sauce, and chiles in a large nonstick saucepan; bring to a boil. Reduce the heat and simmer, covered, until the chicken is tender and cooked through, about 25 minutes. Remove from the heat and let cool.

2. **Meanwhile, combine** the tomatoes, onion, chopped cilantro, garlic, vinegar, oil, and salt in a medium bowl until blended. Set aside.

3. **Preheat the oven** to 425°F. Spray a large nonstick baking sheet with nonstick spray.

4. **Place the tortillas** on the baking sheet. Spread each with the beans, then top with the chicken mixture, scallions, and cheese. Bake until the cheese is melted and bubbly, about 15 minutes. Top each tostada with the tomato mixture, sour cream, and cilantro sprigs.

**PER SERVING:** 358 CALORIES
12g total fat, 4g saturated fat, 87mg cholesterol, 864mg sodium, 27g total carbohydrate, 4g dietary fiber, 33g protein, 195mg calcium

COOK'S HINT COOK'S HINT **time saver** COOK'S HINT COOK'S HINT

To save time, use a deli-bought roasted chicken. Remove the skin and cut the meat into strips so you have about 2 cups of chicken, and reduce the simmering time in step #1 to 5 minutes. This recipe also is a great way to use leftover roast chicken or turkey.

# chinese chicken legs

**4 POINTS** PER SERVING | MAKES 6 SERVINGS

*These legs are spicy and finger-lickin' good! If you want to cut down on the heat, omit the chili paste. A perfect accompaniment to this dish is cool cucumbers tossed with thinly sliced red bell pepper and sprinkled with a little seasoned rice vinegar. Pick up some "sticky rice" at your local Chinese take-out to finish the meal.*

**1. Preheat the oven** to 400°F. Line the bottom of a large baking pan with foil or parchment paper.

**2. Combine** the scallions, barbecue sauce, soy sauce, oyster sauce, honey, sugar, ginger, chili paste, and garlic in a large bowl. Add the chicken legs and toss until well coated.

**3. Place the chicken in the baking pan.** Spoon any remaining sauce over the chicken. Cover loosely with aluminum foil and bake 20 minutes. Remove the foil, and continue baking until the chicken is browned and cooked through and the sauce is thickened, about 20 minutes longer. Sprinkle with the sesame seeds.

**PER SERVING:** 175 CALORIES
3g total fat, 1g saturated fat, 52mg cholesterol, 596mg sodium, 13g total carbohydrate, 1g dietary fiber, 22g protein, 34mg calcium

8 scallions, coarsely chopped (about 1 cup)

⅓ cup prepared barbecue sauce

2 tablespoons reduced-sodium soy sauce

2 tablespoons oyster sauce

2 tablespoons honey

1 tablespoon sugar

2 teaspoons grated peeled fresh ginger

1 teaspoon chili paste or hot pepper sauce

1 garlic clove, minced

2¼ pounds chicken drumsticks, skin removed

2 teaspoons sesame seeds, toasted

COOK'S HINT COOK'S HINT **sesame seeds** COOK'S HINT COOK'S HINT COOK'S HINT

To toast the sesame seeds, place them in a small dry skillet over medium-low heat. Toast, shaking the pan and stirring constantly, until lightly browned and fragrant, 2–3 minutes. Watch them carefully when toasting; seeds can burn quickly. Transfer the seeds to a plate to cool.

# turkey-stuffed cabbage rolls

**8 POINTS** PER SERVING | MAKES 4 SERVINGS

*Stuffed with ground turkey, fragrant basmati rice and mushrooms, these rolls cook long and slow so they are fork-tender and delicious. The stuffing also works nicely in baked stuffed zucchini and tomatoes. To reheat leftovers—if you have any!—steam or microwave them.*

1 (1½-pound)
Savoy cabbage

1 cup basmati rice or
long-grain white rice

2 teaspoons olive oil

½ pound white
mushrooms, sliced

1 onion, finely chopped

¾ pound ground skinless
turkey breast

1 large egg

½ teaspoon salt

1 (26-ounce) jar
marinara sauce

1. **Fill a large saucepot** two-thirds full of water and bring to a boil.

2. **Carefully separate the cabbage leaves,** discarding the tough parts close to the core. With tongs, working in batches, immerse the leaves in the boiling water just until wilted, about 30 seconds. Drain the cabbage. Reserve 8 large leaves; thinly slice the remaining cabbage; set aside.

3. **Meanwhile, bring 2 cups water to a boil** in a medium saucepan. Add the rice. Simmer, covered, until the liquid is absorbed and the rice is tender, about 20 minutes. Fluff the rice with a fork and transfer to a large bowl. Let cool.

4. **Preheat the oven to 325°F.**

5. **Heat the oil** in a large nonstick skillet, then add the mushrooms and onion. Cook, stirring occasionally, until any liquid is absorbed and the vegetables are tender, about 8 minutes. Add the mushroom mixture to the rice. Stir in the turkey, egg, and salt until well mixed. Divide the turkey mixture among the 8 cabbage leaves. Fold in the sides of the leaves over the stuffing, then roll the leaves to enclose the stuffing.

6. **Line the bottom of a large nonstick baking pan** with the remaining sliced cabbage. Place the cabbage rolls, seam-side down, on top. Drizzle with the sauce. Bake, covered, basting occasionally, until the cabbage is fork-tender and the filling is cooked through, 1½–2 hours.

**PER SERVING (2 STUFFED CABBAGE ROLLS): 431 CALORIES**
8g total fat, 2g saturated fat, 104mg cholesterol, 1,187mg sodium, 62g total carbohydrate, 7g dietary fiber, 31g protein, 151mg calcium

# baked turkey and ziti casserole

**7 POINTS** PER SERVING | MAKES 8 SERVINGS

*Give this hearty, satisfying casserole a Tex-Mex flavor by adding canned green chiles and chili powder to the meat mixture and stirring in reduced-fat cheddar instead of the mozzarella cheese.*

1. **Cook the ziti** according to package directions, then drain and set aside. Preheat the oven to 375°F.

2. **Meanwhile, heat the oil** in a large nonstick skillet, then add the turkey, onion, bell pepper, salt, and ground pepper. Cook, stirring often, until all pan juices evaporate and the turkey is browned, about 10 minutes.

3. **Stir in the ziti, marinara sauce, and ricotta.** Spoon the mixture into a large nonstick baking pan. Top with the mozzarella cheese. Bake, uncovered, until the filling is hot and the cheese is melted, 40–50 minutes.

**PER SERVING:** 362 CALORIES
9g total fat, 4g saturated fat, 51mg cholesterol, 663mg sodium, 43g total carbohydrate, 3g dietary fiber, 28g protein, 229mg calcium

12 ounces ziti
or penne

2 teaspoons canola oil

1 pound ground skinless
turkey breast

1 onion, chopped

1 green bell pepper,
seeded and chopped

½ teaspoon salt

¼ teaspoon freshly
ground pepper

1 (24-ounce) jar
marinara sauce

1 cup part-skim ricotta
cheese

1 cup shredded
part-skim mozzarella
cheese

COOK'S HINT COOK'S HINT **leftovers idea** COOK'S HINT COOK'S HINT COOK'S HINT
Once cooked, this dish freezes beautifully. If you have leftovers, wrap in individual portions and pop in the freezer. Then reheat in the microwave.

# turkey and cheddar burgers  [20]

*7 POINTS* PER SERVING | MAKES 4 SERVINGS

*You will be amazed at how tender, juicy, and flavorful these turkey burgers are: grated cheddar cheese, zucchini, and minced onion mixed in with the ground turkey help keep it moist.*

1 pound ground skinless turkey breast

1 small zucchini, shredded

½ cup shredded reduced-fat cheddar cheese

¼ cup minced red onion

¾ teaspoon salt

½ teaspoon freshly ground pepper

¼ cup ketchup

¼ cup reduced-calorie mayonnaise

4 lettuce leaves

4 tomato slices

4 whole-wheat hamburger buns, split and toasted

1. **Heat a nonstick ridged grill pan** over medium-low heat.

2. **Combine** the turkey, zucchini, cheese, onion, salt, and pepper in a bowl until blended. Shape into four patties.

3. **Grill the patties** until browned on the outside and no longer pink in the center, about 7 minutes on each side.

4. **Meanwhile, whisk together** the ketchup and mayonnaise in a small bowl.

5. **Layer the lettuce, burgers, and tomato slices** on the bottoms of the hamburger buns. Top with the ketchup mixture, then the bun tops.

PER SERVING: 348 CALORIES
12g total fat, 4g saturated fat, 80mg cholesterol, 1053mg sodium, 25g total carbohydrate, 4g dietary fiber, 35g protein, 158mg calcium

COOK'S HINT COOK'S HINT **juicier burgers** COOK'S HINT COOK'S HINT COOK'S HINT

Don't be tempted to press the burgers with a spatula when cooking. This common mistake actually robs the burgers of moistness by squeezing out the juices.

# turkey chili verde

**7 POINTS** PER SERVING | MAKES 6 SERVINGS

*Popular in Mexican and Southwestern cuisine, tomatillos look like small green tomatoes. You'll recognize them by their thin, papery covering, which should be removed before using. They are available in Latin-American markets and in the produce section of well-stocked supermarkets. If you can't find fresh tomatillos, substitute drained, canned tomatillos.*

1. **Heat the oil** in a large nonstick saucepan, then add the onion, bell pepper, and garlic. Sauté until softened, about 8 minutes. Add the turkey, chili powder, and cumin. Cook, over medium-high heat, breaking up the turkey with a fork, until the liquid evaporates and the turkey begins to brown, about 6 minutes.

2. **Meanwhile, purée** the tomatillos, chiles, and cilantro in a food processor; add to the turkey mixture. Stir in the broth, beans, and sugar; bring to a boil. Reduce the heat and simmer, covered, until the mixture is thickened and flavors are blended, about 45 minutes.

**PER SERVING (1 CUP): 334 CALORIES**
11g total fat, 3g saturated fat, 51mg cholesterol, 527mg sodium, 33g total carbohydrate, 9g dietary fiber, 27g protein, 128mg calcium

2 teaspoons canola oil

1 onion, finely chopped

1 green bell pepper, seeded and chopped

1 garlic clove, minced

1 pound ground skinless turkey breast

3 tablespoons chili powder

1 teaspoon ground cumin

½ pound tomatillos, husks removed and halved

1 (4½-ounce) can chopped green chiles, drained

½ cup cilantro leaves

2 cups low-sodium chicken broth

2 (15-ounce) cans cannellini (white kidney) beans, rinsed and drained

1 teaspoon sugar

COOK'S HINT **leftover idea** COOK'S HINT COOK'S HINT COOK'S HINT COOK'S HINT COOK'S HINT COOK'S HINT

If you have any leftover turkey or chicken, cut it into small chunks and use it here in place of the ground turkey.

# warm grilled turkey sausage and roasted potato salad

**4 POINTS** PER SERVING | MAKES 6 SERVINGS

*Turkey sausage is a delicious substitute for fattier pork sausage. It's available sweet or hot—either variety works well here, as does low-fat kielbasa.*

3 tablespoons
red wine vinegar

2 tablespoons country-style Dijon mustard

1 tablespoon
extra-virgin olive oil

¾ teaspoon salt

¾ teaspoon freshly
ground pepper

1¼ pounds red potatoes,
scrubbed and cut into
1-inch chunks

1 teaspoon dried thyme

1 pound turkey sausage

4 cups mixed
salad greens

1 (7-ounce) jar roasted
red peppers, drained and
chopped

½ cup sliced red onion

15 small oil-cured black
olives, pitted and
chopped (¼ cup)

1. **Preheat the oven** to 425°F. Spray a nonstick roasting pan with nonstick spray. Whisk together the vinegar, mustard, oil, ¼ teaspoon of the salt and ¼ teaspoon of the ground pepper in a small bowl until blended; set aside.

2. **Combine** the potatoes, thyme, and remaining ½ teaspoon salt, and ½ teaspoon ground pepper in a large bowl. Lightly spray the potatoes with nonstick spray; toss to coat. Arrange the potatoes in the pan in one layer. Roast, stirring occasionally, until the potatoes are tender and browned, about 40 minutes. Transfer the potatoes to a large bowl; set aside.

3. **Spray the broiler rack** with nonstick spray; preheat the broiler. Arrange the sausage on the rack. Broil 7 inches from the heat, turning occasionally, until the sausage is browned and cooked through, about 20 minutes. When the sausage is cool enough to handle, cut diagonally into 1-inch chunks; add to the potatoes. Stir in the salad greens, roasted peppers, onion, and olives. Drizzle with the dressing; toss to coat. Serve at once.

**PER SERVING (GENEROUS 1½ CUPS): 205 CALORIES**
8g total fat, 2g saturated fat, 26mg cholesterol, 915mg sodium, 25g total carbohydrate, 3g dietary fiber, 11g protein, 50mg calcium

COOK'S HINT COOK'S HINT **utensils** COOK'S HINT COOK'S HINT COOK'S HINT COOK'S HINT

Use spring-loaded tongs to turn the sausage when broiling.
Piercing the sausages with a fork will cause all the juices to escape.

# meats

herb-crusted roast beef and vegetables
steak with roasted garlic and chili rub
stuffed flank steak with tomato sauce
warm pasta salad with blue cheese dressing
savory beef loaf with bulgur and sun-dried tomatoes
beefy black bean chili   moroccan meatball stew
veal cutlets with mushrooms and tomatoes
veal curry with rice and peas   glazed pork loin and acorn squash
skewered pork with mushrooms and scallions
pineapple pork fried rice   pork adobo
caribbean callaloo pork stew
roast lamb shanks with lentils   lamb and white bean chili
shepherd's pie   ham and yams in cider sauce
pasta shells with beans, greens, and sausage

# herb-crusted roast beef and vegetables

*6 POINTS* PER SERVING | MAKES 8 SERVINGS

*This lean version of an old-fashioned Sunday supper is a simple way to feed a small crowd. A ripe tomato salad is all you need to round out the menu. Thinly sliced leftover eye round roast also makes a great roast beef sandwich.*

1 cup parsley leaves

¼ cup coarsely chopped chives

1 tablespoon rosemary

2 garlic cloves, minced

2 tablespoons Dijon mustard

1 teaspoon salt

¼ teaspoon freshly ground pepper

1 (2-pound) boneless eye round roast, trimmed of all visible fat

4 teaspoons olive oil

2½ pounds small red potatoes, halved

2 pounds zucchini, trimmed and cut into 2-inch pieces

2 onions, cut into eighths

½ pound baby carrots

1. **Preheat the oven** to 450°F. Spray a large roasting pan with nonstick spray. Mince the parsley, chives, and rosemary together. In a large bowl, combine the herbs with the garlic, mustard, salt, and pepper. Place the beef in the roasting pan. Rub 2 tablespoons of the herb mixture over the top and sides of the beef.

2. **Stir the oil** into the remaining herb mixture. Add the potatoes, zucchini, onions, and carrots to the bowl and toss well. Arrange the vegetables in a single layer around the meat in the roasting pan. (If you can't fit all the vegetables in a single layer, use a separate pan to roast the remainder.) Place the roasting pan in the oven and reduce the oven temperature to 350°F.

3. **Roast the meat and vegetables,** stirring and turning the vegetables occasionally, until the vegetables are tender and the beef reaches an internal temperature of 140°F for medium-rare, about 1 hour and 15 minutes. Let stand 10 minutes before slicing.

PER SERVING: 317 CALORIES
6g total fat, 2g saturated fat, 60mg cholesterol, 411mg sodium, 38g total carbohydrate, 6g dietary fiber, 28g protein, 64mg calcium

COOK'S HINT COOK'S HINT **beef** COOK'S HINT COOK'S HINT COOK'S HINT COOK'S HINT

Eye round and other lean roasts are best cooked and served rare to medium-rare; if a lean cut of meat is overcooked it becomes tough and dry. Test for doneness with an instant-read thermometer: Insert the thermometer into the center of the meat and wait for the temperature indicator to come to a full stop before reading. It's important to realize that meats continue to cook after coming out of the oven, so it's best to remove the meat at a temperature slightly lower than desired, then let it stand at least 10 minutes before slicing.

# steak with roasted garlic and chili rub

*3 POINTS* PER SERVING | MAKES 4 SERVINGS

*To give your steak an Italian, instead of a Southwestern flavor, substitute equal amounts of dried basil for the chili powder and dried thyme for the cumin.*

1. **Preheat the oven** to 400°F. Wrap the garlic in foil and place on a baking sheet; roast until softened, 10–12 minutes. Remove the garlic from the oven. Spray the broiler rack with nonstick spray; preheat the broiler.

2. **When cool enough to handle,** squeeze the garlic from its papery skin into a small bowl. Add the chili powder, cumin, oregano, and salt; stir and mash together. Rub the steak on both sides with the garlic and chili mixture.

3. **Increase the oven temperature to broil.** Broil the steak 4 inches from the heat until done to taste, about 5 minutes on each side for medium.

PER SERVING: 136 CALORIES
4g total fat, 1g saturated fat, 60mg cholesterol, 196mg sodium, 1g total carbohydrate, 0g dietary fiber, 23g protein, 15mg calcium

4 large garlic cloves, unpeeled

1 teaspoon chili powder

½ teaspoon ground cumin

¼ teaspoon dried oregano

¼ teaspoon salt

1 (1-pound) boneless sirloin steak, trimmed of all visible fat

COOK'S HINT COOK'S HINT **vegetables** COOK'S HINT COOK'S HINT COOK'S HINT COOK'S HINT

Double the amount of seasoning rub and toss the extra with chunks of zucchini, scallions, and bell peppers to broil alongside the steak.

# stuffed flank steak with tomato sauce

**6 POINTS** PER SERVING | MAKES 8 SERVINGS

*For total satisfaction, serve with a side dish of mashed potatoes or pasta, and steamed broccoli or green beans.*

2 slices whole-wheat, oatmeal, or oat bran bread, made into crumbs

1 (10-ounce) package frozen chopped kale, thawed and well drained

1 roasted red bell pepper, finely chopped

½ cup shredded part-skim mozzarella cheese

¼ cup grated Parmesan cheese

2 garlic cloves, finely chopped

1 egg white

1¼ teaspoons salt

1 (2-pound) flank steak, trimmed of all visible fat

1 teaspoon olive oil

1 small onion, finely chopped

1 (28-ounce) can crushed tomatoes

¼ teaspoon freshly ground pepper

1. **Preheat the oven** to 400°F. Spray the rack of a roasting pan with nonstick spray.

2. **Combine** the bread crumbs, kale, roasted pepper, mozzarella cheese, Parmesan cheese, 1 of the garlic cloves, the egg white, and ½ teaspoon of the salt in a medium bowl.

3. **With a long, thin knife** held horizontal to your cutting board, split the steak in half lengthwise without cutting all the way through. Open the steak like a book. Sprinkle evenly with the remaining ¾ teaspoon salt. Spread the bread stuffing over the steak, leaving a 1-inch border. Roll the steak up tightly from one long side. Tie with kitchen string at 1-inch intervals. Place the steak on the rack in the roasting pan. Roast 1 hour. Remove from the oven and let stand 15 minutes, then cut crosswise into ½-inch slices.

4. **Meanwhile, to prepare the tomato sauce,** heat the oil in a nonstick saucepan, then add the onion and the remaining garlic clove. Sauté until golden, 7–10 minutes. Add the tomatoes and ground pepper; bring to a boil. Reduce the heat and simmer, stirring occasionally, until slightly thickened, about 30 minutes. Serve with the steak slices.

**PER SERVING** (⅛ OF THE STEAK AND SCANT ½ CUP SAUCE): 271 CALORIES
11g total fat, 5g saturated fat, 71mg cholesterol, 728mg sodium, 11g total carbohydrate, 3g dietary fiber, 31g protein, 181mg calcium

COOK'S HINT COOK'S HINT **time saver** COOK'S HINT COOK'S HINT
To save time, use frozen or jarred roasted bell peppers.

# warm pasta salad
# with blue cheese dressing

***7 POINTS*** PER SERVING | MAKES 6 SERVINGS

*You can transform this pasta salad into a potato salad by substituting a pound of freshly boiled, then thickly sliced red potatoes for the pasta. Either way, a crisp green salad will round out the meal. It's best to eat this dish as soon as it's made or the pasta will soak up all the dressing.*

**1. Cook the pasta** according to package directions. Combine the yogurt, mayonnaise, blue cheese, salt, and pepper in a large bowl.

**2. Heat a large nonstick skillet.** Swirl in the oil, then add the garlic. Sauté until fragrant, 30 seconds. Add the beef in two batches and cook, until just browned, about 2 minutes.

**3. Drain the pasta well** and add to the bowl with the yogurt dressing. Add the steak and tomatoes and toss to coat. Serve at once.

**PER SERVING (GENEROUS 1 CUP): 323 CALORIES**
9g total fat, 3g saturated fat, 40mg cholesterol, 324mg sodium, 39g total carbohydrate, 2g dietary fiber, 22g protein, 144mg calcium

2 cups penne

1 cup plain nonfat yogurt

2 tablespoons low-fat mayonnaise

2 ounces blue cheese, finely crumbled

¼ teaspoon salt

⅛ teaspoon freshly ground pepper

2 teaspoons olive oil

1 garlic clove, minced

1 (12-ounce) round steak, trimmed of all visible fat and thinly sliced

½ pint cherry tomatoes, halved

# savory beef loaf with bulgur and sun-dried tomatoes

**5 POINTS** PER SERVING | MAKES 4 SERVINGS

*Bulgur is wheat that has been steamed, dried, and ground to a fine, medium, or coarse texture. It is used most often in Middle Eastern cooking to make salads and stews, or it is served as a side dish like rice or barley. This meatloaf goes well with mashed potatoes or corn on the cob and a vegetable medley on the side.*

⅓ cup finely ground bulgur

¼ cup sun-dried tomato pieces (not oil-packed)

½ cup warm water

1 pound lean ground beef (10% or less fat)

⅓ cup plain nonfat yogurt

2 scallions, finely chopped

1 garlic clove, finely chopped

1 egg white

½ teaspoon dried thyme

¼ teaspoon salt

⅛ teaspoon freshly ground pepper

**1.** Preheat the oven to 375°F. Spray a small baking pan with nonstick spray.

**2.** Combine the bulgur, sun-dried tomatoes, and warm water in a large bowl; let soak 10 minutes.

**3.** Add the beef, yogurt, scallions, garlic, egg white, thyme, salt, and pepper to the bulgur mixture; mix well. Shape into a 4 x 8-inch loaf and place in the baking pan. Bake until an instant-read thermometer inserted in the center of the loaf registers 160°F.

PER SERVING: 244 CALORIES
8g total fat, 3g saturated fat, 65mg cholesterol, 307mg sodium, 13g total carbohydrate, 3g dietary fiber, 28g protein, 65mg calcium

COOK'S HINT COOK'S HINT **variation** COOK'S HINT COOK'S HINT COOK'S HINT COOK'S HINT

This versatile seasoned beef and bulgur combination makes great hamburgers for grilling or broiling. Or try crumbling any leftovers into tomato sauce to use as a topping for pasta.

# beefy black bean chili

*7 POINTS* PER SERVING | MAKES 6 SERVINGS

*This basic ground beef chili is jazzed up with a garnish of tomato, avocado, and tortilla chips. You could also add chopped red onions or scallions and a sprinkling of cilantro to the garnish. Serve as is, or over rice.*

1. **Heat the oil** in a large nonstick skillet over medium heat, then add the onion. Sauté until softened, 3–5 minutes. Add the garlic, chili powder, cumin, and oregano. Sauté, stirring constantly, 1 minute longer. Add the beef and brown, breaking it apart with a spoon, about 5 minutes.

2. **Stir in** the stewed tomatoes, beans, and corn. Simmer, uncovered, stirring occasionally, until the flavors are blended, about 20 minutes. Serve with the tomato, avocado, and tortilla chips.

**PER SERVING (1⅓ CUPS): 346 CALORIES**
10g total fat, 3g saturated fat, 43mg cholesterol, 448mg sodium, 42g total carbohydrate, 9g dietary fiber, 26g protein, 101mg calcium

2 teaspoons olive oil

1 onion, finely chopped

2 garlic cloves, minced

1 tablespoon chili powder

1 teaspoon ground cumin

½ teaspoon
dried oregano

1 pound lean ground beef
(10% or less fat)

2 (14½-ounce) cans
stewed tomatoes

1 (19-ounce) can black
beans, rinsed and drained

1 (14½-ounce) can
no-salt-added corn
kernels, drained

1 large ripe tomato,
chopped

¼ ripe avocado,
finely chopped

32 baked tortilla chips

# moroccan meatball stew

**4 *POINTS*** PER SERVING | MAKES 4 SERVINGS

*Paprika, a powdered blend of dried red peppers, is a staple seasoning in Central European cuisine. Unless labeled hot, the paprika sold in supermarkets is usually mild and somewhat sweet. Serve this stew over couscous, with sautéed zucchini and red bell peppers on the side.*

½ pound lean ground beef (10% or less fat)

½ pound lean ground veal

2 tablespoons minced cilantro

2½ teaspoons paprika

2 teaspoons ground cumin

1 teaspoon salt

¼ teaspoon freshly ground pepper

1 teaspoon olive oil

1 onion, finely chopped

1 garlic clove, minced

1 ripe tomato, seeded and chopped

½ (6-ounce) can tomato paste

¾ cup water

1 tablespoon chopped parsley, to garnish

1. **Combine** the beef, veal, 1 tablespoon of the cilantro, 1½ teaspoons of the paprika, 1 teaspoon of the cumin, ½ teaspoon of the salt, and ⅛ teaspoon of the pepper in a large bowl. Shape into 24 one-inch balls.

2. **Heat a large nonstick skillet.** Swirl in the oil, then add the onion and garlic. Sauté until softened, 3–5 minutes. Stir in the tomato, tomato paste, water, the remaining 1 tablespoon cilantro, 1 teaspoon paprika, 1 teaspoon cumin, ½ teaspoon salt, and ⅛ teaspoon pepper; bring to a boil. Add the meatballs, reduce the heat and simmer, covered, until the meatballs are cooked and the sauce thickens, 30–45 minutes. Garnish with the parsley just before serving.

PER SERVING: 204 CALORIES
8g total fat, 3g saturated fat, 73mg cholesterol, 819mg sodium, 9g total carbohydrate, 2g dietary fiber, 24g protein, 45mg calcium

# veal cutlets with mushrooms and tomatoes [20]

*4 POINTS* PER SERVING | MAKES 4 SERVINGS

*For everyday cooking, use readily available white mushrooms called for in this recipe. To make it special, use exotic, more flavorful mushrooms, such as chanterelle, shiitake, or cèpe mushrooms. You also can substitute 1 cup cherry tomatoes for regular tomatoes if you prefer.*

**1. Place the cutlets** on a sheet of wax paper and sprinkle with the flour, ¼ teaspoon of the salt, and $\frac{1}{16}$ teaspoon of the pepper to lightly coat. Heat a large nonstick skillet. Swirl in the oil, then add the cutlets. Sauté until golden brown, about 2 minutes on each side. Transfer the cutlets to a plate and keep warm.

**2. Spray the same skillet** with nonstick spray, then add the mushrooms, garlic, and the remaining ¼ teaspoon salt and $\frac{1}{16}$ teaspoon pepper. Sauté, stirring often, until the mushrooms are golden, about 2 minutes. Add the wine and cook until the liquid evaporates, about 3 minutes. Stir in the tomatoes, broth, and basil. Simmer until slightly thickened, about 5 minutes. Swirl in the butter until blended. Return the cutlets to the skillet and simmer until just heated through, about 1 minute.

**PER SERVING: 182 CALORIES**
8g total fat, 3g saturated fat, 77mg cholesterol, 375mg sodium, 8g total carbohydrate, 1g dietary fiber, 20g protein, 31mg calcium

1 pound veal cutlets

1 tablespoon all-purpose flour

½ teaspoon salt

⅛ teaspoon freshly ground pepper

2 teaspoons olive oil

½ pound white mushrooms, sliced

1 garlic clove, minced

¼ cup dry white wine

2 ripe tomatoes, seeded and diced

½ cup low-sodium chicken broth

2 tablespoons minced fresh basil or 1½ teaspoons dried

1 teaspoon butter

# veal curry with rice and peas

***8 POINTS*** PER SERVING | MAKES 4 SERVINGS

*Don't let the long ingredient list of this recipe scare you—it's mostly spices. This is a very simple dish to prepare, and the spicy sauce is so rich and flavorful, you won't need a fancy side dish. Serve with plain steamed cauliflower, carrots, or spinach. You can substitute bite-size pieces of chicken breast or pork tenderloin for the veal.*

1 cup plain nonfat yogurt

2 tablespoons coconut milk

1 jalapeño pepper, seeded and minced (wear gloves to prevent irritation)

1 tablespoon curry powder

1 teaspoon minced peeled fresh ginger

1 garlic clove, minced

¼ teaspoon salt

¼ teaspoon ground cloves

⅛ teaspoon ground cardamom

1 pound veal cutlets, cut into 1-inch pieces

1 cup aromatic long-grain white rice, such as basmati or texmati

1 cup frozen peas, partially thawed

2 teaspoons canola oil

1 onion, finely chopped

1 tablespoon all-purpose flour

1. **Combine** the yogurt, coconut milk, jalapeño pepper, curry powder, ginger, garlic, salt, cloves, and cardamom in a large bowl. Add the veal and stir to coat. Cover and marinate 30 minutes at room temperature or overnight in the refrigerator.

2. **Meanwhile, cook the rice** according to package directions, adding the peas during the last 5 minutes of the cooking time.

3. **Heat a large nonstick skillet.** Swirl in the oil, then add the onion. Sauté until softened, 3–5 minutes. Sprinkle with the flour and cook, stirring constantly, 1 minute. Stir in the veal with the yogurt marinade. Simmer over very low heat, stirring occasionally, until the veal is just cooked through, 7–8 minutes. (Do not allow the yogurt mixture to boil.) Serve with the rice and peas.

PER SERVING (1 CUP VEAL MIXTURE AND SCANT 1 CUP RICE MIXTURE):
419 CALORIES
9g total fat, 3g saturated fat, 75mg cholesterol, 287mg sodium, 56g total carbohydrate, 4g dietary fiber, 28g protein, 181mg calcium

COOK'S HINT COOK'S HINT **leftovers** COOK'S HINT COOK'S HINT COOK'S HINT

If you have leftover cooked rice, reheat 2 cups rice with the peas and ¼ cup water. Cover the pan and cook until the rice and peas are heated through, 5–7 minutes.

# glazed pork loin and acorn squash

**7 POINTS** PER SERVING | MAKES 4 SERVINGS

*Round out this sweet pork and squash with the contrasting bite of braised kale, collard greens, or broccoli rabe. Finish with a comforting serving of applesauce.*

1. **Preheat the oven** to 425°F. Line a large roasting pan with foil and lightly spray the foil with nonstick spray. Rub the pork with 1 teaspoon of the sage, ¼ teaspoon of the salt, ⅛ teaspoon of the pepper, and the garlic. Place in the roasting pan and roast 20 minutes.

2. **Sprinkle the squash** with the remaining ¼ teaspoon salt and ⅛ teaspoon pepper. Place the squash, cut-sides down, around the pork and roast about 30 minutes longer.

3. **Combine** the orange juice, maple syrup, and the remaining ½ teaspoon sage in a small bowl. Turn the squash halves cut-side up. Baste the pork loin and the squash with the orange-maple glaze. Roast until the squash are cooked through and the pork reaches an internal temperature of 155–160°F, 15–20 minutes longer, basting two or three times with the glaze. Let stand 10 minutes before slicing. (You can leave the squash in the turned-off oven to keep warm while the pork stands.)

**PER SERVING:** 343 CALORIES
9g total fat, 3g saturated fat, 72mg cholesterol, 344mg sodium, 40g total carbohydrate, 7g dietary fiber, 28g protein, 114mg calcium

1 pound boneless center-cut pork loin, trimmed of all visible fat

1½ teaspoons dried sage, crumbled

½ teaspoon salt

¼ teaspoon freshly ground pepper

2 garlic cloves, minced

2 small acorn squash, halved and seeded

¼ cup orange juice

2 tablespoons maple syrup

COOK'S HINT COOK'S HINT **safety first** COOK'S HINT COOK'S HINT COOK'S HINT COOK'S HINT

Pork always should be cooked to an internal temperature of 160°F. However, you don't want to overcook a pork roast or it will get dry. The best way to ensure a safe, moist, and tasty roast is to cook it to an internal temperature of 155°F, then remove the roast from the oven and let it stand for 10 minutes before slicing and serving. The internal temperature will rise to 160°F while the roast stands.

# skewered pork with mushrooms and scallions

**4 POINTS** PER SERVING | MAKES 4 SERVINGS

*It's easier to cut thin slices from a pork tenderloin or any raw meat or poultry if you put it in the freezer first for 15–20 minutes. Serve these tasty, tender pork kebabs with an aromatic rice such as brown basmati. For easy clean-up, line the broiler pan with foil before broiling the skewers.*

½ cup water

3 tablespoons reduced-sodium soy sauce

2 teaspoons minced peeled fresh ginger

3 garlic cloves, minced

1 tablespoon sugar

1 tablespoon rice wine vinegar or white wine vinegar

1 pound pork tenderloin, trimmed and cut into 16 thin slices

¼ pound shiitake mushrooms

8 scallions, trimmed to 4-inch lengths

1 tablespoon toasted sesame seeds

1. **Combine** the water, soy sauce, ginger, garlic, sugar, and vinegar in a large zip-close plastic bag; add the pork, mushrooms, and scallions. Squeeze out the air and seal the bag; turn to coat the pork and vegetables. Refrigerate, turning the bag occasionally, at least 30 minutes or up to 12 hours.

2. **Spray the broiler rack** with nonstick spray; preheat the broiler. Loosely skewer the pork, mushrooms, and scallions onto eight 9-inch metal skewers. Place the skewers on the broiler rack and broil 5 inches from the heat, until cooked through, about 4 minutes on each side.

3. **Meanwhile, pour the marinade** into a small saucepan and boil, stirring constantly, 3 minutes. Pour over the cooked pork and vegetables. Sprinkle with sesame seeds before serving.

**PER SERVING:** 203 CALORIES
6g total fat, 2g saturated fat, 72mg cholesterol, 509mg sodium, 9g total carbohydrate, 2g dietary fiber, 28g protein, 39mg calcium

COOK'S HINT COOK'S HINT **safety first** COOK'S HINT COOK'S HINT COOK'S HINT COOK'S HINT

If a marinade for meat, poultry, or fish is to be used during cooking or as a sauce, it must be boiled at a rolling boil (that is, one that cannot be stirred down) for at least 3 minutes to kill any bacteria.

# pineapple pork fried rice [20]

**8 POINTS** PER SERVING | MAKES 4 SERVINGS

*This one-dish meal is flavored with typical Thai seasonings, including garlic, ginger, cilantro, chile pepper, and nam pla (fish sauce). If you can't find fish sauce, substitute ½ teaspoon anchovy paste or mashed anchovy, stirred into 2 tablespoons of water. Or, you can omit this ingredient altogether and stir the tomato paste into 2 tablespoons of water.*

**1. Heat the oil** in a large nonstick skillet over medium heat, then add the pork. Sauté until lightly browned, 2–3 minutes. Add the scallions, garlic, ginger, jalapeño pepper, salt, and ground pepper; sauté until fragrant and the pork is cooked through, about 2 minutes longer.

**2. Combine** the nam pla and tomato paste in a small bowl; stir into the skillet along with the rice, tomatoes, and pineapple. Cook, stirring gently, until the mixture is heated through, about 5 minutes. Stir in the cilantro just before serving.

**PER SERVING (1½ CUPS): 362 CALORIES**
12g total fat, 3g saturated fat, 72mg cholesterol, 378mg sodium, 34g total carbohydrate, 3g dietary fiber, 29g protein, 31mg calcium

2 teaspoons canola oil

1 pound lean pork loin or tenderloin, trimmed of all visible fat and cut into ¾-inch cubes

2 scallions, finely chopped

1 large garlic clove, minced

1 tablespoon minced peeled fresh ginger

½ jalapeño pepper, seeded and minced (wear gloves to prevent irritation)

½ teaspoon salt

⅛ teaspoon freshly ground pepper

2 tablespoons fish sauce (nam pla), optional

1 tablespoon tomato paste

2 cups cooked brown or white rice

3 plum tomatoes, seeded and diced

½ small pineapple, peeled and cubed

1 tablespoon minced cilantro

COOK'S HINT COOK'S HINT COOK'S HINT **time saver** COOK'S HINT COOK'S HINT COOK'S HINT COOK'S HINT

When cooking rice, cook extra to have on hand in the refrigerator for recipes such as this. Cooked rice keeps in the refrigerator for up to 5 days.

# pork adobo

**5 POINTS** PER SERVING | MAKES 4 SERVINGS

*This is a classic dish from the Philippines that could also be made using chunks of boneless chicken or veal, instead of the pork. Serve in individual bowls over hot cooked rice with a spinach, tomato, and mushroom salad on the side.*

1 pound boneless center-cut pork loin, trimmed of all visible fat and cut into 1½-inch cubes

1 cup water

¼ cup cider vinegar

2 tablespoons reduced-sodium soy sauce

3 garlic cloves, minced

1 small bay leaf

¼ teaspoon salt

1. **Combine** the pork, water, vinegar, soy sauce, garlic, bay leaf, and salt in a medium saucepan. Let stand 30 minutes.

2. **Bring the mixture to a boil.** Reduce the heat and simmer, covered, until the meat is very tender, about 1 hour. Remove the bay leaf before serving.

PER SERVING (GENEROUS 1 CUP): 197 CALORIES
9g total fat, 3g saturated fat, 72mg cholesterol, 490mg sodium, 2g total carbohydrate, 0g dietary fiber, 26g protein, 13mg calcium

# caribbean callaloo pork stew

***4 POINTS*** PER SERVING | MAKES 6 SERVINGS

*Callaloo, a green vegetable widely used in Caribbean cooking, is the edible leaves of the taro root. Fresh callaloo can usually be found in Caribbean and Asian food markets. If you can't find it, substitute kale, collard greens, or Swiss chard. Callaloo is also the name of a gumbo-like soup or stew that contains the greens along with okra and any of a variety of meats and seafood, usually some type of pork and either crab or shrimp.*

**1. Remove and discard** any thick stems from the callaloo and coarsely chop. Combine the callaloo, broth, okra, pork, onion, bay leaf, jalapeño pepper, garlic, salt, thyme, and ground pepper in a large saucepot; bring to a boil. Reduce the heat and simmer, covered, until the pork and vegetables are very tender, about 1 hour.

**2. Add the shrimp, lemon, and hot sauce,** if using. Cook until the shrimp are just opaque, about 5 minutes. Remove the bay leaf before serving. Serve the stew in individual bowls over the rice.

**PER SERVING (1½ CUPS STEW AND ½ CUP RICE): 243 CALORIES**
4g total fat, 1g saturated fat, 60mg cholesterol, 491mg sodium, 32g total carbohydrate, 4g dietary fiber, 19g protein, 140mg calcium

COOK'S HINT COOK'S HINT **variation** COOK'S HINT COOK'S HINT COOK'S HINT
For variety, you can substitute lean ham or chicken breast for the pork and fresh lump crabmeat for the shrimp.

1 pound fresh callaloo, kale, collard greens, or Swiss chard, cleaned

4 cups low-sodium chicken broth

1 (10-ounce) box frozen cut okra, thawed

½ pound boneless pork loin, trimmed of all visible fat and cut into 1-inch cubes

1 onion, finely chopped

1 bay leaf

1 jalapeño pepper, seeded and minced (wear gloves to prevent irritation)

1 large garlic clove, minced

1 teaspoon salt

½ teaspoon dried thyme

⅛ teaspoon freshly ground pepper

½ pound large shrimp, peeled and deveined

1 lemon, thinly sliced

½ teaspoon hot pepper sauce (optional)

3 cups cooked white rice

# roast lamb shanks with lentils

**8 POINTS** PER SERVING | MAKES 4 SERVINGS

*Make this a comforting and satisfying meal by serving it with a side dish of couscous or aromatic rice, and a simple carrot-zucchini sauté.*

4 (7-ounce) lamb shanks, trimmed

1 teaspoon dried rosemary

1 teaspoon dried oregano

½ teaspoon salt

¼ teaspoon freshly ground pepper

1 cup water

1 cup brown or green lentils, picked over, rinsed, and drained

2 cups low-sodium chicken broth

1 (14½-ounce) can tomatoes in juice, cut up

1 large garlic clove, minced

**1. Preheat the oven** to 350°F. Place the lamb shanks in a small roasting pan. Rub evenly with ½ teaspoon each of the rosemary and oregano. Sprinkle with ¼ teaspoon of the salt and ⅛ teaspoon of the pepper. Add the water to the pan; cover tightly with foil. Roast until very tender, 1½–2 hours.

**2. Meanwhile, combine** the lentils, broth, tomatoes, garlic, remaining ½ teaspoon each of the rosemary and oregano, remaining ¼ teaspoon salt and ⅛ teaspoon pepper in a medium saucepan; bring to a boil. Reduce the heat and simmer, covered, until the lentils are tender, 30–45 minutes.

**3. Transfer the lamb shanks to a plate.** Drain and discard the liquid and fat from the roasting pan. Spoon the lentil mixture into the roasting pan, top with the shanks, and return the roasting pan to the oven. Roast, uncovered, until the lentils are heated through, about 15 minutes.

PER SERVING (1 LAMB SHANK AND ¾ CUP LENTILS): 414 CALORIES
11g total fat, 4g saturated fat, 98mg cholesterol, 566mg sodium, 34g total carbohydrate, 12g dietary fiber, 45g protein, 76mg calcium

COOK'S HINT COOK'S HINT **lamb** COOK'S HINT COOK'S HINT COOK'S HINT COOK'S HINT

Inexpensive lamb shanks lend themselves to slow roasting and braising, so the meat becomes very tender and falls easily from the bone. You can tell a lamb shank is properly cooked when a fork inserted into the meaty part meets no resistance on its way in or out.

# lamb and white bean chili

**5 POINTS** PER SERVING | MAKES 6 SERVINGS

*This is a mild chili: spicy, but not spicy-hot. Like most chilies, it's even better when reheated and served the next day. Serve over brown rice or warm cornbread wedges with butternut squash cubes.*

**1. Cook the bacon** in a large, deep nonstick skillet or saucepan until crisp. Drain and wipe the fat from the skillet and drain the bacon on a paper towel. Reheat the skillet and swirl in 1 teaspoon of the oil. Add the lamb in 2 or 3 batches and cook until lightly browned on all sides, about 3 minutes. Transfer the lamb to a plate.

**2. Swirl the remaining 1 teaspoon oil** into the skillet, then add the onion. Cook until softened, 3–5 minutes. Add the garlic, chili powder, and cumin; cook until fragrant, about 1 minute. Stir in the crushed tomatoes, tomato paste, water, thyme, oregano, bay leaf, and jalapeño pepper; bring to a boil. Reduce the heat and simmer until the lamb is very tender, about 1 hour. Stir in the beans and simmer 10 minutes longer. Remove the bay leaf before serving.

**PER SERVING (1 CUP): 271 CALORIES**
9g total fat, 3g saturated fat, 56mg cholesterol, 536mg sodium, 24g total carbohydrate, 6g dietary fiber, 25g protein, 114mg calcium

2 slices bacon

2 teaspoons olive oil

1 pound boneless lamb shoulder, trimmed of all visible fat and cut into 1-inch cubes

1 onion, finely chopped

2 garlic cloves, minced

1 tablespoon chili powder

2 teaspoons ground cumin

1 (28-ounce) can crushed tomatoes

½ (6-ounce) can tomato paste

1 cup water

2 teaspoons dried thyme

2 teaspoons dried oregano

1 bay leaf, broken in half

1 jalapeño pepper, seeded and minced (wear gloves to prevent irritation)

1 (15-ounce) can cannellini (white kidney) beans, rinsed and drained

COOK'S HINT COOK'S HINT **chili** COOK'S HINT COOK'S HINT COOK'S HINT

Commonly available jalapeño peppers range from mild to hot, but there's no way to tell how hot they are until you taste them. To increase the heat of a bland jalapeño, leave in some of the seeds. Or you can kick up the heat by adding a little ground cayenne, a pinch of crushed red pepper, or a dash of hot pepper sauce. For a hot chili with smoky flavor, add a small chipotle pepper.

# shepherd's pie

**5 *POINTS*** PER SERVING | MAKES 6 SERVINGS

*Leave the peels on the potatoes to boost the fiber in this classic lamb casserole. If you like, add a tablespoon of chopped chives to the potato mixture while mashing or sprinkle with paprika before baking.*

3 large potatoes
(1½ pounds),
cut in chunks

1 teaspoon olive oil

1 large onion,
finely chopped

2 garlic cloves, minced

½ pound lean ground beef
(10% or less fat)

½ pound lean
ground lamb

1 (14½-ounce) can diced
tomatoes in juice

1 cup frozen peas,
thawed

1 teaspoon salt

¼ teaspoon freshly
ground pepper

½ teaspoon
dried oregano

½ teaspoon dried thyme

½ cup plain nonfat yogurt

1 teaspoon butter

1. **Preheat the oven** to 375°F. Cook the potatoes in water to cover in a large pot until tender.

2. **Meanwhile, heat a large nonstick skillet.** Swirl in the oil, then add the onion and garlic. Sauté until softened, 3–5 minutes. Add the beef and lamb and brown, breaking it apart with a spoon, about 5 minutes. Drain all excess fat from the skillet.

3. **Stir in** the tomatoes, peas, ½ teaspoon of the salt, ⅛ teaspoon of the pepper, the oregano, and thyme; bring to a boil. Reduce the heat and simmer, stirring occasionally, about 10 minutes.

4. **Drain the potatoes** and return them to the saucepan. Mash in the yogurt, butter, the remaining ½ teaspoon salt and ⅛ teaspoon pepper.

5. **Spread the meat mixture** in a 10-inch deep-dish pie plate or other 1½-quart baking dish. Spread the mashed potatoes evenly over the meat. Bake until the potatoes begin to brown and the filling is bubbly, about 20 minutes. Let stand 10 minutes before serving.

PER SERVING: 269 CALORIES
7g total fat, 2g saturated fat, 44mg cholesterol, 581mg sodium, 33g total carbohydrate, 5g dietary fiber, 20g protein, 87mg calcium

COOK'S HINT COOK'S HINT **removing fat** COOK'S HINT COOK'S HINT COOK'S HINT COOK'S HINT

To drain the fat from the meat mixture, after step #2, spoon the meat into a colander. Toss and press the mixture gently with a spatula. Wipe the remaining fat from the skillet with a paper towel before returning the meat mixture to the skillet and continuing to cook.

# ham and yams in cider sauce

*5 POINTS* PER SERVING | MAKES 4 SERVINGS

*Round out this easy Southern favorite with two classic side dishes: coleslaw and steamed collard greens.*

1. **Cover the yams with water** in a large saucepan and bring to a boil. Boil until just tender, 30 to 40 minutes. Drain, peel, and slice ¼-inch thick.

2. **Heat a large nonstick skillet.** Add the ham pieces and cook until lightly browned, about 1 minute on each side.

3. **Whisk together** the cider, flour, and cloves in a small bowl until smooth. Pour into the skillet and add the yams. Simmer gently, stirring often and turning the yams in the sauce, until the sauce is thickened, about 5 minutes.

PER SERVING: 248 CALORIES
5g total fat, 2g saturated fat, 45mg cholesterol, 1034mg sodium, 31g total carbohydrate,
3g dietary fiber, 19g protein, 36mg calcium

1 pound yams
or sweet potatoes

1 (12-ounce) lean ham
steak, cut into four pieces

1 cup apple cider

2 teaspoons
all-purpose flour

⅛ teaspoon ground cloves

# pasta shells with beans, greens, and sausage [20]

**8 POINTS** PER SERVING | MAKES 6 SERVINGS

*A small amount of chicken broth, seasoned with garlic and sage, serves as a light sauce for this tasty pasta dish. Toasted slices of Italian bread, topped with chopped roasted bell pepper or chopped ripe tomatoes, would be a perfect side dish.*

3 cups small pasta shells

8 ounces sweet or hot Italian sausage, casings removed

2 garlic cloves, minced

2 teaspoons dried sage

1 (19-ounce) can cannellini (white kidney) beans, rinsed and drained

3 cups torn spinach leaves

2 cups low-sodium chicken broth

½ teaspoon salt

⅛ teaspoon freshly ground pepper

1. **Cook the pasta** according to package directions until slightly firm.

2. **Meanwhile, heat a large nonstick skillet** over medium-high heat, then add the sausage and brown, breaking it apart with a spoon, about 3 minutes. Transfer the sausage to a paper towel-lined plate to drain.

3. **Add the garlic and sage** to the same skillet and sauté until fragrant, about 30 seconds. Add the beans, spinach, and broth; bring to a boil. Reduce the heat and simmer until the spinach is just tender, about 5 minutes. Add the drained pasta, sausage, salt, and pepper. Simmer until just heated through, about 3 minutes.

**PER SERVING (1½ CUPS): 413 CALORIES**
7g total fat, 2g saturated fat, 15mg cholesterol, 558mg sodium, 68g total carbohydrate, 7g dietary fiber, 20g protein, 107mg calcium

COOK'S HINT COOK'S HINT **pasta** COOK'S HINT COOK'S HINT COOK'S HINT COOK'S HINT COOK'S HINT

Pasta shapes are often chosen to match the type of sauce they are paired with. When a recipe calls for a short, stubby pasta such as small shells, you can substitute any pasta with a similar size and shape such as elbows, rotelle, radiatore, twists, orecchiette (little ears), or even farfalle (bow-ties).

honey-lime salmon with confetti corn salad  salmon au poivre
pan-seared tuna with fennel and orange relish
ginger swordfish with orange-avocado salsa
flounder florentine  halibut with spicy tomatoes and capers
easy crusty cod
red snapper with black beans, corn, and mango
cajun catfish on greens  poached sole with parsley-caper sauce
roasted whole trout, baby carrots, and zucchini  tuna patties
stir-fried shrimp and vegetables

shrimp and tomato flambé  jambalaya
spicy shrimp and lobster linguine
broiled lobster tails with plums
garlic scallop broil with ouzo and feta cheese
corn cioppino

# fish & shellfish

# honey-lime salmon
# with confetti corn salad

*6 POINTS* PER SERVING | MAKES 4 SERVINGS

*The zesty lime, pungent garlic, and sweet honey are a perfect foil for the rich salmon. If you like, arrange the corn salad on a bed of mixed greens to serve with the salmon.*

1 teaspoon grated
lime zest

¼ cup fresh lime juice

1 tablespoon canola oil

1 garlic clove, minced

2 teaspoons honey

¾ teaspoon salt

½ teaspoon freshly
ground pepper

4 (4-ounce) salmon fillets

2 cups fresh or thawed
frozen corn kernels

1 red bell pepper, seeded
and finely chopped

½ cup chopped red onion

¼ cup chopped parsley

**1. Combine** the lime zest, lime juice, oil, garlic, honey, salt, and ground pepper in a small bowl. Put 3 tablespoons of the lime mixture in a large zip-close plastic bag; add the salmon. Squeeze out the air and seal the bag; turn to coat the fish. Refrigerate, turning the bag occasionally, about 30 minutes. Set the remaining dressing aside.

**2. Spray the broiler rack** with nonstick spray; preheat the broiler. Combine the corn, bell pepper, onion, parsley, and the remaining dressing in a medium bowl.

**3. Transfer the salmon** from the marinade (discard the marinade) to the broiler rack. Broil 5 inches from the heat until the salmon is just opaque in the center and lightly browned on the outside, about 4 minutes on each side. Serve with the corn salad.

**PER SERVING (1 SALMON FILLET AND A GENEROUS ½ CUP SALAD):**
275 CALORIES
10g total fat, 2g saturated fat, 75mg cholesterol, 403mg sodium, 23g total carbohydrate, 3g dietary fiber, 27g protein, 31mg calcium

COOK'S HINT COOK'S HINT **perfect fish** COOK'S HINT COOK'S HINT COOK'S HINT COOK'S HINT

For moist, tender fish, cook it until it just turns opaque in the center and not a minute longer. The rule of thumb is to cook fish fillets and steaks 8–10 minutes per inch of thickness.

Herb-Crusted Roast Beef and Vegetables

Moroccan Meatball Stew. Opposite: Pineapple Pork Fried Rice.

Ginger Swordfish with Orange-Avocado Salsa. Opposite: Caribbean Callaloo Pork Stew.

Red Snapper with Black Beans, Corn, and Mango. Opposite: Roasted Whole Trout, Baby Carrots, and Zucchini.

Spicy Shrimp and Lobster Linguine

# salmon au poivre

**4 POINTS** PER SERVING | MAKES 4 SERVINGS

*Coarsely ground black pepper infuses the salmon with a welcome spiciness in this simple, yet delicious dish. Buy a salmon fillet, about 1-inch thick throughout, in one, 1-pound piece, then skin it and cut it into 4 pieces. Or, have your fishmonger do the work for you. A tossed green salad of frisee lettuce with orange sections makes a refreshing accompaniment.*

**1. Place the salmon** in a shallow, snug-fitting nonreactive dish; add the lemon juice, garlic, and salt; turn the salmon to coat both sides. Let stand 5 minutes.

**2. Spread the pepper on a plate.** Lightly press the salmon into the pepper, coating both sides.

**3. Spray a nonstick skillet** or a nonstick ridged grill pan with nonstick spray and set over medium heat. Add the salmon and cook until it is just opaque in the center, 4–5 minutes on each side.

PER SERVING: 176 CALORIES
7g total fat, 2g saturated fat, 75mg cholesterol, 216mg sodium, 3g total carbohydrate, 1g dietary fiber, 25g protein, 35mg calcium

4 (4-ounce) salmon fillets (1-inch thick), skin removed

2 tablespoons fresh lemon juice

1 large garlic clove, minced

½ teaspoon salt

3 tablespoons coarsely ground black pepper

COOK'S HINT COOK'S HINT **salmon** COOK'S HINT COOK'S HINT COOK'S HINT COOK'S HINT COOK'S HINT

You can cook the salmon with or without the skin. Removing it allows more flavor from the marinade and the black pepper to penetrate the fish. If you prefer to leave the skin on, avoid eating it because of its extra fat.

# pan-seared tuna with fennel and orange relish [20]

*4 POINTS* PER SERVING | MAKES 4 SERVINGS

*Tuna is excellent when simply cooked, as it is here. We prefer it cooked rare, or medium-rare with it still a touch red in the center. Simply increase the cooking time, if you prefer your tuna more well-done. The fennel and orange relish can be made ahead of time and kept in the refrigerator for up to 3 days.*

½ fennel bulb, very thinly sliced (about 4 cups)

1 teaspoon grated orange zest

1 navel orange, sectioned

⅓ cup finely chopped red onion

¼ cup white wine vinegar

1 tablespoon chopped fennel tops

¾ teaspoon salt

4 (5-ounce) yellow fin tuna steaks, ¾–inch thick

½ teaspoon ground cumin

¼ teaspoon freshly ground pepper

1 teaspoon olive oil

1. **Combine** the fennel, orange zest, orange sections, onion, vinegar, fennel tops, and ¼ teaspoon of the salt. Cover and refrigerate at least 10 minutes.

2. **Meanwhile, sprinkle the tuna** with the remaining ½ teaspoon salt, the cumin, and pepper. Heat the oil in a nonstick skillet, then add the tuna. Cook until browned on the outside but still a little red in the center, 2–3 minutes on each side. Serve with the relish.

PER SERVING: 196 CALORIES
3g total fat, 1`g saturated fat, 78mg cholesterol, 603mg sodium, 13g total carbohydrate, 3g dietary fiber, 29g protein, 84mg calcium

COOK'S HINT COOK'S HINT oranges COOK'S HINT COOK'S HINT COOK'S HINT COOK'S HINT

To section an orange, use a sharp paring knife and slice away the top and bottom ends of the orange. Place the orange on a chopping board and slice away the rind, removing all of the pith. Working over a large bowl to catch the juices, cut the orange sections out from between the membranes, letting each section fall into the bowl. Discard any seeds.

# ginger swordfish
## with orange-avocado salsa

**6 POINTS** PER SERVING | MAKES 4 SERVINGS

*Swordfish is a perfect fish for broiling or grilling because it is more substantial than a delicate fillet. If you prefer, you can substitute another firm-flesh fish such as tuna for the swordfish. Serve with brown rice or boiled red-skinned potatoes.*

1. **Combine** the fish, lemon juice, oil, ginger, garlic, and salt in a large zip-close plastic bag. Squeeze out the air and seal the bag; turn to coat the fish. Refrigerate, turning the bag occasionally, 1 hour.

2. **Spray the broiler rack** with nonstick spray; preheat the broiler. Meanwhile to prepare the salsa, combine the orange sections, orange juice, cilantro, onion, and hot pepper sauce in a medium bowl, then gently stir in the avocado.

3. **Transfer the swordfish** from the marinade (discard the marinade) to the broiler rack and broil 5 inches from the heat, until just opaque in the center, about 4 minutes on each side. Serve with the salsa.

**PER SERVING (1 STEAK WITH ½ CUP SALSA): 287 CALORIES**
15g total fat, 3g saturated fat, 75mg cholesterol, 145mg sodium, 13g total carbohydrate, 4g dietary fiber, 26g protein, 49mg calcium

4 (5-ounce) swordfish steaks

2 tablespoons fresh lemon juice

1 tablespoon extra-virgin olive oil

2 teaspoons minced peeled fresh ginger

1 garlic clove, minced

¼ teaspoon salt

2 navel oranges, sectioned

3 tablespoons orange juice

¼ cup chopped cilantro

3 tablespoons finely chopped red onion

¼ teaspoon hot pepper sauce

1 avocado, peeled, pitted, and chopped

# flounder florentine

**5 POINTS** PER SERVING | MAKES 4 SERVINGS

*Mild-tasting flounder takes well to baking with the delicate flavors of lemon and nutmeg. The mushrooms and spinach add interest, while the cheese and crumb topping adds visual appeal and texture.*

2 teaspoons butter

¼ pound mushrooms, trimmed and sliced

4 (5-ounce) flounder fillets

½ teaspoon salt

¼ teaspoon freshly ground pepper

⅛ teaspoon nutmeg

1 (10-ounce) package frozen leaf spinach, thawed and squeezed dry

¼ cup dry white wine, or chicken broth

1 tablespoon fresh lemon juice

½ cup fresh bread crumbs

¼ cup shredded cheddar cheese

1. **Preheat the oven** to 450°F. Spray a 9-inch square baking dish with nonstick spray.

2. **Melt the butter** in a medium skillet, then add the mushrooms. Sauté until golden, about 5 minutes.

3. **Lay the fish on wax paper;** sprinkle with ¼ teaspoon of the salt, ⅛ teaspoon of the pepper, and the nutmeg. Top each fillet with a layer of spinach and mushrooms; sprinkle with the remaining ¼ teaspoon salt and ⅛ teaspoon pepper. Roll up the fish fillets and place seam-side down in the baking dish. Sprinkle with the wine and lemon juice.

4. **Combine** the bread crumbs and cheese in a small bowl; carefully spoon directly on top of the fish rolls. Bake uncovered, until the flounder is just opaque in the center and the crumbs are golden, about 15 minutes. Serve the fish with the pan juices.

**PER SERVING:** 243 CALORIES
7g total fat, 3g saturated fat, 82mg cholesterol, 615mg sodium, 14g total carbohydrate, 2g dietary fiber, 30g protein, 160mg calcium

COOK'S HINT COOK'S HINT **frozen fish** COOK'S HINT COOK'S HINT COOK'S HINT COOK'S HINT

Frozen fish, which is usually flash frozen within minutes of catching it, is often just as good and sometimes better than some fresh fish, which may have been in the market for several days. Keep the frozen fish in your freezer until the day before you need it, then thaw in the refrigerator overnight. Or, thaw the wrapped frozen fish in cold water, allowing one hour for every pound of fish.

# halibut with spicy tomatoes and capers

*4 POINTS* PER SERVING | MAKES 4 SERVINGS

*This is an easy, light skillet dinner with Mexican flavors. It really shines when served alongside roasted potatoes and steamed zucchini.*

**1. Heat the oil** in a large skillet, then add the onion. Sauté until translucent, 3–5 minutes. Add the garlic and jalapeño pepper and sauté until fragrant, about 1 minute. Add the tomatoes, capers, and salt; bring to a boil. Reduce the heat and simmer, uncovered, until the sauce is slightly thickened, about 15 minutes.

**2. Stir in the parsley and oregano.** Add the halibut, spooning the sauce over it; cover and simmer until the halibut is just opaque in the center, about 8 minutes. Serve with the lime wedges.

PER SERVING: 215 CALORIES
5g total fat, 1g saturated fat, 75mg cholesterol, 702mg sodium, 15g total carbohydrate, 3g dietary fiber, 30g protein, 96mg calcium

2 teaspoons olive oil

1 onion, sliced

3 garlic cloves, minced

1 jalapeño pepper, seeded and chopped (wear gloves to prevent irritation)

1 (28-ounce) can diced tomatoes

2 tablespoons drained tiny capers

¼ teaspoon salt

¼ cup chopped parsley

1 tablespoon chopped fresh oregano, or 1 teaspoon dried

1¼ pounds halibut or cod fillets

1 lime, cut into 4 wedges

# easy crusty cod [20]

*3 POINTS* PER SERVING | MAKES 4 SERVINGS

*This dish is a family favorite, filled with comforting familiar flavors.*
*Serve with mashed potatoes and peas.*

1 pound cod or halibut
fillet, cut into 4 pieces

½ cup chopped parsley

2 scallions, finely
chopped

2 tablespoons
all-purpose flour

2 teaspoons
fresh lemon juice

2 teaspoons extra-virgin
olive oil

¼ teaspoon salt

¼ teaspoon freshly
ground pepper

1. **Preheat the oven** to 500°F. Spray a 6 x 10-inch baking dish with cooking spray. Place the fish in the baking dish.

2. **Combine** the parsley, scallions, flour, lemon juice, oil, salt, and pepper in a small bowl. Spoon the mixture directly on top of the fish. Bake, uncovered until the fish is just opaque in the center and lightly browned and crisp on top, about 10 minutes.

PER SERVING: 144 CALORIES
4g total fat, 1g saturated fat, 60mg cholesterol, 244mg sodium, 4g total carbohydrate,
1g dietary fiber, 22g protein, 33mg calcium

COOK'S HINT COOK'S HINT **buying fish** COOK'S HINT COOK'S HINT COOK'S HINT COOK'S HINT

When buying fresh fish fillets or steaks, look for fish with a fresh mild odor, a firm texture that springs back when pressed with a finger, and a moist appearance.

# red snapper with black beans, corn, and mango

**4 POINTS** PER SERVING | MAKES 6 SERVINGS

*Mango, cilantro, and lime make a magical combination in this healthy salad. Add delicately flavored red snapper to the mix and you have a truly delightful experience. Serve with baked tortilla chips.*

1. **Preheat the broiler.** Spray a shallow baking dish with nonstick spray. Combine the lime zest, lime juice, oil, garlic, oregano, chili powder, and salt in a small bowl.

2. **Combine** the beans, corn, mango, cilantro, and 3 tablespoons of the lime juice mixture in a medium bowl.

3. **Place the snapper fillets** in the baking dish; spoon the remaining lime juice mixture over the fillets. Broil 5 inches from the heat until the fish is just opaque in the center, 7–8 minutes.

4. **Arrange the mesclun** on a serving platter; spoon the bean mixture on top. Arrange the snapper on top and drizzle any pan juices over all.

**PER SERVING (1 PIECE SNAPPER AND ¾ CUP SALAD): 213 CALORIES**
4g total fat, 1g saturated fat, 40mg cholesterol, 298mg sodium, 26g total carbohydrate, 6g dietary fiber, 20g protein, 81mg calcium

2 teaspoons grated lime zest

¼ cup fresh lime juice

1 tablespoon extra-virgin olive oil

1 garlic clove, minced

½ teaspoon oregano

½ teaspoon chili powder

¼ teaspoon salt

1 (15-ounce) can black beans, rinsed and drained

1 cup fresh or thawed frozen corn kernels

1 ripe mango, peeled and chopped

¼ cup chopped cilantro

1 pound red snapper fillets, cut into 6 pieces

6 cups mesclun

# cajun catfish on greens [20]

*4 POINTS* PER SERVING | MAKES 4 SERVINGS

*Catfish is a firm-fleshed fish with a slightly sweet flavor. Here, Cajun seasoning and lime give it a Southwestern flair. Serve with boiled red-skinned potatoes, seasoned with salt, pepper, and chopped parsley.*

¼ cup yellow cornmeal

3 tablespoons
all-purpose flour

2 teaspoons
Cajun seasoning

½ teaspoon coarsely
ground black pepper

¼ + ⅛ teaspoon salt

1 large egg

1 pound catfish fillets, cut
into 4 pieces

1 bunch arugula,
trimmed, rinsed, and
patted dry

1 teaspoon grated
lime zest

1 tablespoon fresh
lime juice

2 teaspoons olive oil

1 small garlic clove,
minced

Pinch sugar

1. **Preheat the oven** to 500°F. Spray a baking sheet with nonstick spray. Combine the cornmeal, flour, Cajun seasoning, pepper, and ¼ teaspoon of the salt on a plate.

2. **Lightly beat the egg** in a shallow dish; add the fish, turning to coat both sides. Lift the fish from the egg and coat it with the cornmeal mixture.

3. **Arrange the fish** on the baking sheet. Lightly spray the tops with nonstick spray and bake, without turning, until just opaque in the center and crisp and golden on the outside, about 10 minutes.

4. **Arrange the arugula** on a large platter. Combine the lime zest, lime juice, oil, garlic, sugar, and the remaining ⅛ teaspoon salt in a small bowl; sprinkle over the arugula. Top with the fish.

**PER SERVING: 203 CALORIES**
5g total fat, 1g saturated fat, 109mg cholesterol, 506mg sodium, 10g total carbohydrate, 1g dietary fiber, 28g protein, 67mg calcium

COOK'S HINT COOK'S HINT **lemon** COOK'S HINT COOK'S HINT COOK'S HINT COOK'S HINT

Remove any fishy odors from your hands and cutting board by rubbing them with a cut lemon.

# poached sole
# with parsley-caper sauce

*3 POINTS* PER SERVING | MAKES 4 SERVINGS

*Poaching fish works beautifully in the microwave because it keeps the fish moist and tender. One word of caution: don't ignore the standing instructions as the food continues to cook during this time.*

**1. Spray a 10-inch square** microwavable dish with a lid with nonstick spray. Add the fish and sprinkle with the lemon juice, salt, and pepper; dot with the butter. Cover the dish with the lid and microwave on High until the fish is just opaque in the center, 5–6 minutes, then let it stand, covered, for 1 minute. Drain the liquid from the fish into a cup. Cover the fish to keep it warm.

**2. Meanwhile, mix the flour** with 2 tablespoons of the milk to a smooth paste in a medium saucepan. Stir in the remaining milk and the fish liquid. Cook, stirring constantly, until the mixture boils and thickens. Stir in the parsley and capers. Pour the sauce over the fish.

PER SERVING: 143 CALORIES
3g total fat, 2g saturated fat, 59mg cholesterol, 471mg sodium, 6g total carbohydrate, 0g dietary fiber, 21g protein, 84mg calcium

1 pound sole fillets, cut into 4 pieces

1 tablespoon fresh lemon juice

½ teaspoon salt

½ teaspoon freshly ground pepper

2 teaspoons butter

2 tablespoons all-purpose flour

¾ cup fat-free milk

½ cup chopped parsley

1 tablespoon tiny capers, rinsed and drained

COOK'S HINT COOK'S HINT **cheese** COOK'S HINT COOK'S HINT COOK'S HINT COOK'S HINT COOK'S HINT

This dish is delicious as is, but if you have cheese lovers in your house, sprinkle the sauce-covered fish with ½ cup shredded reduced-fat cheddar cheese (add *1 POINT* per serving) and broil under a preheated broiler until the cheese is golden, about 3 minutes.

# roasted whole trout, baby carrots, and zucchini

**7 POINTS** PER SERVING | MAKES 4 SERVINGS

*Roasting foods coaxes out their sweetness and intensifies their flavors. You can substitute 2 cups broccoli florets, asparagus (cut into 2-inch lengths), or any other quick-cooking, no-POINTS vegetable for the zucchini, if you prefer.*

4 small (8-ounce) whole boneless rainbow trout, cleaned, heads and tails removed

1 teaspoon salt

¼ teaspoon freshly ground pepper

½ cup coarsely chopped parsley

5 teaspoons chopped fresh rosemary or 1¼ teaspoons dried

2 lemons, thinly sliced

1 bag (1 pound) baby carrots

2 small zucchini, cut lengthwise into quarters

2 tablespoons sliced almonds

**1. Preheat the oven** to 450°F. Spray a large roasting pan with cooking spray. Lay the trout on a sheet of wax paper; sprinkle the cavities with ½ teaspoon of the salt and ⅛ teaspoon of the pepper. Divide the parsley, 4 teaspoons of the rosemary, and the lemon slices among the cavities; place the fish in the roasting pan.

**2. Add the carrots** and zucchini to the pan; spread into one single layer. Lightly spray the trout and vegetables with cooking spray and sprinkle the vegetables with the remaining 1 teaspoon rosemary, ½ teaspoon salt, and ⅛ teaspoon pepper. Roast until the trout is almost cooked through, 15–20 minutes. Increase the oven temperature to broil. Sprinkle the trout with the almonds and broil 5 inches from the heat until the trout is just opaque in the center, the skin is browned, and the vegetables are tender, 3–4 minutes.

**PER SERVING:** 359 CALORIES
13g total fat, 3g saturated fat, 131mg cholesterol, 742mg sodium, 14g total carbohydrate, 4g dietary fiber, 45g protein, 72mg calcium

COOK'S HINT COOK'S HINT **handling fish** COOK'S HINT COOK'S HINT COOK'S HINT

If you lay the fish on a sheet of wax paper while you season it, you'll find you have less to clean up aferwards. Leftover trout is delicious cold the next day.

# tuna patties [20]

*3 POINTS* PER SERVING | MAKES 4 SERVINGS

*Pantry-shelf items are the basis for these easy patties. If you like, make them into open-faced sandwiches by placing the patties on toasted English muffin halves, topped with a lettuce leaf and slices of ripe tomato.*

1. **Combine** the tuna, bread crumbs, scallions, pimientos, egg, Worcestershire sauce, and salt in a medium bowl. Shape into 4 patties, about 4 inches in diameter.

2. **Heat the oil** in a large nonstick skillet, then add the patties. Cook until golden brown and cooked through, about 4 minutes on each side.

PER SERVING: 159 CALORIES
5g total fat, 1g saturated fat, 74mg cholesterol, 493mg sodium, 8g total carbohydrate, 1g dietary fiber, 21g protein, 34mg calcium

2 (6-ounce) cans water-packed tuna, drained and flaked

2 slices whole-wheat bread, made into crumbs

3 scallions, chopped or ¼ cup finely chopped onion

¼ cup chopped drained pimientos

1 large egg

2 teaspoons Worcestershire sauce

¼ teaspoon salt

2 teaspoons canola oil

# stir-fried shrimp and vegetables

*4 POINTS* PER SERVING | MAKES 6 SERVINGS

*This shrimp dish is guaranteed to become a weeknight staple, as well as a favorite for friends. The trick to a successful stir-fry is to have all the ingredients prepared ahead of time. Then, the actual cooking time will take only minutes.*

1 tablespoon cornstarch

2 tablespoons reduced-sodium soy sauce

1 cup low-sodium vegetable or chicken broth

2 tablespoons finely chopped peeled fresh ginger

¼ teaspoon crushed red pepper

1 tablespoon Asian (dark) sesame oil

3 garlic cloves, minced

2 tablespoons sesame seeds

5 cups broccoli florets

1 red bell pepper, seeded and cut into strips

1 yellow bell pepper, seeded and cut into strips

1 bunch scallions, trimmed and cut into 2-inch lengths

1 pound large shrimp, peeled and deveined

3 cups cooked brown rice

**1. Combine** the cornstarch and the soy sauce to a smooth paste in a medium bowl. Stir in the broth, ginger, and crushed red pepper.

**2. Heat a wok** or large nonstick skillet over high heat until a drop of water sizzles. Swirl in the oil, then add the garlic and sesame seeds. Stir-fry until fragrant, about 30 seconds. Add the broccoli, red and yellow bell peppers, and scallions. Stir-fry 4–5 minutes. Add the shrimp and stir-fry until just opaque in the center and the vegetables are tender-crisp, 3–4 minutes.

**3. Stir the cornstarch mixture** into the wok and cook, stirring constantly, until the mixture simmers and thickens, about 2 minutes. Serve with the rice.

PER SERVING (1⅓ CUPS SHRIMP AND VEGETABLES AND ½ CUP RICE): 228 CALORIES
6g total fat, 1g saturated fat, 71mg cholesterol, 317mg sodium, 32g total carbohydrate, 5g dietary fiber, 14g protein, 76mg calcium

# shrimp and tomato flambé

*7 POINTS* PER SERVING | MAKES 4 SERVINGS

*This dish is so easy and delicious, igniting it with brandy only gilds the lily.*
*Serve with a crusty French baguette and a tossed leafy green salad.*

1. Heat a large nonstick skillet. Swirl in 1 teaspoon of the oil, then add the
onion and garlic. Sauté until golden, about 7 minutes. Add the tomatoes,
wine, salt, and pepper; bring to a boil. Reduce the heat and simmer until the
sauce is slightly thickened, about 10 minutes.

2. Meanwhile, cook the pasta according to package directions; drain and
toss with the remaining 1 teaspoon oil; keep warm.

3. Add the shrimp and basil to the tomato sauce. Cook until the shrimp
are just opaque in the center, 4–5 minutes.

4. Heat the brandy in a small saucepan (do not boil); ignite and pour over
the shrimp. Serve with the pasta and cheese.

PER SERVING: 374 CALORIES
6g total fat, 2g saturated fat, 111mg cholesterol, 776mg sodium, 55g total carbohydrate,
4g dietary fiber, 24g protein, 172mg calcium

2 teaspoons extra-virgin
olive oil

1 large onion, chopped

3 garlic cloves, minced

1 can (28-ounce) diced
tomatoes, drained

2 tablespoons dry
white wine

½ teaspoon salt

½ teaspoon coarsely
ground pepper

½ pound bow-tie pasta

1 pound large shrimp,
peeled and deveined

2 tablespoons chopped
fresh basil, or
2 teaspoons dried

2 tablespoons brandy

¼ cup shredded
Parmesan cheese

COOK'S HINT COOK'S HINT flambé COOK'S HINT COOK'S HINT COOK'S HINT COOK'S HINT COOK'S HINT

Flambés can be fun, when you do them right. Here's how: The food to be
flamed should be hot and the brandy or liqueur should be warmed
to just hot, although not simmering. Ignite the brandy with a long-handled
lighter just as you're about to pour it over the food.

# jambalaya

*5 POINTS* PER SERVING | MAKES 6 SERVINGS

*Even if you don't call Louisiana home, this hearty one-pot meal, so simple to make, will probably become a family favorite. To save prep time, buy two (8-ounce) packages of precut fresh broccoli florets from the produce section of your supermarket. To save cooking time, substitute white rice for the brown, but simmer for only 15 to 20 minutes.*

2 teaspoons olive oil

1 large onion, chopped

2 garlic cloves, minced

1 green bell pepper, seeded and chopped

1 cup brown rice

2 cups low-sodium chicken broth

1 (14½-ounce) can Mexican-style stewed tomatoes

2 bay leaves

½ pound skinless boneless chicken breasts, cut into pieces

1 tablespoon chopped fresh thyme, or 1 teaspoon dried

½ pound medium shrimp, peeled and deveined

4 cups broccoli florets

2 ounces sliced baked ham, cut into strips

1. **Heat a nonstick Dutch oven.** Swirl in the oil, then add the onion and garlic. Sauté until golden, about 7 minutes. Add the bell pepper and rice and sauté until lightly browned, 3–4 minutes. Add the broth, tomatoes, and bay leaves; bring to a boil. Reduce the heat and simmer, covered, until the rice is almost tender, about 35 minutes.

2. **Add the chicken and thyme.** Simmer, covered, 5 minutes. Add the shrimp, broccoli, and ham. Simmer, covered, until the shrimp are just opaque, the chicken is cooked through, and the rice is tender, 8–10 minutes. Remove the bay leaves and fluff the mixture with a fork.

PER SERVING (GENEROUS 1 CUP): 264 CALORIES
5g total fat, 1g saturated fat, 62mg cholesterol, 435mg sodium, 35g total carbohydrate, 5g dietary fiber, 20g protein, 74mg calcium

COOK'S HINT COOK'S HINT **fresh fish** COOK'S HINT COOK'S HINT COOK'S HINT COOK'S HINT

Buy fresh fish the day you're going to use it. When you get home, place in a zip-close plastic bag and refrigerate. If you don't use it by the next day, double wrap the package in plastic wrap, then place in a zip-close plastic bag and freeze for up to 6 months.

# spicy shrimp and lobster linguine

**7 POINTS** PER SERVING | MAKES 6 SERVINGS

*A spicy tomato sauce full of shrimp and lobster makes for spectacular, yet easy entertaining. You can make the sauce a few hours ahead of time, cover it and let it sit on the stove. Then reheat the sauce and add the lobster and shrimp a few minutes before you're ready to eat.*

1. **Heat the oil** in a very large nonstick skillet, then add the onions and garlic. Sauté until golden, about 10 minutes. Add the tomatoes, wine, oregano, crushed pepper, salt, sugar, and ground pepper; bring to a boil. Reduce the heat and simmer, uncovered, until the flavors are blended and the sauce is slightly thickened, about 15 minutes.

2. **Meanwhile, remove the meat** from the lobster tail and cut it into ½–inch pieces. Add the lobster and the shrimp to the sauce and simmer, uncovered, until the shrimp and lobster are just opaque, about 5 minutes.

3. **Meanwhile, cook the linguine** according to package directions; drain and place in a large serving bowl. Toss at once with the sauce and sprinkle with the parsley.

**PER SERVING (SCANT 2 CUPS): 375 CALORIES**
4g total fat, 1g saturated fat, 98mg cholesterol, 641mg sodium, 58g total carbohydrate, 5g dietary fiber, 25g protein, 108mg calcium

1 tablespoon olive oil

3 onions, chopped

6 garlic cloves, chopped

1 (28-ounce) can diced tomatoes

¼ cup dry red wine

2 tablespoons chopped fresh oregano, or 2 teaspoons dried

½ teaspoon crushed red pepper

½ teaspoon salt

¼ teaspoon sugar

¼ teaspoon coarsely ground black pepper

1 lobster tail (about ½ pound)

1 pound large shrimp, peeled and deveined

¾ pound linguine

¼ cup chopped parsley

COOK'S HINT COOK'S HINT **lobster** COOK'S HINT COOK'S HINT COOK'S HINT COOK'S HINT

To pry the meat out of the lobster tail, cut away the soft undercover with scissors and ease away the meat from the shell with your fingers.

# broiled lobster tails with plums

**4 POINTS** PER SERVING | MAKES 4 SERVINGS

*Guests or family will feel like they're getting the star treatment with this impressive dish. Sweetly flavored with port wine and Chinese five-spice powder, this recipe is delightful served with fresh steamed asparagus.*

4 (5-ounce) lobster tails

2 tablespoons fresh lemon juice

2 teaspoons olive oil

2 teaspoons port wine

½ teaspoon Chinese five-spice powder

1 garlic clove, minced

¼ teaspoon salt

4 plums, pitted and halved

1. With scissors, remove the soft undercover of the lobster tails; crack through the hard upper shells with a cleaver, press down to lie flat. Place lobster, shell-side down, in a shallow nonreactive baking dish.

2. Combine the lemon juice, oil, port wine, five-spice powder, garlic, and salt in a small bowl; pour over the lobster tails. Cover and refrigerate at least 30 minutes or up to 2 hours.

3. Spray the broiler rack with nonstick spray; preheat the broiler. Transfer the lobster tails from the marinade to the broiler rack (discard the marinade). Arrange the plum halves on the rack with the lobster. Broil, 5 inches from the heat, until the lobster is just opaque in the center and the plums are heated through, 10–12 minutes.

PER SERVING: 194 CALORIES
2g total fat, 0g saturated fat, 106mg cholesterol, 629mg sodium, 11g total carbohydrate, 1g dietary fiber, 31g protein, 94mg calcium

# garlic scallop broil with ouzo and feta cheese [20]

**4 POINTS** PER SERVING | MAKES 4 SERVINGS

*Ouzo is a sweet, clear, anise-flavored liqueur from Greece.*
*Serve this special scallop dish with rice and fresh steamed green beans.*

**1. Preheat the broiler.** Heat the oil in a large nonstick skillet, then add the garlic. Sauté until fragrant, about 30 seconds. Add the tomatoes, wine, and pepper; bring to a boil. Reduce the heat and simmer, uncovered, until the flavors are blended, about 10 minutes. Add the scallops and simmer until just opaque in the center, about 5 minutes. Stir in the scallions and parsley.

**2. Turn the mixture** into a 6 x 10-inch baking dish. Sprinkle with the ouzo and feta cheese. Broil until the cheese is lightly browned and melted, about 2 minutes.

PER SERVING: 183 CALORIES
8g total fat, 3g saturated fat, 35mg cholesterol, 360mg sodium, 9g total carbohydrate, 1g dietary fiber, 19g protein, 187mg calcium

1 tablespoon extra-virgin olive oil

4 garlic cloves, finely chopped

2 plum tomatoes, chopped

⅓ cup dry white wine, or chicken broth

¼ teaspoon freshly ground pepper

1 pound sea scallops

1 bunch scallions, cut diagonally into 2-inch lengths

½ cup chopped parsley

1 tablespoon ouzo liqueur

2 ounces feta cheese, crumbled

COOK'S HINT COOK'S HINT **variation** COOK'S HINT COOK'S HINT COOK'S HINT COOK'S HINT COOK'S HINT

If you prefer not to use alcohol in a recipe, you can usually substitute an equal amount of water or broth.

# corn cioppino

*3 POINTS* PER SERVING | MAKES 6 SERVINGS

*Cioppino is the favorite fish stew of San Francisco. Our version adds corn for extra flavor, crunch, and fiber. It is particularly delicious and comforting served with sourdough bread to soak up the juices.*

2 teaspoons extra-virgin olive oil

1 large onion, chopped

2 celery stalks, chopped

3 garlic cloves, minced

1 (14½-ounce) can diced tomatoes

2 cups low-sodium vegetable broth, or bottled clam juice

¼ cup dry white wine

2 tablespoons chopped fresh marjoram, or 2 teaspoons dried

¼ teaspoon crushed red pepper

2 cups fresh or thawed frozen corn kernels

½ pound mussels, scrubbed and debearded

½ pound halibut fillets, cut into chunks

½ pound large shrimp, peeled and deveined

¼ pound cooked lump crabmeat, picked over

½ cup chopped flat-leaf parsley

1. Heat a nonstick Dutch oven. Swirl in the oil, then add the onion, celery, and garlic. Sauté until softened and lightly browned, about 10 minutes. Add the tomatoes, broth, wine, marjoram, and red pepper; bring to a boil. Reduce the heat and simmer, covered, until the flavors blend, about 10 minutes.

2. Add the corn and return to a boil. Add the mussels, halibut, and shrimp; return to a boil. Reduce the heat and simmer until the mussel's open and the shrimp are just opaque, 4–5 minutes. Discard any mussels that don't open. Add the crabmeat and parsley and simmer 30 seconds.

PER SERVING (1⅓ CUPS): 173 CALORIES
3g total fat, 1g saturated fat, 78mg cholesterol, 616mg sodium, 19g total carbohydrate, 3g dietary fiber, 19g protein, 84mg calcium

COOK'S HINT COOK'S HINT mussels COOK'S HINT COOK'S HINT COOK'S HINT

The hairy filaments that protrude from a mussel are known as a "beard." To remove, pinch the filaments between thumb and forefinger and pull firmly. After buying mussels, discard those with broken shells or shells that do not close tightly when gently tapped. Since mussels can be sandy, soak them in a bowl of cold water for 2–3 minutes. Repeat, using fresh water until there is no more sand in the bowl. Then scrub them with a stiff brush under cold running water.

# vegetarian

eggplant parmesan meatless moussaka
amaranth and feta-stuffed red peppers gorgonzola pizzettas
grilled vegetable quesadillas
fettuccine with white beans and roasted peppers
broccoli rabe and polenta pie quinoa, rice, and carrot fritters
root vegetable mash with caramelized onions
easy pierogies and peppers
broiled polenta with ratatouille curried bean burgers
rice, lentil, and spinach pilaf
peanutty tempeh and vegetable stir-fry
warm kamut taboulleh root vegetable cassoulet
lentil, corn, and sweet pepper chili
vegetable tagine with walnuts and prunes
roasted tofu, asparagus, and radishes

# eggplant parmesan

*5 POINTS* PER SERVING | MAKES 6 SERVINGS

*Traditional Eggplant Parmesan is a rare indulgence for those of us who are watching our POINTS. Yet this simple "oven-fried" version eliminates most of the fat by using nonstick spray and baking the eggplant. To help brown the eggplant, remember to lightly mist it with nonstick spray just before baking. For best flavor, use olive oil cooking spray.*

2 large eggs

2 tablespoons fat-free milk

1 cup Italian-seasoned dry bread crumbs

1 (1¾ to 2-pound) eggplant, unpeeled and cut into ¼-inch slices

2 teaspoons extra-virgin olive oil

1 large onion, finely chopped

4 garlic cloves, minced

1 (28-ounce) can crushed tomatoes

1 (14½-ounce) can diced tomatoes

¼ cup dry red wine

2 tablespoons minced fresh basil, or 2 teaspoons dried

½ teaspoon salt

½ teaspoon freshly ground pepper

¼ teaspoon sugar

1 cup shredded part-skim mozzarella cheese

3 tablespoons grated Parmesan cheese

**1.** Preheat the oven to 375°F. Spray 2 baking sheets and a 9 x 13-inch baking dish with nonstick spray.

**2.** Lightly beat the eggs and milk in a shallow bowl. Place the bread crumbs in another shallow bowl. Dip the eggplant in the egg mixture, then in the bread crumbs and arrange in one layer on the baking sheets. Lightly spray the eggplant with nonstick spray. Bake until the eggplant is softened and lightly browned, about 25 minutes.

**3.** Meanwhile, heat a nonstick Dutch oven. Swirl in the oil, then add the onion and garlic. Sauté until golden, about 7 minutes. Add the crushed tomatoes, diced tomatoes, wine, basil, salt, pepper, and sugar; bring the mixture to a boil. Reduce the heat and simmer, uncovered, until slightly thickened, about 15 minutes.

**4.** Spoon about one third of the tomato sauce in the bottom of the baking dish. Top with a layer of half of the eggplant, then another one third of the sauce, then another layer of the remaining eggplant, then the remaining sauce. Sprinkle with the mozzarella and Parmesan cheeses and bake, uncovered, until the dish is hot and bubbling and the cheese is golden, about 20 minutes. Let stand 5 minutes before serving.

**PER SERVING:** 275 CALORIES
10g total fat, 4g saturated fat, 84mg cholesterol, 863mg sodium, 34g total carbohydrate, 6g dietary fiber, 14g protein, 308mg calcium

# meatless moussaka

**5 POINTS** PER SERVING | MAKES 4 SERVINGS

*This vegetarian moussaka is just as rich in savory, creamy flavor and as satisfying as the traditional Greek version made with lamb. We use Textured Vegetable Protein (TVP) which is made from soybeans, to replace the meat. You can find TVP in some supermarkets and most health food stores. If you prefer, substitute 1 cup cooked and drained lentils for the TVP.*

1. **Preheat the oven** to 375°F. Spray an 8 x 12-inch baking dish with nonstick spray. Spray a large baking sheet with nonstick spray. Arrange the eggplant slices on the baking sheet in a single layer and bake until softened, about 20 minutes.

2. **Meanwhile, heat a large nonstick saucepan.** Swirl in the oil, then add the onion and garlic. Sauté until golden, about 7 minutes. Add the tomatoes, TVP, bell pepper, wine, cinnamon, salt, and ground pepper; bring to a boil. Reduce the heat and simmer, uncovered, until almost all of the liquid has evaporated, about 25 minutes. Stir in the parsley.

3. **Blend the flour** with 3 tablespoons of the milk in a small saucepan until smooth; blend in the remaining milk. Cook, stirring constantly, until the mixture boils and thickens, about 3 minutes. Remove the mixture from the heat. Beat the egg and nutmeg in a small bowl; stir about ½ cup of the hot milk mixture into the egg, then return to the saucepan and mix well.

4. **Arrange the eggplant** in the baking dish; top with the tomato mixture and spread smooth. Top with the milk mixture and spread smooth. Sprinkle with the cheese and bake until hot in the center and golden on top, about 20 minutes. Let stand 5 minutes before serving.

**PER SERVING:** 272 CALORIES
7g total fat, 3g saturated fat, 65mg cholesterol, 921mg sodium, 34g total carbohydrate, 7g dietary fiber, 20g protein, 402mg calcium

1 (1-pound) eggplant, unpeeled and cut into ¼-inch slices

1 teaspoon olive oil

1 onion, finely chopped

3 garlic cloves, minced

1 (28-ounce) can diced tomatoes

½ cup TVP (textured vegetable protein)

1 green bell pepper, seeded and chopped

¼ cup dry red wine

½ teaspoon cinnamon

½ teaspoon salt

½ teaspoon freshly ground pepper

3 tablespoons finely chopped parsley

3 tablespoons all-purpose flour

1½ cups fat-free milk

1 large egg

⅛ teaspoon nutmeg

½ cup shredded Parmesan cheese

# amaranth and feta-stuffed red peppers

**4 POINTS** PER SERVING | MAKES 4 SERVINGS

*Amaranth, a protein-rich grain which adds a nutty flavor to foods, can be found in health-food stores. It is good mixed with other grains, such as rice or bulgur, which cook in about 20 minutes.*

1 teaspoon canola oil

1 onion, finely chopped

1 cup low-sodium vegetable broth

⅓ cup amaranth, rinsed

⅓ cup long-grain white rice

1 cup drained, rinsed canned chickpeas

½ cup finely chopped flat leaf parsley

1 teaspoon grated lemon zest

½ teaspoon freshly ground pepper

⅛ teaspoon salt

2 large red bell peppers, split in half lengthwise and seeded

1 ounce feta cheese, cubed

1. **Preheat the oven** to 350°F. Spray an 8 x 12-inch baking dish with nonstick spray. Heat the oil in a large nonstick saucepan, then add the onion. Sauté until translucent, 3–5 minutes.

2. **Add the broth,** amaranth, and rice; bring to a boil. Reduce the heat and simmer, covered, until the amaranth and rice are tender, and all of the liquid is absorbed, about 20 minutes. Stir in the chickpeas, parsley, lemon zest, ground pepper, and salt.

3. **Spoon the amaranth mixture** into the bell pepper shells and arrange them in the baking dish. Cover tightly with foil and bake until the bell peppers are softened and the filling is heated through, about 30 minutes.

4. **Remove the baking dish** from the oven and preheat the broiler. Remove the foil from the baking dish. Push the cheese cubes part-way through the filling and broil 5 inches from the heat until the cheese is lightly browned, 2–3 minutes.

PER SERVING: 243 CALORIES
5g total fat, 2g saturated fat, 6mg cholesterol, 271mg sodium, 42g total carbohydrate, 7g dietary fiber, 9g protein, 107mg calcium

# gorgonzola pizzettas

**8 POINTS** PER SERVING | MAKES 4 SERVINGS

*Made in the town located outside Milan of the same name, Gorgonzola is one of Italy's great cheeses. It's especially wonderful when melted, as it is here on these mini-pizza (called pizzetta). On its own, try it with fresh sliced pears or apples.*

1. **Preheat the oven** to 450°F. Spray a baking sheet with nonstick spray.

2. **Spread the flat breads** with the ricotta cheese; top with the tomato halves and the basil. Sprinkle with the Gorgonzola. Place the pizzettas on the baking sheet and bake until hot and the cheese browns, about 7 minutes.

PER SERVING: 384 CALORIES
12g total fat, 7g saturated fat, 39mg cholesterol, 692mg sodium, 47g total carbohydrate, 3g dietary fiber, 21g protein, 393mg calcium.

4 (7-inch) flat or pita breads

1½ cups part-skim ricotta cheese

16 grape or cherry tomatoes, halved

20 basil leaves, thinly sliced

2 ounces Gorgonzola cheese, crumbled (about ½ cup)

COOK'S HINT COOK'S HINT COOK'S HINT **microwave version** COOK'S HINT COOK'S HINT

If you prefer, you can microwave the pizzettas, one at a time, on High until hot and the cheese melts, about 2 minutes.

# grilled vegetable quesadillas

*4 POINTS* PER SERVING | MAKES 4 SERVINGS

*Colorful grilled vegetables and zippy pepper-Jack cheese make a lively and satisfying filling for these quesadillas.*

1 small zucchini, sliced lengthwise into 4 slices

1 small yellow squash, sliced lengthwise into 4 slices

1 red bell pepper, seeded and cut into 8 pieces

1 green bell pepper, seeded and cut into 8 pieces

1 small red onion, peeled and cut into 4 slices

8 (6-inch) corn tortillas

1 cup shredded reduced-fat pepper-Jack cheese

**1. Preheat the broiler.** Line the broiler pan with foil; spray the foil with nonstick spray. Place the zucchini, yellow squash, red and green bell peppers, and the red onion on the broiler pan in a single layer. Broil 5 inches from the heat, until lightly charred, about 7 minutes on each side.

**2. Preheat the oven** to 450°F. Spray a baking sheet with nonstick spray. Arrange the vegetables on 4 of the tortillas. Top with the cheese and the remaining tortillas; lightly spray the tortilla tops with nonstick spray.

**3. Place the quesadillas** on the baking sheet and bake until hot and the cheese melts, about 7 minutes.

**PER SERVING: 228 CALORIES**
6g total fat, 3g saturated fat, 15mg cholesterol, 236mg sodium, 33g total carbohydrate, 5g dietary fiber, 13g protein, 324mg calcium

COOK'S HINT COOK'S HINT **microwave** COOK'S HINT COOK'S HINT COOK'S HINT COOK'S HINT

You need the broiler to cook the vegetables, but after you assemble the quesadillas it's just as easy to use the microwave—the result is surprisingly good and moist. Simply microwave the quesadillas, one at a time, on High, until hot and the cheese melts, about 1½ minutes.

# fettuccine with white beans and roasted peppers

*7 POINTS* PER SERVING | MAKES 6 SERVINGS

*Serve this rustic melange of pasta, beans, multi-colored roasted bell peppers, and cheese with a mixed green salad. If you're pressed for time, substitute a 12-ounce jar of drained, roasted red peppers for the fresh peppers.*

1. **Preheat the broiler.** Line a baking sheet with foil; spray the foil with nonstick spray. Arrange the peppers on the baking sheet in a single layer. Broil 5 inches from the heat, until the skin is lightly charred, about 7 minutes on each side; keep warm.

2. **Meanwhile, cook the fettuccine** according to package directions; drain, reserving ⅓ cup of the cooking liquid. Keep the fettuccine warm with the reserved liquid in a large serving bowl.

3. **Heat the beans,** parsley, and lemon juice in a medium saucepan, stirring gently to avoid breaking up the beans. Add the bean mixture to the fettuccine along with roasted peppers and the mozzarella cheese, then toss gently. Serve with ground pepper.

**PER SERVING (1½ CUPS): 343 CALORIES**
9g total fat, 5g saturated fat, 53mg cholesterol, 371mg sodium, 46g total carbohydrate, 8g dietary fiber, 21g protein, 329mg calcium

1 large red bell pepper, seeded and quartered

1 orange bell pepper, seeded and quartered

1 yellow bell pepper, seeded and quartered

½ pound fettuccine

1 (19-ounce) can cannellini (white kidney) beans, rinsed and drained

¼ cup finely chopped parsley

1 tablespoon fresh lemon juice

8 ounces part-skim mozzarella cheese, cut into chunks

Freshly ground pepper

COOK'S HINT COOK'S HINT **substitute** COOK'S HINT COOK'S HINT COOK'S HINT COOK'S HINT

If you prefer, you can substitute an equal amount of chickpeas for the cannellini beans.

# broccoli rabe and polenta pie

***3 POINTS*** PER SERVING | MAKES 6 SERVINGS

*Broccoli rabe is a powerhouse of vitamins and minerals, but be forewarned: It has an assertive, slightly bitter taste that needs to be tamed. Here, pungent garlic, sweet bell pepper, savory Parmesan cheese, and creamy polenta (yellow cornmeal) all work together to mellow this tasty vegetable.*

2 teaspoons extra-virgin olive oil

1 onion, finely chopped

4 garlic cloves, minced

1 bunch broccoli rabe, cleaned and chopped

1 large red bell pepper, seeded and chopped

¾ cup low-sodium vegetable broth

¼ teaspoon crushed red pepper

3½ cups water

1½ teaspoons salt

1 cup yellow cornmeal

⅓ cup shredded Parmesan cheese

**1. Preheat the oven** to 375°F. Spray a 10-inch pie dish with nonstick spray. Heat a large deep nonstick skillet. Swirl in the oil, then add the onion and garlic. Sauté until golden, about 7 minutes. Add the broccoli rabe, bell pepper, broth, and crushed red pepper. Cook, uncovered, stirring frequently, until the broccoli rabe is wilted and tender and most of the liquid has evaporated, about 12 minutes.

**2. Meanwhile, to make the polenta,** bring the water and salt to a boil in a large nonstick saucepan. Reduce the heat to simmer, then stirring constantly, slowly add the cornmeal in a thin steady stream. Cook over low heat, stirring frequently, until very thick, about 10 minutes. Spread the polenta in the bottom of the pie dish.

**3. Spoon the broccoli rabe mixture** over the polenta and spread smooth. Sprinkle with the cheese and bake until heated through and browned on top, about 20 minutes. Let stand 5 minutes before serving.

**PER SERVING:** 162 CALORIES
4g total fat, 1g saturated fat, 4mg cholesterol, 710mg sodium, 26g total carbohydrate, 5g dietary fiber, 7g protein, 165mg calcium

COOK'S HINT COOK'S HINT **creamy polenta** COOK'S HINT COOK'S HINT COOK'S HINT

The key to smooth lump-free polenta? Constant stirring while slowly adding the cornmeal to the water. Here's a neat trick to ensure you don't add too much cornmeal at once: grab a handful and sift it through your fist.

# quinoa, rice, and carrot fritters

*5 POINTS* PER SERVING | MAKES 4 SERVINGS

*Quinoa, pronounced KEY-nwa, is a traditional grain indigenous to the Andes. It is an excellent source of protein because, unlike all other grains, quinoa contains all the essential amino acids needed to make a complete protein. Remember to rinse quinoa grains thoroughly under cold running water for 1–2 minutes before cooking to remove the bitter outer coating.*

1. **Bring the broth to a boil** in a medium saucepan. Add the quinoa and rice. Reduce the heat and simmer, covered, 15 minutes. Uncover and simmer until all the liquid is absorbed, about 5 minutes.

2. **Heat 1 teaspoon of the oil** in a large nonstick skillet, then add the onion. Sauté until translucent, 3 to 5 minutes.

3. **Combine** the carrots, eggs, flour, flax seeds, salt, and pepper in a medium bowl. Add the cooked quinoa mixture and the sautéed onion and mix well.

4. **Heat the remaining 1 teaspoon oil** on a nonstick griddle or in a large nonstick skillet. Drop the batter onto the griddle in ¼-cup measures, 4–6 fritters at a time. Cook until golden, about 3 minutes on each side.

**PER SERVING (4 FRITTERS): 284 CALORIES**
7g total fat, 1g saturated fat, 106mg cholesterol, 357mg sodium, 46g total carbohydrate, 4g dietary fiber, 9g protein, 56mg calcium

2 cups low-sodium vegetable broth

½ cup quinoa, rinsed and drained

½ cup long-grain white rice

2 teaspoons canola oil

1 onion, finely chopped

2 carrots, shredded

2 large eggs, lightly beaten

3 tablespoons all-purpose flour

2 teaspoons ground flax seeds

½ teaspoon salt

½ teaspoon freshly ground pepper

COOK'S HINT COOK'S HINT **flax** COOK'S HINT COOK'S HINT COOK'S HINT COOK'S HINT

Flax seeds can be found in most health food stores. They are a good source of omega-3 fatty acids and have recently been celebrated for their cholesterol-lowering benefits. They are digested and absorbed more easily when they are ground. The best way to grind them is in a spice or coffee grinder. Other good vegetarian sources of omega-3s are green leafy vegetables, canola oil, soybeans, and walnuts.

# root vegetable mash with caramelized onions

**5 POINTS** PER SERVING | MAKES 4 SERVINGS

*This is vegetarian comfort food at its best. The sweet parsnips spiked with a hint of nutmeg add delicious depth to ordinary carrots, onions, and chickpeas. If you can find the naturally sweet Vidalia onion, substitute the 2 yellow onions with 1 large Vidalia onion and omit the sugar. Serve with steamed spinach.*

1 pound carrots, peeled and cut into 1-inch chunks

1 (½-pound) parsnip, peeled and cut into 1-inch chunks

2 teaspoons butter

2 yellow onions, coarsely chopped

1 teaspoon packed brown sugar

½ teaspoon salt

⅛ teaspoon freshly ground pepper

Pinch nutmeg

1 (19-ounce) can chickpeas, rinsed and drained

1. Place the carrots and parsnip in a large saucepan with enough water to cover; bring to a boil. Reduce the heat and simmer, covered, until the vegetables are tender, about 15 minutes. Drain, reserving ⅓ cup of the cooking liquid. Cover the vegetables and the reserved liquid and keep warm.

2. Meanwhile, to caramelize the onions, melt the butter in a large nonstick skillet over medium heat. Add the onions and cook, stirring occasionally, until light golden, about 6 minutes. Reduce the heat to low, stir in the brown sugar and cook, stirring occasionally, until the onions are golden brown and well softened, about 12 minutes.

3. Pulse the vegetables with the reserved liquid, the salt, pepper, and nutmeg in a food processor until the vegetables are mashed and smooth.

4. Stir the chickpeas into the onions and cook until heated through, about 3 minutes. Mound the mashed vegetables in the center of a shallow serving dish and surround with the chickpea mixture.

PER SERVING (½ CUP EACH VEGETABLES AND CHICKPEA MIXTURE):
293 CALORIES
5g total fat, 2g saturated fat, 5mg cholesterol, 591mg sodium, 54g total carbohydrate, 11g dietary fiber, 11g protein, 109mg calcium

COOK'S HINT COOK'S HINT **butter** COOK'S HINT COOK'S HINT COOK'S HINT COOK'S HINT

Don't shy away from butter if you're trying to lose weight. Even a small amount adds wonderful, rich flavor to this dish. We recommend that you <u>don't</u> substitute oil or margarine.

# easy pierogies and peppers [20]

*6 POINTS* PER SERVING | MAKES 3 SERVINGS

*Keep a bag of pepper stir-fry and a package of pierogies on hand in the freezer to make this quick-fix dinner any time. It takes less than 10 minutes preparation time. Substitute potato and onion pierogies for the potato and cheddar pierogies, if you prefer, and serve with a sprinkling of Parmesan cheese.*

1. **Spray a large nonstick skillet** with nonstick spray and set over high heat. Add the pepper stir-fry and sauté until lightly browned, 10–12 minutes. At first the frozen peppers and onions will give off water, but continue cooking them until the water evaporates and they brown lightly.

2. **Meanwhile, cook the pierogies** in boiling water until thawed, 3–5 minutes. Drain, reserving ¼ cup of the cooking liquid. Keep the pierogies warm.

3. **Add the reserved cooking liquid,** the tomato sauce, oregano, fennel, salt, and ground pepper to the pepper stir-fry, and simmer 1 minute. Serve the pierogies with the sauce.

**PER SERVING (4 PIEROGIES WITH ¾ CUP PEPPERS): 332 CALORIES**
7g total fat, 3g saturated fat, 65mg cholesterol, 1139mg sodium, 55g total carbohydrate, 5g dietary fiber, 14g protein, 179mg calcium

1 (1-pound) bag frozen pepper stir-fry (green, red, yellow bell peppers, and onions)

1 (16.9-ounce) package frozen potato and cheddar pierogies

1 (8-ounce) can tomato sauce

1 tablespoon finely chopped fresh oregano, or 1 teaspoon dried

2 teaspoons fennel seeds, toasted and ground

½ teaspoon salt

½ teaspoon coarsely ground pepper

COOK'S HINT COOK'S HINT **fennel seeds** COOK'S HINT COOK'S HINT COOK'S HINT COOK'S HINT

To toast and grind the fennel seeds, place them in a small dry skillet over medium-low heat. Toast, shaking the pan and stirring constantly, until lightly browned and fragrant, 2–3 minutes. Watch them carefully when toasting; seeds can burn quickly. Transfer the seeds to a spice grinder and grind to a powder. Or grind with a mortar and pestle, or pound the seeds between two clean kitchen towels with a mallet until finely crushed.

# broiled polenta with ratatouille

*3 POINTS* PER SERVING | MAKES 6 SERVINGS

*For a more substantial meal, stir two 15-ounce cans rinsed and drained kidney beans or chickpeas into the ratatouille during the last 5 minutes of cooking (½ cup of the beans will add 1 POINT per serving).*

8 sun-dried tomato halves (not packed in oil)

1 tablespoon olive oil

1 large onion, coarsely chopped

5 garlic cloves, finely chopped

1 (¾-pound) eggplant, unpeeled and cubed

1 (½-pound) zucchini, cubed

1 green bell pepper, seeded and cut into 1-inch pieces

1 red bell pepper, seeded and cut into 1-inch pieces

1 (28-ounce) can crushed tomatoes

1 teaspoon sugar

½ teaspoon salt

¼ teaspoon freshly ground pepper

¼ cup finely chopped fresh basil, or 1 tablespoon dried

1 (16-ounce) tube refrigerated polenta

¼ cup grated Parmesan cheese

1. Soak the sun-dried tomatoes in warm water to cover until softened, about 15 minutes. Drain, discarding the liquid, then chop the tomatoes.

2. Meanwhile, heat a nonstick Dutch oven. Swirl in the oil, then add the onion and garlic. Sauté until golden, about 7 minutes. Add the eggplant, zucchini, green and red bell peppers, tomatoes, sugar, salt, ground pepper, and the chopped sun-dried tomatoes; bring to a boil, stirring occasionally. Reduce the heat and simmer, covered, until the vegetables are softened and the flavors are developed, about 30 minutes. Stir in the basil, during the last 2 to 3 minutes of cooking.

3. Meanwhile, preheat the broiler and spray a baking sheet with nonstick spray. Cut the polenta into 12 crosswise slices; arrange on the baking sheet. Sprinkle with the cheese and broil 5 inches from the heat until hot and the cheese is golden, about 4 minutes.

4. Serve the ratatouille with the broiled polenta rounds.

PER SERVING (GENEROUS 1 CUP RATATOUILLE AND 2 POLENTA ROUNDS): 156 CALORIES
4g total fat, 1g saturated fat, 3mg cholesterol, 634mg sodium, 26g total carbohydrate, 5g dietary fiber, 6g protein, 120mg calcium

# curried bean burgers

5 POINTS PER SERVING | MAKES 4 SERVINGS

*These burgers are flavorful and moist just as they are. If you have a craving for a cheeseburger, place a thin slice of reduced-fat cheddar or Swiss cheese over each burger after flipping it, allowing the cheese to melt while the burger finishes cooking. Serve in whole-wheat buns with lettuce and tomato, or with a side dish of crunchy coleslaw.*

1. **Heat a large nonstick skillet.** Swirl in 2 teaspoons of the oil, then add the onion. Sauté until golden, about 7 minutes. Add the fennel, curry powder, coriander, salt, and pepper; sauté until the fennel is softened and the mixture is fragrant, 4–5 minutes.

2. **Transfer the mixture** to a food processor, then add the beans, bread crumbs, egg, almonds, and parsley; pulse until coarsely chopped. Shape into 4 burgers.

3. **Heat a large nonstick skillet.** Swirl in the remaining 2 teaspoons oil, then add the burgers. Cook until golden on the outside and cooked through to the center, 3–4 minutes on each side.

PER SERVING: 251 CALORIES
11g total fat, 2g saturated fat, 53mg cholesterol, 730mg sodium, 31g total carbohydrate, 7g dietary fiber, 11g protein, 84mg calcium

4 teaspoons olive oil

1 onion, finely chopped

1 cup finely chopped fennel or celery

1 teaspoon curry powder

1 teaspoon ground coriander

½ teaspoon salt

½ teaspoon freshly ground pepper

1 (15-ounce) can red or white kidney beans, rinsed and drained

4 slices 7-grain bread, made into crumbs (2 cups)

1 large egg

¼ cup sliced almonds

¼ cup coarsely chopped parsley or fennel tops

COOK'S HINT COOK'S HINT **texture** COOK'S HINT COOK'S HINT COOK'S HINT COOK'S HINT COOK'S HINT

Don't fret if the bean mixture seems too soft—it lends moistness to the finished burgers. If you find the uncooked bean mixture a little too soft to handle, refrigerate for 30 minutes before shaping it into burgers.

# rice, lentil, and spinach pilaf

*6 POINTS* PER SERVING | MAKES 4 SERVINGS

*It takes only 5 minutes to assemble the ingredients for this vegan dish. The rice and lentil combination forms a complete protein, while the spinach and cranberries add vitamins and minerals. Serve with sesame breadsticks.*

1 teaspoon olive oil

2 shallots, minced

¾ cup basmati brown rice

2¼ cups low-sodium vegetable broth

½ cup lentils, picked over, rinsed, and drained

1 (10-ounce) package frozen chopped spinach, thawed and squeezed dry

½ cup dried cranberries

¼ teaspoon salt

¼ teaspoon freshly ground pepper

¼ cup pine nuts

1. **Heat the oil** in a large nonstick saucepan, then add the shallots. Sauté until softened, 3–4 minutes. Add the rice and sauté, until the rice is lightly browned, about 3 minutes.

2. **Add the broth** and lentils; bring the mixture to a boil. Reduce the heat and simmer, covered, 30 minutes. Stir in the spinach, cranberries, salt, and pepper; simmer, covered, until the rice is tender, 10–15 minutes. Fluff the mixture with a fork and stir in the nuts.

PER SERVING (GENEROUS 1 CUP): 333 CALORIES
7g total fat, 1g saturated fat, 0mg cholesterol, 212mg sodium, 60g total carbohydrate, 11g dietary fiber, 12g protein, 108mg calcium

COOK'S HINT COOK'S HINT **pine nuts** COOK'S HINT COOK'S HINT COOK'S HINT COOK'S HINT COOK'S HINT

For added flavor, toast the pine nuts in a small nonstick skillet over medium-low heat, shaking the pan and stirring constantly until golden and fragrant, about 2 minutes. To thaw the spinach quickly, place it in a microwavable bowl and microwave on High for 2 minutes, stirring once, until thawed.

Broiled Polenta with Ratatouille

Roasted Tofu, Asparagus, and Radishes. Opposite: Braised Leeks and Shiitake Mushrooms.

Carrot Cake with Cream Cheese Frosting. Opposite: Confetti Corn Cakes.

Chocolate Angel Food Cake with Macerated Strawberries. Opposite: Creamy Brown Rice Pudding.

Apricot Pistachio Biscotti

# peanutty tempeh and vegetable stir-fry

*6 POINTS* PER SERVING | MAKES 6 SERVINGS

*Tempeh is made from fermented soy bean curds. It has a firmer texture than plain soy bean curds (tofu) and a slightly nutty, smoky flavor. Like other soy products, tempeh may help reduce the risk of heart disease.*

1. **Bring the water to a boil** in a medium saucepan. Add the tempeh; reduce the heat and simmer until softened, about 5 minutes; drain.

2. **Heat a large nonstick skillet** or wok over high heat until a drop of water sizzles. Swirl in the oil, then add the green beans, sugar snap peas, bell pepper, and jalapeño pepper. Stir-fry until the vegetables are crisp-tender, about 5 minutes.

3. **Meanwhile, mix the broth,** peanut butter, soy sauce, and ginger in a small bowl; stir into the vegetables. Add the scallions and cook, stirring constantly, until the vegetables are well coated with the peanut sauce and the scallions are just softened, about 2 minutes. Serve over the rice.

**PER SERVING:** 302 CALORIES
11g total fat, 2g saturated fat, 0mg cholesterol, 272mg sodium, 39g total carbohydrate, 9g dietary fiber, 15g protein, 93mg calcium

COOK'S HINT COOK'S HINT COOK'S HINT **ginger** COOK'S HINT COOK'S HINT COOK'S HINT

To enhance the ginger flavor, top the stir-fry with slices of pickled ginger, available in the produce section of some supermarkets or in Asian food stores.

2 cups water

1 (8-ounce) package tempeh, cut into ¼-inch strips

2 teaspoons peanut oil

½ pound green beans, trimmed

½ pound fresh sugar snap peas

1 red bell pepper, seeded and cut into ¼-inch strips

1 jalapeño pepper, seeded and finely chopped (wear gloves to prevent irritation)

1 cup low-sodium vegetable broth

¼ cup smooth peanut butter

2 tablespoons reduced-sodium soy sauce

1 tablespoon grated peeled fresh ginger

1 bunch scallions (white parts and 2 inches of the green parts), cut into 2-inch lengths

3 cups cooked brown rice

# warm kamut taboulleh

**7 POINTS** PER SERVING | MAKES 4 SERVINGS

*Kamut (kah-MOOT) is a high-protein wheat which can be found in health food stores. Its name comes from the ancient Egyptian word for wheat. It takes 1½ hours to cook, but if you prefer you can substitute bulgur wheat (the traditional grain used in this dish), which cooks in a speedier 25 minutes. Serve with toasted whole-wheat pita breads, cut into triangles.*

3 cups water

1 cup kamut

1 (15-ounce) can chickpeas, rinsed and drained

3 tablespoons fresh lemon juice

1 tablespoon olive oil

1 garlic clove, minced

¾ teaspoon salt

½ teaspoon freshly ground pepper

1 pint yellow cherry or grape tomatoes, halved

1 red bell pepper, seeded and chopped

1 bunch scallions, trimmed and thinly sliced

½ cup chopped, peeled cucumber

½ cup coarsely chopped flat-leaf parsley

**1. Bring the water to a boil** in a medium saucepan. Add the kamut; reduce the heat and simmer, covered, until softened, about 1¼ hours. Uncover and simmer until all of the liquid is evaporated, about 15 minutes.

**2. Place the kamut in a large bowl.** Add the chickpeas, lemon juice, oil, garlic, salt, and ground pepper. Stir in the tomatoes, bell pepper, scallions, cucumber, and parsley. Serve at once, or cover and refrigerate for up to 2 days.

PER SERVING (SCANT 2 CUPS): 342 CALORIES
7g total fat, 1g saturated fat, 0mg cholesterol, 650mg sodium, 61g total carbohydrate, 12g dietary fiber, 14g protein, 87mg calcium

COOK'S HINT COOK'S HINT **variation** COOK'S HINT COOK'S HINT COOK'S HINT COOK'S HINT

For a non-vegan version of this dish, add one ounce crumbled feta cheese and omit the salt.

# root vegetable cassoulet

**4 POINTS** PER SERVING | MAKES 6 SERVINGS

*Cassoulet originates from Carcassonne in the Languedoc region of France, and is traditionally made with meats, sausages, beans, and fresh herbs. Here, our meatless, vegan version is flavorful, vegetable-packed, and easy.*

**1. Heat a nonstick Dutch oven.** Swirl in the oil, then add the onion and garlic. Sauté until golden, about 7 minutes. Add the carrots, celery, turnip, and parsnip and sauté 2 minutes.

**2. Stir in the beans and broth** and bring the mixture to a boil. Reduce the heat and simmer, covered, until the vegetables are tender and the flavors are blended, about 30 minutes. Stir in the parsley, marjoram, pepper, and salt.

PER SERVING (SCANT 1½ CUPS): 238 CALORIES
1g total fat, 0g saturated fat, 0mg cholesterol, 457mg sodium, 44g total carbohydrate, 11g dietary fiber, 14g protein, 157mg calcium

1 teaspoon extra-virgin olive oil

1 large onion, finely chopped

4 garlic cloves, finely chopped

2 carrots, finely chopped

2 celery stalks, sliced

½ small turnip, peeled and finely chopped

1 parsnip, peeled and finely chopped

2 (19-ounce) cans cannellini (white kidney) beans, rinsed and drained

1 cup low-sodium vegetable broth

¼ cup chopped parsley

1 tablespoon finely chopped fresh marjoram, or 1 teaspoon dried

½ teaspoon freshly ground pepper

¼ teaspoon salt

COOK'S HINT COOK'S HINT **garlic** COOK'S HINT COOK'S HINT COOK'S HINT

To make easy work of peeling garlic, separate the cloves from the bulb, then place them on a cutting board. Using the flat side of a large cutting knife, lightly smash the cloves. Discard the skins and chop the garlic as usual.

# lentil, corn, and sweet pepper chili

*5 POINTS* PER SERVING | MAKES 6 SERVINGS

*You can't get more comfort-in-a-bowl than this on a winter's night.*
*It is delicious served with cornbread or baked tortilla chips.*

2 teaspoons extra-virgin olive oil

1 large onion, finely chopped

1 (28-ounce) can crushed tomatoes

1 cup low-sodium vegetable broth

1½ cups lentils, picked over, rinsed, and drained

2 cups fresh or frozen corn kernels

1 large red bell pepper, seeded and chopped

1 (4½-ounce) can chopped green chiles, drained

1 teaspoon ground cumin

1 teaspoon ground coriander

½ teaspoon salt

¼ cup finely chopped cilantro

1. **Heat a nonstick Dutch oven.** Swirl in the oil, then add the onion. Sauté until golden, about 7 minutes. Add the tomatoes, broth, and lentils; bring to a boil. Reduce the heat and simmer, covered, 20 minutes.

2. **Add the corn,** bell pepper, chiles, cumin, coriander, and salt. Return the mixture to a boil. Reduce the heat and simmer, covered, until the lentils and vegetables are tender, about 15 minutes. Stir in the cilantro.

PER SERVING (SCANT 1½ CUPS): 265 CALORIES
3g total fat, 0g saturated fat, 0mg cholesterol, 590mg sodium, 49g total carbohydrate, 15g dietary fiber, 16g protein, 80mg calcium

COOK'S HINT COOK'S HINT **hot and sweet** COOK'S HINT COOK'S HINT COOK'S HINT COOK'S HINT

For extra heat, serve with jalapeño or hot pepper sauce. For extra sweetness, stir in ½ cup raisins during the last 5 minutes of cooking.

# vegetable tagine with walnuts and prunes

**8 POINTS** PER SERVING | MAKES 4 SERVINGS

*In Morocco, a long-simmering stew is called a tagine, which is also the name for the earthenware pots in which the stews are cooked. Serve this exotic stew with flat breads or pita breads to catch all the delicious juices.*

**1. Preheat the oven** to 350°F. Heat an ovenproof nonstick Dutch oven. Swirl in the oil, then add the onions and coriander. Sauté until golden and fragrant, about 7 minutes. Add the squash, carrot, fennel, chickpeas, tomatoes, broth, prunes, and cayenne; bring to a boil.

**2. Cover the Dutch oven** and bake until the vegetables are tender and the flavors are blended, about 45 minutes. Stir in the walnuts and parsley.

PER SERVING (SCANT 2 CUPS): 389 CALORIES
11g total fat, 1g saturated fat, 0mg cholesterol, 375mg sodium, 69g total carbohydrate, 14 Fib, 12g protein, 186mg calcium

2 teaspoons extra-virgin olive oil

2 onions, thinly sliced

1 teaspoon ground coriander

1 small butternut squash, peeled and cut into 1-inch cubes

1 large carrot, peeled and cut into ¼-inch slices

½ fennel bulb, trimmed and cut into ½-inch chunks

1 (15-ounce) can chickpeas, rinsed and drained

1 (14½-ounce) can diced tomatoes

½ cup low-sodium vegetable broth

½ cup chopped pitted prunes

⅛ teaspoon cayenne

⅓ cup coarsely chopped walnuts

¼ cup finely chopped parsley

COOK'S HINT COOK'S HINT **dried fruit** COOK'S HINT COOK'S HINT COOK'S HINT

What's the fastest, least messy way to cut up dried fruit, such as dates, apricots, figs, and prunes? Use kitchen shears.

# roasted tofu, asparagus, and radishes

*2 POINTS* PER SERVING | MAKES 4 SERVINGS

*If you're tofu-phobic, you'll get over it once you try this flavorful dish.*
*Pop a baking pan of small, red-skinned potatoes, halved or quartered and sprayed*
*with cooking spray, into the oven to roast alongside the tofu and vegetables.*

2 tablespoons
balsamic vinegar

1 tablespoon
extra-virgin olive oil

3 garlic cloves,
finely chopped

1 tablespoon finely
chopped fresh rosemary,
or 1 teaspoon dried

1 teaspoon grated
lemon zest

½ teaspoon salt

¼ teaspoon freshly
ground pepper

1 pound reduced-fat firm
tofu, cut into 1-inch cubes

1 bunch asparagus,
trimmed and cut into
2-inch lengths

1 (6-ounce) bag radishes,
trimmed

1 small red onion,
cut into 4 wedges

1. **Preheat the oven** to 400°F. Spray a nonstick roasting pan, large enough to hold all the vegetables and tofu in a single layer, with nonstick spray.

2. **Combine** the vinegar, oil, garlic, rosemary, lemon zest, salt, and pepper in a large bowl. Add the tofu, asparagus, radishes, and onion; toss gently to coat.

3. **Turn the mixture** into the roasting pan and spread into one layer. Roast until the vegetables are tender and lightly browned, turning once, 20–25 minutes.

PER SERVING: 106 CALORIES
5g total fat, 1g saturated fat, 0mg cholesterol, 356mg sodium, 9g total carbohydrate,
3g dietary fiber, 9g protein, 58mg calcium

COOK'S HINT COOK'S HINT **roasted vegetables** COOK'S HINT COOK'S HINT COOK'S HINT

Before tossing the vegetables with the seasonings, pat them dry with paper towels. Also make sure all of the items are in a single layer in the roasting pan to prevent the vegetables from steaming, and encourage them to brown and caramelize.

# sides

mashed potatoes with roasted garlic spicy louisiana potatoes
spinach, onion, and potato hash
mashed potatoes and celeriac maple-roasted root vegetables
green bean and tomato sauté
roasted asparagus and red peppers
braised leeks and shiitake mushrooms
spicy italian-style broccoli stir-fried sesame bok choy
caramelized pearl onions, fennel, and brussels sprouts
eggplant tomato tian warm red cabbage sauté
herbed cherry tomatoes two-apple slaw
greek feta pilaf vegetable fried rice
citrus-scented snap pea and carrot couscous
confetti corn cakes creamy blue cheese polenta
herbed quinoa with peas and scallions
rosemary-scented barley with beets
southwestern corn skillet warm three-bean salad
white beans with sage

# mashed potatoes
# with roasted garlic

*2 POINTS* PER SERVING | MAKES 6 SERVINGS

*Roasting, rather than boiling, the potatoes helps to give this
classic side dish a lighter, fluffier texture.*

1½ pounds baking
potatoes, scrubbed

7 garlic cloves, peeled

⅓ cup low-fat (1%) milk

2 tablespoons butter

½ teaspoon salt

¼ teaspoon freshly
ground pepper

**1. Preheat the oven** to 425°F.

**2. Pierce the potatoes** several times with a fork. Wrap the garlic in foil.
Place the potatoes and garlic on a baking sheet. Bake until the potatoes pierce
easily with a fork and the garlic is softened, about 45 minutes. Let cool until
comfortable to handle, about 10 minutes.

**3. Slit the potatoes** with a knife and using a spoon, scoop out the flesh;
transfer to a bowl. Mash the garlic with a fork and combine in a small
saucepan with the milk, butter, salt, and pepper. Heat the garlic mixture
until hot. Pour over the potatoes and mash until smooth.

**PER SERVING (SCANT ½ CUP): 111 CALORIES**
4g total fat, 2g saturated fat, 11mg cholesterol, 230mg sodium, 17g total carbohydrate,
1g dietary fiber, 2g protein, 28mg calcium

# spicy louisiana potatoes

***2 POINTS*** PER SERVING | MAKES 6 SERVINGS

*If your family tends to like dishes on the mild side, cook these spicy potatoes with ½ teaspoon of the Cajun seasoning. Those who like a little extra spice can sprinkle on more.*

**1. Preheat the oven** to 425°F. Spray a baking sheet with nonstick spray.

**2. Combine** the potatoes with cold water to cover by 2 inches in a medium saucepan; bring to a boil. Cook 7 minutes. Drain the potatoes, transfer to a large bowl, and toss with the onion, oil, Cajun seasoning, lemon juice, salt, and pepper. Arrange on the baking sheet in a single layer. Bake, until the potatoes are tender and crisp around the edges, stirring once, about 30 minutes.

**PER SERVING** (⅔ CUP): 127 CALORIES
2g total fat, 0g saturated fat, 0mg cholesterol, 238mg sodium, 25g total carbohydrate, 3g dietary fiber, 2g protein, 14mg calcium

1½ pounds red bliss potatoes, cut into ¼-inch wedges

1 red onion, cut into 8 wedges

1 tablespoon olive oil

1½ teaspoons Cajun seasoning

1 tablespoon fresh lemon juice

¼ teaspoon salt

¼ teaspoon freshly ground pepper

COOK'S HINT COOK'S HINT **variation** COOK'S HINT COOK'S HINT COOK'S HINT COOK'S HINT

To make spicy French fries, substitute baking potatoes, cut into ¼-inch sticks, and omit the lemon juice, onion, and the boiling step. Bake the potatoes in a single layer on a baking sheet, sprayed with nonstick spray, until crisp and golden, about 15 minutes on each side.

# spinach, onion, and potato hash [20]

**3 POINTS** PER SERVING | MAKES 4 SERVINGS

*A hint of curry and fennel add depth of flavor and a slight Indian touch to this dish.*

2 tablespoons reduced-calorie stick margarine

2 onions, thinly sliced

1 tablespoon sugar

½ teaspoon fennel seeds, lightly crushed

2 (15-ounce) cans sliced potatoes, drained

2 teaspoons paprika

1 teaspoon curry powder

1 (10-ounce) package frozen chopped spinach, thawed and squeezed dry

¼ cup water

½ teaspoon salt

**1.** Melt the margarine in a large nonstick skillet over medium-high heat, then add the onions, sugar, and fennel. Sauté until golden, 7–8 minutes. Reduce the heat to medium, then add the potatoes, paprika, and curry powder. Cook, stirring frequently, until the potatoes are browned and tender, 8–10 minutes.

**2.** Stir in the spinach, water, and salt; cook until the liquid evaporates and the spinach is heated through, about 3 minutes.

**PER SERVING (1 CUP): 173 CALORIES**
4g total fat, 1g saturated fat, 0mg cholesterol, 818mg sodium, 33g total carbohydrate, 7g dietary fiber, 5g protein, 96mg calcium

COOK'S HINT COOK'S HINT **fennel seeds** COOK'S HINT COOK'S HINT COOK'S HINT COOK'S

To crush fennel seeds, place then in a zip-close plastic bag on a cutting board. Tap lightly with a meat mallet or the bottom of a heavy skillet until lightly crushed.

# mashed potatoes and celeriac

***3 POINTS*** PER SERVING | MAKES 6 SERVINGS

*Celeriac, also known as celery root or celery knob, has a flavor similar to a combination of celery and parsley. It can be eaten raw, roasted, or sautéed.*

1. **Combine** the potatoes, celeriac, and onions in a pot with enough water to cover by 2 inches; bring to a boil. Reduce the heat and simmer 15 minutes. Add the garlic and cook 5 minutes longer; drain.

2. **Transfer the mixture** to a food processor or blender. Add the milk, butter, salt, and pepper; process until smooth.

PER SERVING (⅔ CUP): 150 CALORIES
4g total fat, 2g saturated fat, 11mg cholesterol, 379mg sodium, 26g total carbohydrate, 3g dietary fiber, 3g protein, 59mg calcium

1¼ pounds baking potatoes, peeled and cut into 1-inch pieces

¾ pound celeriac, peeled and cut into 1-inch pieces

2 onions, chopped

6 garlic cloves, peeled

⅓ cup fat-free milk

2 tablespoons butter

¾ teaspoon salt

¼ teaspoon freshly ground pepper

COOK'S HINT COOK'S HINT **garlic** COOK'S HINT COOK'S HINT COOK'S HINT

For a sweet, roasted-garlic flavor, substitute 6 cloves of roasted garlic for the boiled garlic and add it to the food processor when you purée the mixture.

# maple-roasted root vegetables

*1 POINT* PER SERVING | MAKES 6 SERVINGS

*Yukon gold potatoes, parsnips, and rutabaga make great additions or substitutions to this wonderful autumnal mix. The hint of maple syrup helps to accentuate the natural sweetness in the vegetables.*

1 pound white turnips, peeled and cut into 1½-inch chunks

1 pound sweet potatoes, peeled and cut into 1½-inch chunks

2 large carrots, peeled and cut into 1½-inch chunks

1 large yellow onion, peeled and quartered, root end left intact

2 tablespoons maple syrup

1 teaspoon salt

¾ teaspoon cinnamon

¼ teaspoon freshly ground pepper

⅛ teaspoon nutmeg

1. **Preheat the oven** to 425°F. Spray a large roasting pan with nonstick spray.

2. **Combine the turnips,** sweet potatoes, carrots, onion, maple syrup, salt, cinnamon, pepper, and nutmeg in a large bowl; toss well to coat. Arrange in a single layer in the roasting pan.

3. **Roast,** stirring occasionally, until the vegetables are tender and lightly browned, about 45 minutes.

**PER SERVING** (⅔ CUP): 102 CALORIES
0g total fat, 0g saturated fat, 0mg cholesterol, 436mg sodium, 25g total carbohydrate, 4g dietary fiber, 2g protein, 49mg calcium

# green bean and tomato sauté [20]

*1 POINT* PER SERVING | MAKES 4 SERVINGS

*Here's a simple Italian favorite—green beans and tomatoes, seasoned to perfection. To give the dish a different feel, substitute 1 pint of cherry or grape tomatoes, halved, for the chopped plum tomatoes.*

**1. Bring a large pot** of lightly salted water to a boil. Add the green beans, return to a boil and cook until crisp-tender, about 3 minutes. Drain.

**2. Heat the oil** in a large nonstick skillet over medium-high heat, then add the garlic and shallot. Sauté until fragrant, about 1 minute. Add the tomatoes and sugar; sauté until slightly softened, about 2 minutes. Add the green beans, vinegar, basil, salt, and pepper. Sauté until heated through, about 2 minutes.

**PER SERVING (1 CUP): 81 CALORIES**
4g total fat, 1g saturated fat, 0mg cholesterol, 305mg sodium, 12g total carbohydrate, 4g dietary fiber, 2g protein, 65mg calcium

1 pound green beans, trimmed and halved

1 tablespoon extra-virgin olive oil

2 garlic cloves, minced

1 large shallot, finely chopped

3 plum tomatoes, seeded and chopped

2 teaspoons sugar

1 teaspoon balsamic vinegar

½ teaspoon dried basil

½ teaspoon salt

⅛ teaspoon freshly ground pepper

COOK'S HINT COOK'S HINT **green beans** COOK'S HINT COOK'S HINT COOK'S HINT COOK'S HINT

When buying green beans look for a bright green color and crisp pods that easily snap in two. Take care not to overcook the beans, otherwise they will become soggy and lose their vibrant color.

# roasted asparagus and red peppers

**1 POINT** PER SERVING | MAKES 4 SERVINGS

*Roasting vegetables is an easy way to maximize flavor without adding a lot of fat. The high heat of roasting helps to caramelize the natural sugars in the vegetables, which brings out their sweetness.*

1 pound asparagus, trimmed and fibrous stalks peeled

1 large red bell pepper, seeded and cut into ½-inch strips

1 tablespoon fresh lemon juice

1 teaspoon olive oil

½ teaspoon salt

¼ teaspoon crushed red pepper

1 teaspoon grated lemon zest

**1. Preheat the oven** to 400°F. Spray a nonstick baking sheet with nonstick spray.

**2. Combine** the asparagus and bell pepper strips in a large bowl; spray with nonstick spray. Add the lemon juice, oil, salt, and crushed red pepper; toss well to coat.

**3. Arrange the vegetables** on the baking sheet. Bake until tender, shaking the pan occasionally, 15–18 minutes. Transfer the vegetables to a bowl and toss with the lemon zest.

**PER SERVING:** 39 CALORIES
2g total fat, 0g saturated fat, 0mg cholesterol, 295mg sodium, 5g total carbohydrate, 2g dietary fiber, 2g protein, 16mg calcium

# braised leeks and
# shiitake mushrooms [20]

***1 POINT*** PER SERVING | MAKES 4 SERVINGS

*Shiitake mushrooms, once considered exotic, are now widely cultivated
in the United States. They are available in most supermarket produce sections
and add a wonderful earthy flavor to soups, stir-fries, and vegetable dishes.*

**1. Cut the leeks in half** lengthwise then cut crosswise into 2-inch pieces.

**2. Melt the butter** in a large skillet over medium-high heat, then add the leeks
and mushrooms. Sauté until the vegetables begin to soften, about 5 minutes.
Add the broth, salt, thyme, and pepper. Reduce the heat and simmer, covered,
until the vegetables are tender, about 12 minutes. Uncover and simmer until
most of the liquid evaporates, about 3 minutes.

**PER SERVING (½ CUP): 64 CALORIES**
3g total fat, 2g saturated fat, 8mg cholesterol, 330mg sodium, 8g total carbohydrate,
2g dietary fiber, 3g protein, 54mg calcium

3 leeks, white and
light green parts only,
cleaned

1 tablespoon butter

½ pound shiitake
mushrooms, stems
removed, thickly sliced

½ cup fat-free
low-sodium chicken broth

½ teaspoon salt

¼ teaspoon dried thyme

⅛ teaspoon freshly
ground pepper

COOK'S HINT COOK'S HINT **leeks** COOK'S HINT COOK'S HINT COOK'S HINT COOK'S HINT

Leeks often pick up sand between their layers as they grow. To clean,
trim the dark green tops (reserve them for when you're making soup stock)
and the roots, leaving the root end intact to hold the layers together.
Slice the leek lengthwise, fan open the layers, and rinse thoroughly under
running water.

# spicy italian-style broccoli [20]

*1 POINT* PER SERVING | MAKES 4 SERVINGS

*This tasty side dish can easily become a salad. Simply chill and toss with mixed baby greens, chopped bell pepper, and sliced red onion and cucumber.*

6 cups broccoli florets

3 tablespoons prepared fat-free Italian-style dressing

3 tablespoons shaved Parmesan cheese

¼ teaspoon crushed red pepper

1. Bring a large pot of lightly salted water to a boil. Add the broccoli and return to a boil. Cook 3 minutes; drain.

2. Transfer the broccoli to a large bowl; add the dressing, cheese and crushed red pepper. Toss well to coat and serve at once or at room temperature.

PER SERVING (1 CUP): 66 CALORIES
2g total fat, 1g saturated fat, 4mg cholesterol, 458mg sodium, 9g total carbohydrate, 4g dietary fiber, 7g protein, 140mg calcium

COOK'S HINT COOK'S HINT **variation** COOK'S HINT COOK'S HINT COOK'S HINT COOK'S HINT

For an easy pasta salad, combine Spicy Italian-Style Broccoli with ¼ cup fat-free Italian-style dressing, 8 ounces chilled, cooked spiral pasta, and ½ cup each chopped red bell pepper, celery, and red onion (generous 2 cups has *4 POINTS*).

# stir-fried sesame bok choy [20]

*1 POINT* PER SERVING | MAKES 4 SERVINGS

*Bok choy is a versatile, mild-tasting vegetable that can be used in soups, salads, and other vegetable dishes.*

1. **Heat a large nonstick skillet** or wok over medium-high heat until a drop of water sizzles. Pour in the oil and swirl to coat the pan, then add the garlic, ginger, and crushed red pepper; stir-fry until fragrant, about 30 seconds.

2. **Add the bok choy and cook,** stirring often, 3 minutes. Stir in the broth, soy sauce, sugar, and cornstarch; bring to a boil stirring constantly. Cook, until thickened, about 1 minute. Remove from the heat and sprinkle with the sesame seeds.

**PER SERVING (½ CUP): 50 CALORIES**
2g total fat, 0g saturated fat, 0mg cholesterol, 415mg sodium, 7g total carbohydrate, 2g dietary fiber, 3g protein, 183mg calcium

1 teaspoon Asian (dark) sesame oil

1 garlic clove, minced

1 teaspoon minced peeled fresh ginger

¼ teaspoon crushed red pepper

1½ pounds baby bok choy, cleaned and cut into bite-size pieces

¼ cup low-sodium chicken broth

2 tablespoons reduced-sodium soy sauce

1 teaspoon sugar

½ teaspoon cornstarch

1 teaspoon sesame seeds

# caramelized pearl onions, fennel, and brussels sprouts

**2 POINTS** PER SERVING | MAKES 4 SERVINGS

*Members of the cabbage family, Brussels sprouts, a cruciferous vegetable, are high in vitamins A and C, and are a decent source of iron.*

1 (10-ounce) container Brussels sprouts, halved

1½ tablespoons butter

2 cups frozen whole onions, thawed

½ medium fennel bulb, thinly sliced (about 2 cups)

2 tablespoons sugar

½ teaspoon salt

⅛ teaspoon freshly ground pepper

**1.** Bring a medium saucepan of lightly salted water to a boil. Add the Brussels sprouts and return to a boil; cook 3 minutes. Drain.

**2.** Melt the butter in a large nonstick skillet over medium heat, then add the onions, fennel, and sugar. Cook until golden brown, stirring occasionally, 12–14 minutes. Add the Brussels sprouts, salt, and pepper; cook 2–3 minutes until heated through.

**PER SERVING (¾ CUP): 126 CALORIES**
5g total fat, 3g saturated fat, 12mg cholesterol, 359mg sodium, 20g total carbohydrate, 6g dietary fiber, 4g protein, 51mg calcium

COOK'S HINT COOK'S HINT **make-ahead** COOK'S HINT COOK'S HINT COOK'S HINT COOK'S HINT

This is a great make-ahead dish. Simply store in an airtight container in the refrigerator for up to 3 days. To reheat, transfer to a skillet over medium heat and cook until heated through, stirring occasionally, about 5–7 minutes.

# eggplant tomato tian

**2 POINTS** PER SERVING | MAKES 6 SERVINGS

*Tian is French for a shallow earthenware casserole, but it also refers to any food prepared in the dish. The flavors in this dish are traditional to the Provence region of France.*

1. **Preheat the oven** to 450°F. Spray 2 nonstick baking sheets and a 7 x 11-inch baking dish with nonstick spray.

2. **Arrange the eggplant slices** on the baking sheets. Lightly spray the eggplant with nonstick spray. Bake until softened, 12–15 minutes.

3. **Meanwhile, spray a large nonstick skillet** with nonstick spray and set over medium-high heat, then add the onions, garlic, and sugar. Sauté, stirring occasionally, until softened and lightly browned, 8–10 minutes. Remove from the heat and stir in the capers.

4. **Arrange the eggplant** in the bottom of the baking dish. Sprinkle with 2 tablespoons of the basil, ½ teaspoon of the salt, and ¼ teaspoon of the pepper. Top with the onion mixture. Sprinkle with the remaining basil, ¼ teaspoon salt, and ¼ teaspoon pepper. Arrange the tomato slices, slightly overlapping, in a single layer on top. Drizzle with the olive oil and top with the cheese.

5. **Bake until heated through** and the cheese is light golden, 25–30 minutes.

PER SERVING: 123 CALORIES
5g total fat, 1g saturated fat, 3mg cholesterol, 418mg sodium, 19g total carbohydrate, 5g dietary fiber, 4g protein, 86mg calcium

1 (1½-pound) eggplant, cut into ¼-inch slices

3 onions, thinly sliced

4 garlic cloves, minced

1 tablespoon sugar

1 tablespoon drained capers, chopped

¼ cup chopped basil

¾ teaspoon salt

½ teaspoon freshly ground pepper

1 pound plum tomatoes, cut into ¼-inch slices

1 tablespoon extra-virgin olive oil

¼ cup grated Parmesan cheese

COOK'S HINT COOK'S HINT **leftovers** COOK'S HINT COOK'S HINT COOK'S HINT COOK'S HINT

Leftover tian makes a wonderful topping for pasta: Roughly chop 2 cups leftover tian and combine with an 8-ounce can of tomato sauce in a medium saucepan. Cook over medium heat until hot, then season with salt and pepper to taste. Serve over your favorite pasta.

# warm red cabbage sauté [20]

*1 POINT* PER SERVING | MAKES 6 SERVINGS

*Similar to pickled cabbage, this sweet-and-sour dish works wonderfully with pork, veal, or chicken.*

1 tablespoon canola oil

1 pound red cabbage, thinly sliced (about 6 cups)

1 onion, thinly sliced

3 tablespoons sugar

3 tablespoons cider vinegar

1 teaspoon caraway seeds

1 Granny Smith apple, peeled, cored, and finely chopped

½ teaspoon salt

⅛ teaspoon freshly ground pepper

**Heat the oil** in a large nonstick skillet over medium-high heat, then add the cabbage, onion, and sugar. Cook, stirring occasionally, until the cabbage wilts, 7–8 minutes. Stir in the vinegar and caraway seeds; cook 3 minutes. Add the apple, salt, and pepper; cook until the apple is heated through, about 2 minutes.

**PER SERVING (⅔ CUP): 85 CALORIES**
3g total fat, 0g saturated fat, 0mg cholesterol, 208mg sodium, 16g total carbohydrate, 3g dietary fiber, 1g protein, 43mg calcium

COOK'S HINT COOK'S HINT **time saver** COOK'S HINT COOK'S HINT COOK'S HINT COOK'S HINT

To save time, buy pre-sliced red cabbage in the produce section of most supermarkets.

# herbed cherry tomatoes [20]

*1 POINT* PER SERVING | MAKES 4 SERVINGS

*The simple technique of roasting brings out the natural sweetness of cherry tomatoes.*

1. **Preheat the oven** to 400°F. Spray a shallow roasting pan or jelly-roll pan with nonstick spray.

2. **Combine the tomatoes and oil** in a large bowl; toss well. Spray lightly with nonstick spray and toss to coat. Add the garlic, sugar, basil, oregano, rosemary, thyme, salt, and pepper. Transfer to the roasting pan.

3. **Roast until the tomatoes** just begin to soften and crack, 8–10 minutes.

**PER SERVING** (¾ CUP): 56 CALORIES
2g total fat, 0g saturated fat, 0mg cholesterol, 453mg sodium, 10g total carbohydrate, 2g dietary fiber, 2g protein, 16mg calcium

2 pints cherry or grape tomatoes

1 teaspoon olive oil

2 garlic cloves, minced

1 teaspoon sugar

1 tablespoon chopped fresh basil, or ¾ teaspoon dried

1 teaspoon chopped fresh oregano, or ¼ teaspoon dried

1 teaspoon chopped fresh rosemary, or ¼ teaspoon dried

½ teaspoon chopped fresh thyme, or ⅛ teaspoon dried

¾ teaspoon salt

¼ teaspoon freshly ground pepper

COOK'S HINT COOK'S HINT **variation** COOK'S HINT COOK'S HINT COOK'S HINT COOK'S HINT

Instead of using the roasted tomatoes as a side dish, stir them into 8 ounces of your favorite cooked pasta. Top with a little grated Parmesan cheese and you've got a wonderful, no-fuss dinner for 4.

# two-apple slaw [20]

*2 POINTS* PER SERVING | MAKES 6 SERVINGS

*For an added kick, add ½ cup of golden raisins that have been plumped
in 3 tablespoons of cider vinegar for 10 minutes, then drained.*

2 Granny Smith apples,
peeled, cored, and
thinly sliced

2 Golden Delicious
apples, peeled, cored,
and thinly sliced

3 carrots, peeled
and shredded

2 scallions,
finely chopped

⅓ cup low-fat
mayonnaise

⅓ cup nonfat plain yogurt

2 tablespoons
cider vinegar

1 tablespoon sugar

½ teaspoon celery seeds

¼ teaspoon salt

¼ teaspoon freshly
ground pepper

1. **Combine** the apples, carrots, and scallions in a large bowl.

2. **Combine** the mayonnaise, yogurt, vinegar, sugar, celery seeds, salt, and
pepper in a medium bowl. Pour the mayonnaise mixture over the apple
mixture and toss well.

**PER SERVING (GENEROUS 1 CUP): 126 CALORIES**
5g total fat, 1g saturated fat, 5mg cholesterol, 222mg sodium, 21g total carbohydrate,
3g dietary fiber, 2g protein, 48mg calcium

COOK'S HINT COOK'S HINT **flavor** COOK'S HINT COOK'S HINT COOK'S HINT COOK'S HINT

For truly great flavor, make this slaw the night before to allow
all the flavors to blend, then stir in ¼ cup of chopped basil or cilantro.

# greek feta pilaf

*4 POINTS* PER SERVING | MAKES 6 SERVINGS

*Traditionally feta cheese is made from either sheep or goat milk.
With an assertively tart and slightly salty taste, just a small amount
of the cheese helps to add a lot of flavor to any dish.*

1. **Heat the oil** in a nonstick saucepan over medium-high heat, then add the onion, bell pepper, and garlic. Sauté until softened, 3–5 minutes. Add the rice and sauté until coated with oil, about 1 minute. Add the broth, salt, and pepper; bring to a boil. Reduce the heat and simmer, covered, until the liquid is absorbed, about 20 minutes. Let stand 5 minutes.

2. **Fluff with a fork** and stir in the cheese, dill, and lemon zest; cover and let stand 5 minutes.

**PER SERVING (⅔ CUP): 188 CALORIES**
5g total fat, 2g saturated fat, 11mg cholesterol, 354mg sodium, 30g total carbohydrate, 1g dietary fiber, 6g protein, 81mg calcium

2 teaspoons olive oil

1 onion, chopped

1 small red bell pepper, seeded and chopped

2 garlic cloves, minced

1 cup long-grain white rice

2 cups fat-free, low-sodium chicken broth

½ teaspoon salt

⅛ teaspoon freshly ground pepper

½ cup crumbled feta cheese

2 tablespoons chopped dill

2 teaspoons grated lemon zest

COOK'S HINT COOK'S HINT **variation** COOK'S HINT COOK'S HINT COOK'S HINT COOK'S HINT

To make this dish with an Italian twist, substitute ¼ cup chopped basil for the dill and ¼ cup grated Parmesan cheese for the feta cheese.

# vegetable fried rice [20]

*3 POINTS* PER SERVING | MAKES 6 SERVINGS

*Mirin is a sweet wine made from rice and is essential to Japanese cooking.
It can be found in the ethnic foods section of most large supermarkets. Although
not traditional in Chinese cooking, it adds a nice bit of sweetness to fried rice.*

2 large eggs,
lightly beaten

2 teaspoons Asian (dark)
sesame oil

2 garlic cloves, minced

1 teaspoon minced
peeled fresh ginger

2 cups cooked
brown rice

1½ cups frozen mixed
vegetables, thawed

2 scallions, chopped

2 tablespoons reduced-
sodium soy sauce

1 tablespoon mirin wine

¼ teaspoon salt

**1. Spray a large nonstick skillet** with nonstick spray and set over medium-high
heat. Add the eggs and cook, stirring occasionally, until firm, 2–3 minutes.
Transfer the eggs to a small bowl.

**2. Heat the oil** in the same skillet, then add the garlic and ginger.
Sauté until fragrant, about 30 seconds. Add the rice and mixed vegetables
and cook until hot, stirring occasionally, 3–5 minutes. Stir in the eggs,
scallions, soy sauce, mirin, and salt; cook until hot, about 2 minutes.

PER SERVING (½ CUP): 131 CALORIES
4g total fat, 1g saturated fat, 71mg cholesterol, 332mg sodium, 19g total carbohydrate,
2g dietary fiber, 5g protein, 34mg calcium

COOK'S HINT COOK'S HINT **leftovers** COOK'S HINT COOK'S HINT COOK'S HINT COOK'S HINT

This is a great dish to make with leftover, cold cooked rice because
the grains are drier and tend not to break during cooking.

# citrus-scented snap pea and carrot couscous [20]

*5 POINTS* PER SERVING | MAKES 4 SERVINGS

*Couscous, made from semolina, is the staple grain of North African countries. It is widely available in the United States in a "par-cooked" form. The great advantage to par-cooked couscous is that it takes only 5 minutes to cook.*

1. **Heat the oil** in a medium saucepan over medium-high heat, then add the carrot and cook 1 minute. Add the snap peas and almonds; cook until crisp-tender, about 1 minute. Transfer to a bowl and keep warm.

2. **Return the saucepan** to the heat and add the orange juice, salt, and pepper; bring to a boil. Add the couscous and remove from the heat. Cover and let stand 5 minutes. Fluff with a fork, then stir in the vegetables, raisins, basil, and lemon zest.

PER SERVING (SCANT 1 CUP): 256 CALORIES
5g total fat, 1g saturated fat, 0mg cholesterol, 304mg sodium, 46g total carbohydrate, 4g dietary fiber, 7g protein, 55mg calcium

2 teaspoons olive oil

1 carrot, peeled and thinly sliced

1 cup fresh sugar snap peas

3 tablespoons sliced almonds

1 cup orange juice

½ teaspoon salt

⅛ teaspoon freshly ground pepper

¾ cup couscous

¼ cup golden raisins

¼ cup chopped basil

½ teaspoon grated lemon zest

# confetti corn cakes [20]

4 POINTS PER SERVING | MAKES 6 SERVINGS

*These tasty cakes transform into a great brunch entrée when topped with nonfat sour cream and a slice of smoked salmon. Serve with a salad of sliced red onion and tomatoes, and a sprinkling of capers.*

¾ cup yellow cornmeal

¾ cup all-purpose flour

1 tablespoon sugar

¾ teaspoon salt

½ teaspoon dried basil

¼ teaspoon baking soda

¼ teaspoon freshly ground pepper

2 large eggs, lightly beaten

1⅓ cups fat-free buttermilk

1 (7-ounce) can whole kernel corn, drained

⅓ cup chopped red bell pepper

2 scallions, finely chopped

1 cup nonfat sour cream

1. **Combine** the cornmeal, flour, sugar, salt, basil, baking soda, and ground pepper in a large bowl. Combine the eggs and buttermilk in another bowl. Stir the egg mixture into the cornmeal mixture just until blended. Stir in the corn, bell pepper, and scallions.

2. **Spray a nonstick skillet** or griddle with nonstick spray; set over medium heat until a drop of water sizzles. Pour the batter by ¼ cup measures into the skillet. Cook just until bubbles begin to appear at the edges of the corn cakes, 2–3 minutes. Flip and cook 2 minutes longer. Repeat with the remaining batter, making a total of 12 corn cakes. Serve with sour cream.

**PER SERVING (2 CAKES): 226 CALORIES**
3g total fat, 1g saturated fat, 74mg cholesterol, 543mg sodium, 40g total carbohydrate, 2g dietary fiber, 10g protein, 171mg calcium

COOK'S HINT COOK'S HINT COOK'S HINT **appetizer** COOK'S HINT COOK'S HINT COOK'S HINT COOK'S HINT

For a great hors d'oeuvre, make quarter-size corn cakes and top with a dollop of nonfat sour cream.

# creamy blue cheese polenta [20]

***3 POINTS*** PER SERVING | MAKES 6 SERVINGS

*In northern Italy, polenta is a staple and is served either creamy
or firm. When made firm it is often cut into squares and fried or grilled.
It can even be served for breakfast.*

**Combine** the water, milk, salt, and pepper in a large saucepan; bring
to a boil over medium-high heat. Pour the polenta into the boiling liquid in
a slow steady stream, whisking constantly. Cook, stirring constantly,
until the polenta is thick and creamy, about 5 minutes. Stir in the blue
cheese and Parmesan cheese until combined. Serve at once.

**PER SERVING (⅔ CUP): 161 CALORIES**
5g total fat, 3g saturated fat, 12mg cholesterol, 504mg sodium, 22g total carbohydrate,
2g dietary fiber, 8g protein, 183mg calcium

3 cups water

2 cups low-fat (1%) milk

¾ teaspoon salt

¼ teaspoon freshly
ground pepper

1 cup instant polenta

2 ounces blue cheese,
crumbled

2 tablespoons grated
Parmesan cheese

COOK'S HINT COOK'S HINT **make ahead** COOK'S HINT COOK'S HINT COOK'S HINT
To make this dish ahead of time, prepare as above, then transfer to
an airtight container and refrigerate for up to 2 days. To reheat, combine
the polenta with ½ cup fat-free or low-fat milk and ½ cup water.
Heat gently over medium heat, stirring constantly, until creamy and hot.

# herbed quinoa
# with peas and scallions

**4 *POINTS*** PER SERVING | MAKES 4 SERVINGS

*Quinoa is coated with a naturally-occurring bitter outer coating. While not harmful, it should be eliminated by simply rinsing the grain under cold running water before cooking.*

1 cup quinoa, rinsed

1 cup orange juice

¾ cup water

2 teaspoons ground cumin

½ teaspoon salt

2 teaspoons extra-virgin olive oil

1 garlic clove, minced

1 cup frozen peas, thawed

3 scallions, chopped

¼ cup chopped basil

3 tablespoons chopped cilantro

2 teaspoons grated orange zest

1. **Combine** the quinoa, orange juice, water, cumin, and ¼ teaspoon of the salt in a medium saucepan; bring to a boil. Reduce the heat and simmer, covered, until all of the liquid is absorbed, 15–18 minutes.

2. **Meanwhile, heat the oil** in a nonstick skillet over medium-high heat, then add the garlic. Sauté until fragrant, about 30 seconds. Add the peas, scallions, and the remaining ¼ teaspoon salt. Sauté until heated through, about 2 minutes.

3. **Transfer the quinoa** to a bowl and stir in the pea mixture, basil, cilantro, and orange zest; mix well. Serve at once or at room temperature.

**PER SERVING:** 242 CALORIES
5g total fat, 1g saturated fat, 0mg cholesterol, 332mg sodium, 42g total carbohydrate, 5g dietary fiber, 8g protein, 64mg calcium

# rosemary-scented barley with beets [20]

***4 POINTS*** PER SERVING | MAKES 6 SERVINGS

*Barley is a delicious grain that has been used for thousands of years. We're partial to the modern-day variety of quick-cooking barley—it cooks in a mere 15 minutes.*

**1. Bring the water to a boil** in a medium saucepan, then add the barley. Reduce the heat and simmer, covered, until the liquid evaporates, 10–12 minutes. Remove from the heat and let stand 5 minutes.

**2. Meanwhile, heat the oil** in a large nonstick skillet over medium-high heat, then add the onion, shallot, garlic, sugar, and rosemary. Sauté until golden, 5–7 minutes. Add the mushrooms and sauté until golden, about 6 minutes. Add the beets and cook until heated through, about 1 minute. Remove from the heat and add the barley, salt, and pepper; toss well to combine.

**PER SERVING (GENEROUS ¾ CUP): 197 CALORIES**
5g total fat, 1g saturated fat, 0mg cholesterol, 337mg sodium, 35g total carbohydrate, 7g dietary fiber, 5g protein, 29mg calcium

2 cups water

1 cup quick-cooking barley

2 tablespoons olive oil

1 onion, thinly sliced

1 large shallot, thinly sliced

3 garlic cloves, sliced

1 tablespoon sugar

2 teaspoons chopped rosemary

1 (10-ounce) package white mushrooms, quartered

1 (8¼-ounce) can whole beets, drained and chopped

¾ teaspoon salt

⅛ teaspoon freshly ground pepper

COOK'S HINT COOK'S HINT **beets** COOK'S HINT COOK'S HINT COOK'S HINT

For a more intense beet flavor, substitute two cooked small fresh beets for the canned beets. Simply simmer the beets in a pot of boiling water until tender, about 20 minutes. Drain; let cool slightly, then peel and chop.

# southwestern corn skillet [20]

**2 POINTS** PER SERVING | MAKES 4 SERVINGS

*You can easily make this side dish into a vegetarian entrée by adding
a can of rinsed and drained black beans along with the cherry tomatoes.
Serve over steaming hot rice.*

1 tablespoon corn oil

1 onion, chopped

1 garlic clove, minced

1 jalapeño pepper,
seeded and finely
chopped (wear gloves to
prevent irritation)

1 (10-ounce) package
frozen corn kernels,
thawed

1 medium zucchini,
chopped

1 medium green bell
pepper, seeded and
chopped

½ teaspoon ground cumin

1 cup cherry tomatoes,
halved

2 tablespoons
chopped cilantro

¾ teaspoon salt

¼ teaspoon freshly
ground pepper

**Heat the oil** in a large nonstick skillet over medium-high heat, then add
the onion, garlic, and jalapeño pepper. Sauté until softened, 3–5 minutes.
Add the corn, zucchini, bell pepper, and cumin; sauté until softened,
7-8 minutes. Stir in the cherry tomatoes and sauté until just warmed
through, about 1 minute. Remove from the heat and stir in the cilantro,
salt, and ground pepper.

PER SERVING (1 CUP): 123 CALORIES
4g total fat, 1g saturated fat, 0mg cholesterol, 448mg sodium, 22g total carbohydrate,
4g dietary fiber, 4g protein, 27mg calcium

COOK'S HINT COOK'S HINT **leftovers** COOK'S HINT COOK'S HINT COOK'S HINT COOK'S HINT

Turn any leftovers into soft tacos by mixing 2 cups leftover Southwestern Corn
Skillet with 12 ounces cooked ground turkey breast. Stir in ½ cup prepared
salsa and simmer until heated through. Divide among 4 (6-inch) fat-free flour
tortillas and roll up. Serve with additional salsa (1 taco has **7 POINTS**).

# warm three-bean salad

*3 POINTS* PER SERVING | MAKES 6 SERVINGS

*This quick side dish makes the perfect accompaniment to grilled chicken breasts
or pork tenderloin. It also makes a wonderful picnic salad: Store the salad
in a leak-proof plastic container in the refrigerator overnight or up to 2 days.*

**1. Bring a large pot** of lightly salted water to a boil. Add the yellow wax
beans and green beans; return to a boil. Cook 3 minutes, drain.

**2. Heat the oil** in a large nonstick skillet over medium-high heat, then
add the onion, red and green bell peppers, and basil. Sauté until softened,
3–5 minutes. Add the yellow wax beans and green beans, chickpeas,
sugar, vinegar, salt, and ground pepper; cook until heated through, about
2 minutes.

PER SERVING (GENEROUS ¾ CUP): 179 CALORIES
4g total fat, 0g saturated fat, 0mg cholesterol, 617mg sodium, 31g total carbohydrate,
6g dietary fiber, 7g protein, 67mg calcium

½ pound yellow wax
beans, trimmed and
halved

½ pound green beans,
trimmed and halved

1 tablespoon canola oil

1 small onion, chopped

1 small red bell pepper,
seeded and chopped

1 small green bell
pepper, seeded and
chopped

1 teaspoon dried basil

1 (19-ounce) can
chickpeas, rinsed and
drained

¼ cup sugar

3 tablespoons cider
vinegar

1 teaspoon salt

¼ teaspoon freshly
ground pepper

# white beans with sage [20]

*3 POINTS* PER SERVING | MAKES 4 SERVINGS

*To make this into a main dish entrée, add blanched broccoli or broccoli rabe and serve over pasta. Finish the dish with shaved or grated Parmesan cheese.*

1 tablespoon olive oil

1 onion, chopped

1 medium fennel bulb, chopped

2 garlic cloves, minced

1 (19-ounce) can cannellini (white kidney) beans, rinsed and drained

2 teaspoons dried sage

2 tablespoons fresh lemon juice

1 teaspoon grated lemon zest

¼ teaspoon salt

⅛ teaspoon freshly ground pepper

**Heat the oil** in a large nonstick skillet over medium-high heat, then add the onion, fennel, and garlic. Sauté until softened, 3–5 minutes. Add the cannellini beans and sage; cook 1 minute. Add the lemon juice and cook 1 minute longer. Remove from the heat and stir in the lemon zest, salt, and pepper.

PER SERVING (½ CUP): 190 CALORIES
4g total fat, 1g saturated fat, 0mg cholesterol, 399mg sodium, 32g total carbohydrate, 10g dietary fiber, 9g protein, 85mg calcium

carrot cake with cream cheese frosting
chocolate angel food cake with macerated strawberries
pumpkin spice cake cinnamon-raisin bread pudding
creamy brown rice pudding peanut butter cornflake bars
apple strudel chocolate banana frozen yogurt parfaits
peach sorbet pear ginger crisp
pineapple-topped sour cream cheesecake
strawberries with yogurt and honey
summer pudding rosemary-oatmeal cloverleaf rolls
herbed corn muffins mixed berry muffins
banana bread cherry fudge brownies
apricot pistachio biscotti espresso biscotti

# desserts
## & baked goods

# carrot cake with cream cheese frosting

**5 POINTS** PER SERVING | MAKES 24 SERVINGS

*This decadent layer cake will satisfy all your sweet needs. We've dramatically reduced the amount of oil traditionally called for in this recipe and added applesauce and raisins, both of which help make the cake moist. The traditional cream cheese frosting also is kept low in calories by using nonfat cream cheese.*

3 large eggs

1 cup plain nonfat yogurt

1 cup unsweetened applesauce

1 cup packed light brown sugar

½ cup canola oil

2 tablespoons grated orange zest

1 tablespoon vanilla extract

3½ cups all-purpose flour

1 tablespoon pumpkin pie spice

2 teaspoons baking powder

1 teaspoon baking soda

½ teaspoon salt

3 medium carrots, shredded, about 2 cups

1 cup golden raisins

8 ounces nonfat cream cheese

3 ounces Neufchâtel cheese

1½ cups confectioners' sugar

1. **Preheat the oven** to 375°F. Spray two 9-inch cake pans with nonstick spray and lightly dust with flour.

2. **With an electric mixer at high speed,** beat the eggs, yogurt, applesauce, brown sugar, oil, 1 tablespoon of the orange zest, and the vanilla until blended. In a medium bowl, combine the flour, pumpkin pie spice, baking powder, baking soda, and salt. Add to the egg mixture and mix on low speed just until blended, 2–3 minutes. Stir in the carrots and raisins. Scrape the batter into the pans. Bake until a toothpick inserted in the center comes out clean, 30–35 minutes. Cool in the pans on a rack 10 minutes; remove from the pans and cool completely on the rack.

3. **To prepare the frosting,** with an electric mixer at high speed, beat the nonfat cream cheese, Neufchâtel cheese, confectioners' sugar, and the remaining 1 tablespoon orange zest until blended.

4. **To assemble;** place one cake layer on a plate. Spread with about ½ cup of the frosting and place the second layer on top. Frost the top and sides with the remaining frosting.

**PER SERVING:** 233 CALORIES
6g total fat, 1g saturated fat, 30mg cholesterol, 225mg sodium, 39g total carbohydrate, 1g dietary fiber, 5g protein, 77mg calcium

COOK'S HINT COOK'S HINT **variation** COOK'S HINT COOK'S HINT COOK'S

This yummy carrot cake easily transforms into a delectable zucchini cake by substituting 2 cups of shredded zucchini for the carrots.

# chocolate angel food cake
# with macerated strawberries

*3 POINTS* PER SERVING | MAKES 12 SERVINGS

*This cake may be made a day ahead; simply store, covered, at room temperature. The strawberries can also be prepared a day ahead and refrigerated. If you are not a chocolate fan, but love angel food cake, simply omit the cocoa powder.*

1. Preheat the oven to 350°F.

2. To prepare the cake, combine the flour and cocoa powder in a small bowl; sift twice. With an electric mixer at medium speed, beat the egg whites in a large bowl until thick and foamy. Gradually sprinkle in 1¼ cups of the sugar, the cream of tartar, and salt; continue beating until the egg whites form medium peaks, 3–5 minutes.

3. Add the flour mixture in 3 additions, gently folding each addition into the whites with a rubber spatula until well combined. Fold in the vanilla.

4. Pour the batter into an ungreased 10-inch tube pan or angel food cake pan. Tap the pan lightly on the counter to help remove air bubbles; smooth the top of the batter. Bake until a toothpick inserted in the center comes out clean and the cake begins to pull away from the sides of the pan, 35–40 minutes. Allow the cake to cool completely in pan on a rack. Run a knife around the edge of the cake and remove the side of the pan. Run the knife under the bottom of the cake and the center tube. Invert the cake on to a serving plate.

5. To prepare the strawberries, combine the strawberries, the remaining ¼ cup sugar, the orange juice, and zest in a bowl. Refrigerate 1 hour or overnight, stirring occasionally.

PER SERVING (¹⁄₁₂ CAKE AND GENEROUS ¼ CUP STRAWBERRIES): 169 CALORIES
1g total fat, 0g saturated fat, 0mg cholesterol, 96mg sodium, 38g total carbohydrate, 2g dietary fiber, 4g protein, 14mg calcium

1 cup cake flour
(not self rising)

⅓ cup unsweetened
cocoa powder

10 large egg whites,
at room temperature

1½ cups sugar

1 teaspoon
cream of tartar

¼ teaspoon salt

2 teaspoons
vanilla extract

2 pints strawberries,
stemmed and sliced,
about 6 cups

¼ cup orange juice

1 teaspoon grated
orange zest

COOK'S HINT COOK'S HINT **toast it** COOK'S HINT COOK'S HINT COOK'S HINT

This cake is wonderful toasted in the oven until lightly crisp.
Top with any favorite fruit and fat-free whipped topping, or spread it
with a fruit spread and serve for breakfast.

# pumpkin spice cake

**5 POINTS** PER SERVING | MAKES 20 SERVINGS

*Low-fat baked goods tend to be dry, however, canned pumpkin purée, available in your supermarket baking section, can remedy this too-common problem. Here, it helps keep this cake moist, fresh, and rich-tasting.*

3 cups all-purpose flour

2 cups granulated sugar

1 tablespoon
pumpkin pie spice

1 tablespoon baking
powder

¼ teaspoon salt

4 large eggs

½ cup canola oil

½ cup fat-free milk

1 (15-ounce) can
pumpkin purée

2 teaspoons
vanilla extract

¾ cup confectioners'
sugar

1½ tablespoons fresh
lemon juice

**1. Preheat the oven** to 375°F. Spray a 10-inch Bundt pan with nonstick spray, then lightly dust it with flour.

**2. Combine** the flour, granulated sugar, pumpkin pie spice, baking powder, and salt in a large bowl. Combine the eggs, oil, milk, pumpkin purée, and vanilla in another bowl. Add the egg mixture to the flour mixture; stir just until blended.

**3. Pour the batter** into the pan. Bake until a toothpick inserted in the center comes out clean, 55–60 minutes. Cool in the pan on a rack 15 minutes; remove from the pan and cool on the rack 30 minutes.

**4. Combine** the confectioners' sugar and lemon juice in a bowl. Drizzle over the warm cake and serve at once. Or cool the cake completely on a rack and drizzle with the glaze just before serving.

**PER SERVING:** 230 CALORIES
7g total fat, 1g saturated fat, 43mg cholesterol, 120mg sodium, 41g total carbohydrate, 1g dietary fiber, 4g protein, 64mg calcium

# cinnamon-raisin bread pudding

**5 POINTS** PER SERVING | MAKES 4 SERVINGS

*Readily available cinnamon-raisin swirl bread is a great shortcut ingredient
in this homey dessert. Any leftovers make for a delicious breakfast.*

1. **Preheat the oven** to 350°F. Spray a 1½-quart shallow baking dish with
nonstick spray.

2. **Combine** the milk, eggs, ¼ cup sugar and the vanilla in a large bowl;
mix well. Stir in the bread cubes and let stand 5 minutes, stirring
occasionally. Pour into the baking dish.

3. **Sprinkle the top** with the remaining 1 tablespoon sugar. Bake, uncovered,
until lightly puffed and golden, and a knife inserted in the center comes out
clean, 25–30 minutes. Let stand 15 minutes before serving warm.

**PER SERVING:** 260 CALORIES
4g total fat, 1g saturated fat, 108mg cholesterol, 343mg sodium, 45g total carbohydrate,
1g dietary fiber, 9g protein, 144mg calcium

1 cup fat-free milk

2 large eggs

¼ cup + 1 tablespoon
sugar

½ teaspoon
vanilla extract

8 slices cinnamon-raisin
swirl bread,
cut in 1-inch cubes

COOK'S HINT COOK'S HINT **bread** COOK'S HINT COOK'S HINT COOK'S HINT COOK'S HINT

When making bread puddings of any kind, choose firm-textured bread
such as Italian, French, brick-oven baked, or raisin bread. The bread need
not be fresh—in fact, slightly stale bread is preferable.

# creamy brown rice pudding

**5 POINTS** PER SERVING | MAKES 6 SERVINGS

*Yogurt gives a sweet-tangy flavor to this easy rice pudding, while brown rice (which still has the outer bran attached to the grain, giving it a slight nutritional edge over the traditional white variety) supplies a chewier texture.*

1 quart low-fat
(1%) milk

½ cup sugar

1 teaspoon
vanilla extract

⅛ teaspoon salt

¾ cup quick-cooking
brown rice

½ cup golden raisins

½ cup plain nonfat yogurt

**1. Combine** the milk, sugar, vanilla, and salt in a heavy pot; bring to a simmer over medium-high heat. Stir in the rice and reduce the heat to medium. Simmer, uncovered, 1 hour, stirring occasionally.

**2. Stir in the raisins** and simmer until the rice is tender and the pudding begins to thicken, about 15 minutes longer. Remove from the heat and stir in the yogurt. Serve warm.

**PER SERVING** (½ **CUP**): 271 CALORIES
2g total fat, 1g saturated fat, 7mg cholesterol, 150mg sodium, 54g total carbohydrate, 2g dietary fiber, 9g protein, 255mg calcium

COOK'S HINT COOK'S HINT **variation** COOK'S HINT COOK'S HINT COOK'S HINT COOK'S HINT
For a different zestier flavor, substitute nonfat lemon yogurt
for the plain yogurt and stir in a teaspoon or two of grated lemon zest.

# peanut butter cornflake bars

*3 POINTS* PER SERVING | MAKES 16 SERVINGS

*These bars are ideal for satisfying a sweet-tooth craving. If you like, make the recipe, then freeze each bar individually; remove from the freezer as needed. For a stylish touch, reserve 2 tablespoons of the chocolate chips, melt, then drizzle over the cooled bars.*

1. **Spray an 8-inch square baking dish** with nonstick spray.

2. **Melt the margarine** in a large heavy saucepan over medium heat. Add the marshmallows and cook, stirring constantly, until melted, about 7 minutes. Stir in the peanut butter until smooth. Remove the saucepan from the heat and stir in the corn flakes and chocolate chips. Pour into the baking dish. Press the mixture flat with a sheet of wax paper; cool 30 minutes. Turn out onto a rack and cool 30 minutes longer.

3. **Transfer** to a cutting board and cut into 16 bars.

**PER SERVING (1 BAR): 143 CALORIES**
6g total fat, 1g saturated fat, 0mg cholesterol, 176mg sodium, 22g total carbohydrate, 1g dietary fiber, 2g protein, 5mg calcium

**4 tablespoons light stick margarine**

**4 cups (about 40) marshmallows**

**⅓ cup smooth peanut butter**

**6 cups corn flakes**

**¼ cup mini chocolate chips**

COOK'S HINT COOK'S HINT **substitute** COOK'S HINT COOK'S HINT COOK'S HINT COOK'S HINT COOK'S HINT

Crisp rice cereal or toasted oat cereal are good substitutes for the corn flakes. Or try using a combination of all these equally low-*POINT* cereals.

# apple strudel

*2 POINTS* PER SERVING | MAKES 6 SERVINGS

*Easy-to-use phyllo dough makes light work of this crisp and delicious strudel.*
*If you love pears you can substitute an equal amount for the apples.*
*For a special treat add ¼ cup golden raisins and 2 tablespoons of chopped*
*walnuts to the filling (it adds less than 1 POINT per serving).*

1½ pounds Granny Smith apples, peeled, cored, and cut into ½-inch cubes

2 tablespoons granulated sugar

¼ cup water

1 teaspoon vanilla extract

¾ teaspoon cinnamon

¼ teaspoon ground ginger

4 (12 x 17-inch) sheets phyllo dough, at room temperature

3 tablespoons confectioners' sugar

1 teaspoon orange juice

1. **Preheat the oven** to 350°F. Spray a baking sheet with nonstick spray.

2. **Spray a nonstick skillet** with nonstick spray and set over medium-high heat. Add the apples and granulated sugar; cook, stirring occasionally, about 3 minutes. Stir in the water, vanilla, cinnamon, and ginger. Cook until the apples are tender and the liquid is evaporated, 4–5 minutes. Remove from the heat and cool 10 minutes.

3. **Cover the sheets of phyllo** with plastic wrap to keep them from drying out. Place one sheet on a clean dry work surface. Spray lightly with nonstick spray and top with a second sheet. Repeat with the remaining phyllo sheets. Spoon the apples along one long side of the dough, 2 inches from the edge. Fold the short sides of the dough over the apples and roll up the from the long end jellyroll style. Place on the baking sheet and spray lightly with nonstick spray. Bake until golden and crisp, 17–19 minutes. Cool 10 minutes.

4. **In a small bowl**, combine the confectioners' sugar and orange juice until smooth. Drizzle over the strudel and serve warm.

PER SERVING: 121 CALORIES
0g total fat, 0g saturated fat, 0mg cholesterol, 37mg sodium, 29g total carbohydrate, 2g dietary fiber, 1g protein, 9mg calcium

COOK'S HINT COOK'S HINT phyllo COOK'S HINT COOK'S HINT COOK'S HINT COOK'S HINT
You can find phyllo dough in the freezer section of the supermarket. Make sure it's completely thawed before using.

# chocolate banana
# frozen yogurt parfaits [20]

**5 POINTS** PER SERVING | MAKES 4 SERVINGS

*If you prefer, substitute an equal amount of low-fat graham crackers, vanilla wafers, or your favorite low-fat cookie for the chocolate wafers.*

In each of 4 parfait glasses, place ¼ cup of frozen yogurt, top with 1 tablespoon whipped topping, 3 banana slices, 1 teaspoon chopped pecans, ¼ cup frozen yogurt, 1 crumbled chocolate wafer cookie, 3 banana slices, 1 tablespoon hot fudge, 1 teaspoon chopped pecans, 1 tablespoon whipped topping, and 1 maraschino cherry.

**PER SERVING:** 249 CALORIES
5g total fat, 1g saturated fat, 1mg cholesterol, 110mg sodium, 51g total carbohydrate, 2g dietary fiber, 4g protein, 97mg calcium

2 cups vanilla fat-free
frozen yogurt

½ cup fat-free
whipped topping

1 large banana,
cut into 24 slices

8 teaspoons chopped
pecans, toasted

4 chocolate wafer
cookies

¼ cup fat-free
hot fudge topping

4 maraschino cherries

COOK'S HINT COOK'S HINT **pecans** COOK'S HINT COOK'S HINT COOK'S HINT COOK'S HINT

To toast the pecans, place them in a small dry skillet over medium-low heat. Cook, shaking the pan and stirring constantly, until lightly browned and fragrant, 3–4 minutes. Watch them carefully when toasting; nuts can burn quickly. Transfer the nuts to a plate to cool.

# peach sorbet

*1 POINT* PER SERVING | MAKES 4 SERVINGS

*This refreshing sorbet is a perfect treat on a hot summer's night. It also works as an elegant dessert when served in fine crystal goblets then sprinkled with fresh chopped mint. If you are unable to find peach nectar, substitute an equal amount of peach juice or apricot nectar.*

¼ cup sugar

½ cup water

1½ cups peach nectar

3 tablespoons fresh lemon juice

**1. Combine** the sugar and water in a small saucepan; bring to a boil over high heat; boil 5 minutes. Transfer the mixture to a bowl, then place in the freezer until chilled, 20–25 minutes.

**2. Remove the bowl** from the freezer and stir in the peach nectar and lemon juice; pour into an 8-inch square baking dish and freeze 30 minutes. Remove from the freezer and stir with a fork, making sure to scrape icy parts from the side of the dish. Return to the freezer for 30 minutes, then stir again. Freeze 45 minutes longer.

**3. Transfer the sorbet** to a food processor or blender. Pulse 4–5 times until the sorbet is smooth (be sure not to over process or the sorbet will melt). Serve at once or freeze until ready to use.

**PER SERVING (½ CUP): 66 CALORIES**
0g total fat, 0g saturated fat, 0mg cholesterol, 3mg sodium, 17g total carbohydrate, 1g dietary fiber, 0g protein, 5mg calcium

COOK'S HINT COOK'S HINT **smoother sorbet** COOK'S HINT COOK'S HINT COOK'S HINT

If the sorbet becomes too hard or icy after refreezing, simply allow it to soften in the refrigerator for 20 minutes, or transfer it to the food processor and pulse 4–5 times.

# pear ginger crisp

**5 POINTS** PER SERVING | MAKES 6 SERVINGS

*For added depth of flavor, add 2 tablespoons of finely chopped crystallized ginger to the pear mixture. You can find crystallized or candied ginger in the spice section of most supermarkets or at gourmet specialty food stores.*

1. **Preheat the oven** to 375°F. Spray 8-inch square baking dish with nonstick spray.

2. **Combine** the pears, ¼ cup of the sugar, 1 tablespoon flour, the ginger, ½ teaspoon of the cinnamon, and the vanilla in a bowl. Spoon into the baking dish.

3. **Combine** the remaining ¼ cup sugar, ½ cup flour, ¼ teaspoon cinnamon, the oats, butter, and water in another bowl until crumbs firm. Sprinkle over the pears.

4. **Bake until the filling is bubbling** and the top is golden, 40–50 minutes. Cool on a rack 10 minutes before serving.

**PER SERVING: 240 CALORIES**
6g total fat, 4g saturated fat, 16mg cholesterol, 46mg sodium, 46g total carbohydrate, 3g dietary fiber, 2g protein, 36mg calcium

4 ripe pears, peeled, cored, and thinly sliced

½ cup packed light brown sugar

½ cup + 1 tablespoon all-purpose flour

¾ teaspoon ground ginger

¾ teaspoon cinnamon

½ teaspoon vanilla extract

3 tablespoons quick-cooking rolled oats

3 tablespoons butter, melted

2 teaspoons water

# pineapple-topped sour cream cheesecake

*4 POINTS* PER SERVING | MAKES 20 SERVINGS

*For a chocolate cookie crust, substitute an equal amount of low-fat chocolate graham crackers for the honey grahams.*

10 (2½-inch square) low-fat honey graham crackers, made into fine crumbs

1¼ cups sugar

2 tablespoons butter, melted

1 tablespoon water

8 ounces Neufchâtel cheese

8 ounces nonfat cream cheese

3 large eggs

6 tablespoons all-purpose flour

1½ teaspoons vanilla extract

2 cups vanilla nonfat yogurt

1 cup fat-free sour cream

1 (20-ounce) can pineapple chunks in syrup

1½ tablespoons cornstarch

1. **Preheat the oven** to 350°F. Spray a 9-inch springform pan with nonstick spray.

2. **To prepare the crust,** combine the graham cracker crumbs, ¼ cup of the sugar, the butter, and water in a bowl; pat the mixture into the bottom and 2-inches up the sides of the pan. Bake 10 minutes; cool on a rack. Reduce the oven temperature to 325°F.

3. **To prepare the filling,** purée the Neufchâtel cheese, nonfat cream cheese, eggs, the remaining 1 cup sugar, the flour, and vanilla in a food processor or blender. Transfer to a large bowl and stir in the yogurt and sour cream. Pour the filling into the cooled crust and bake until the cheesecake is almost set, about 1 hour and 5 minutes. Turn off the oven and let the cake stand in the oven 1 hour longer. Cool on a rack 1 hour, then cover and refrigerate 3 hours.

4. **To prepare the topping,** pulse the pineapple chunks and syrup in a food processor until finely chopped. Transfer to a medium saucepan; stir in the cornstarch and bring to a boil over medium-high heat. Cook, stirring occasionally, 1 minute. Transfer to a bowl; cover and refrigerate 2 hours. Spread over the top of the cheesecake.

**PER SERVING: 173 CALORIES**
5g total fat, 3g saturated fat, 45mg cholesterol, 163mg sodium, 27g total carbohydrate, 0g dietary fiber, 6g protein, 89mg calcium

COOK'S HINT COOK'S HINT **make ahead** COOK'S HINT COOK'S HINT

Cheesecakes are great to make ahead, especially if you have company coming. For this recipe, make the cheesecake (without the topping) as directed, cool completely, wrap in a double layer of plastic wrap and then in foil. Refrigerate for up to 3 days or freeze for up to 3 months. Thaw overnight in the refrigerator. Prepare the topping and spread over the cake the day of serving.

# strawberries with yogurt and honey

*3 POINTS* PER SERVING | MAKES 6 SERVINGS

*In Greece, thick, tangy yogurt drizzled with honey and sprinkled with toasted nuts is a traditional dessert. In our delicious version, we use strained nonfat yogurt and add sweet sliced strawberries.*

1. **Line a strainer** or sieve with a paper coffee filter, cheesecloth, or paper towel. Spoon in the yogurt and place over a bowl. Refrigerate for at least 1 hour or overnight to strain.

2. **Divide the berries** among 6 parfait or dessert cups. Top with the strained yogurt, drizzle with the honey, and sprinkle with the nuts. Serve at once.

PER SERVING: 171 CALORIES
4g total fat, 0g saturated fat, 3mg cholesterol, 65mg sodium, 29g total carbohydrate, 2g dietary fiber, 7g protein, 192mg calcium

2 cups plain
nonfat yogurt

1 pint strawberries,
sliced

6 tablespoons honey

½ cup toasted
sliced almonds

# summer pudding

*4 POINTS* PER SERVING | MAKES 6 SERVINGS

*Summer pudding is a traditional English dessert. The classic version contains a variety of berries and red currants. You'll need to remove the crusts from the bread (make them into bread crumbs to use another time).*

**9 slices firm white bread (about 12 ounces), crusts removed**

**2 (12-ounce) bags frozen mixed berries or 5 cups mixed fresh berries**

**½ cup sugar**

**⅓ cup orange juice**

**1 teaspoon grated lemon zest**

1. **Line a 1-quart bowl** with enough plastic wrap to hang over the sides of the bowl by about 3 inches all round. Line the bowl with 7 of the bread slices, trimming to fit just below the rim; reserve the trimmings.

2. **Combine** the fruit, sugar, and orange juice in a medium saucepan; bring to a boil. Cook over medium heat until the fruit is just softened, about 5 minutes. Remove from the heat and stir in the lemon zest.

3. **With a slotted spoon,** transfer the fruit to the prepared bowl; set aside the juice. Top with the remaining 2 slices of bread and the trimmings to cover. Drizzle with ½ cup of the fruit juice. Fold the plastic wrap over the top of the pudding to cover. Place a plate, smaller than the mouth of the bowl, on top of the pudding. Set a weight such as a 28-ounce can on top and refrigerate overnight.

4. **To serve, remove the can.** Invert the pudding onto a serving plate; remove the plastic wrap and cut the pudding into wedges.

PER SERVING: 239 CALORIES
2g total fat, 0g saturated fat, 0mg cholesterol, 232mg sodium, 53g total carbohydrate, 6g dietary fiber, 4g protein, 63mg calcium

# rosemary-oatmeal cloverleaf rolls

**3 POINTS** PER SERVING | MAKES 18 ROLLS

*These deliciously light rolls freeze well and are great to have on hand for any occasion. Simply cool them completely on a rack then transfer to a zip-close plastic bag and freeze. Thaw at room temperature for about 30 minutes. Or thaw in the microwave on High, about 15 seconds for each roll.*

**1. Combine** ¾ cup oats and the boiling water in a small bowl. Let stand 5 minutes.

**2. Combine** the warm water and sugar in a large bowl. Sprinkle in the yeast, and let stand until foamy, about 5 minutes. Stir in the milk and butter.

**3. Combine** 3⅓ cups of the flour, the rosemary, and salt in a bowl. Add to the yeast mixture along with the moistened oats; stir until the dough starts to gather around the spoon. Turn out the dough on a lightly floured surface; knead until the dough is smooth and elastic, about 10 minutes, adding enough of the remaining ⅓ cup flour, 1 tablespoon at a time, to prevent the dough from sticking to hands.

**4. Spray a large bowl** with nonstick spray; put the dough in the bowl. Cover tightly with plastic wrap and let the dough rise in a warm spot until it doubles in size, about 1 hour.

**5. Spray 18 muffin cups** with nonstick spray. Turn out the dough on a lightly floured surface and punch down. Cut into 18 pieces. Divide each piece into 3 and shape each into a ball; place 3 dough balls in each muffin cup. Cover and let rise 30 minutes.

**6. Preheat the oven to 350°F.** Uncover the rolls, brush with beaten egg white mixture, and sprinkle with the remaining 1½ tablespoons oats. Bake until golden and the rolls sound hollow when tapped with fingers, 20–25 minutes. Remove from the pans and cool on a rack 10 minutes. Serve warm or at room temperature.

**PER SERVING:** 132 CALORIES
2g total fat, 1g saturated fat, 4mg cholesterol, 150mg sodium, 24g total carbohydrate, 1g dietary fiber, 4g protein, 29mg calcium

¾ cup + 1½ tablespoons rolled oats

½ cup boiling water

¼ cup warm (105–115°F) water

2 tablespoons sugar

1 envelope active dry yeast

1¼ cups fat-free milk

2 tablespoons butter, melted

3⅔ cups all-purpose flour

1 teaspoon dried rosemary, crumbled

1 teaspoon salt

1 egg white, lightly beaten with 1 tablespoon water

# herbed corn muffins

**2 POINTS** PER SERVING | MAKES 12 SERVINGS

*These savory muffins are an especially nice addition to a Thanksgiving table or midday brunch. For Southwestern flair, add 1 cup of corn kernels and 2 finely chopped seeded jalapeño peppers to the batter before baking.*

1 cup cornmeal

¾ cup all-purpose flour

1½ teaspoons baking powder

¼ teaspoon baking soda

1 teaspoon salt

1 teaspoon dried basil

½ teaspoon dried oregano

¼ teaspoon dried thyme

1 cup fat-free buttermilk

1 large egg, lightly beaten

2½ tablespoons butter, melted

**1. Preheat the oven** to 425°F. Spray a 12-cup muffin pan with nonstick spray.

**2. Combine** the cornmeal, flour, baking powder, baking soda, salt, basil, oregano, and thyme in a medium bowl. Combine the buttermilk, egg, and butter in another bowl. Add the buttermilk mixture to the cornmeal mixture; stir just until blended.

**3. Spoon the batter** into the cups, filling each about two-thirds full. Bake until golden brown and a toothpick inserted in a muffin comes out clean, 18–20 minutes. Cool in the pan on a rack 5 minutes; remove from the pan and cool completely on the rack.

PER SERVING: 107 CALORIES
3g total fat, 2g saturated fat, 25mg cholesterol, 324mg sodium, 16g total carbohydrate, 1g dietary fiber, 3g protein, 64mg calcium

COOK'S HINT COOK'S HINT **leftovers** COOK'S HINT COOK'S HINT COOK'S HINT COOK'S HINT
Use leftovers as a substitute for half or all of the bread in your favorite stuffing recipe.

# mixed berry muffins

**3 POINTS** PER SERVING | MAKES 18 SERVINGS

*Strawberries, blueberries, raspberries, Marionberries—any berry mix will do for these tasty muffins. For an unexpected, yet delicious, twist, stir a teaspoon of chopped fresh thyme in with the dry ingredients.*

**1. Preheat the oven** to 400°F. Spray 18 muffin cups with nonstick spray.

**2. Combine** the whole-wheat flour, all-purpose flour, sugar, baking powder, baking soda, cinnamon, and salt in a large bowl. Combine the buttermilk, eggs, and butter in another bowl. Add the buttermilk mixture to the flour mixture; stir just until blended. Gently fold the berries and zest into the batter.

**3. Spoon the batter into the cups,** filling each about two-thirds full. Bake until golden brown and a toothpick inserted in a muffin comes out clean, 18–20 minutes. Cool in the pan on a rack 5 minutes; remove from the pan and cool completely on the rack.

PER SERVING: 142 CALORIES
4g total fat, 2g saturated fat, 31mg cholesterol, 186mg sodium, 25g total carbohydrate, 3g dietary fiber, 4g protein, 66mg calcium

1½ cups whole-wheat flour

1 cup all-purpose flour

⅔ cup sugar

2 teaspoons baking powder

¾ teaspoon baking soda

½ teaspoon cinnamon

¼ teaspoon salt

1½ cups fat-free buttermilk

2 large eggs, lightly beaten

¼ cup butter, melted

2 cups frozen mixed berries

1 teaspoon grated lemon zest

COOK'S HINT COOK'S HINT freeze a batch COOK'S HINT COOK'S HINT COOK'S HINT

Make a double batch and store the extra muffins in the freezer. You can thaw one in the microwave at a moment's notice for a satisfying breakfast.

# banana bread

**2 POINTS** PER SERVING | MAKES 24 SERVINGS

*For the best flavor, use the ripest bananas possible. If you have overripe bananas that you are not going to eat, just peel them, pop them into a zip-close plastic bag, and freeze them for making bread or muffins another day.*

⅔ cup sugar

⅓ cup butter, softened

2 large eggs

2 ripe bananas, mashed (about 1 cup)

½ cup fat-free buttermilk

¾ teaspoon vanilla extract

1½ cups all-purpose flour

¾ cup toasted wheat germ

1 teaspoon baking powder

½ teaspoon baking soda

½ teaspoon cinnamon

½ teaspoon salt

**1. Preheat the oven** to 350°F. Spray a 4 x 8½-inch nonstick loaf pan with nonstick spray.

**2. With a wooden spoon,** beat the sugar and butter in large bowl until creamy. Add the eggs, bananas, buttermilk, and vanilla; beat until combined. Combine the flour, wheat germ, baking powder, baking soda, cinnamon, and salt in another bowl. Add the flour mixture to the banana mixture; stir just until blended.

**3. Scrape the batter into the pan.** Bake until a toothpick inserted in the center comes out clean, 45–55 minutes. Cool in the pan on a rack 10 minutes; remove from the pan and cool completely on the rack.

**PER SERVING (1 SLICE): 104 CALORIES**
4g total fat, 2g saturated fat, 25mg cholesterol, 123mg sodium, 16g total carbohydrate, 1g dietary fiber, 3g protein, 24mg calcium

COOK'S HINT COOK'S HINT **snacking** COOK'S HINT COOK'S HINT COOK'S HINT COOK'S HINT

For anytime snacking (with built-in portion control), wrap single servings of banana bread in double layers of plastic wrap, then freeze. When ready to use, simply unwrap and toast. Or defrost frozen slices at room temperature.

# cherry fudge brownies

**3 POINTS** PER SERVING | MAKES 16 SERVINGS

*Ideal for after-school (or after-work) snacking, these brownies really satisfy a chocolate craving. The almond extract helps to enhance the sweet cherry flavor, while adding a touch of nuttiness.*

1. **Preheat the oven** to 350°F. Spray an 8-inch square baking pan with nonstick spray.

2. **Combine** the flour, cocoa powder, baking powder, and salt in a large bowl. Combine the granulated sugar, butter, eggs, vanilla extract, and almond extract in another bowl. Add the sugar mixture to the flour mixture; stir just until blended. Fold in the cherries and chocolate chips. Pour the batter into the baking pan.

3. **Bake** until a toothpick inserted in the center comes out almost clean, 28–32 minutes. Cool in the pan on a rack 30 minutes. Cut into 16 bars. Remove from the pan and sprinkle with the confectioners' sugar.

**PER SERVING (1 BROWNIE): 141 CALORIES**
5g total fat, 3g saturated fat, 34mg cholesterol, 86mg sodium, 25g total carbohydrate, 2g dietary fiber, 2g protein, 30mg calcium

¾ cup all-purpose flour

⅔ cup unsweetened cocoa powder

1 teaspoon baking powder

⅛ teaspoon salt

1 cup granulated sugar

¼ cup butter, melted

2 large eggs

1 teaspoon vanilla extract

½ teaspoon almond extract

⅓ cup chopped candied cherries

¼ cup semisweet chocolate chips

2 tablespoons confectioners' sugar

COOK'S HINT COOK'S HINT **sundae** COOK'S HINT COOK'S HINT COOK'S HINT COOK'S HINT

For a special dessert sundae, place a brownie in a bowl and top with a ½-cup scoop of fat-free mint ice cream, a tablespoon of fat-free whipped topping, and a maraschino cherry (**5 POINTS** per sundae).

# apricot pistachio biscotti

*1 POINT* PER SERVING | MAKES 36 SERVINGS

*The combination of ground ginger, pistachios, and chewy dried apricots give these twice-baked treats a North African twist. Serve them with your favorite fresh berries and herbed tea. They also are prefect for dunking into a steaming cup of tea or coffee.*

2¼ cups all-purpose flour

½ cup shelled
pistachio nuts, chopped

½ cup chopped
dried apricots

2 teaspoons
baking powder

½ teaspoon
ground ginger

¼ teaspoon salt

1 cup sugar

2 large eggs

6 tablespoons apricot
nectar or orange juice

½ teaspoon
vanilla extract

1. **Preheat the oven** to 350°F. Spray 2 baking sheets with nonstick spray.

2. **Combine** the flour, pistachios, apricots, baking powder, ginger, and salt in a large bowl. Whisk the sugar, eggs, nectar, and vanilla in a medium bowl until frothy. Add the sugar mixture to the flour mixture; stir just until blended.

3. **Gather the dough** with lightly floured hands and transfer to a lightly floured surface. Divide the dough in two and work each into a 1¾ x 15-inch log about 1 inch high. Transfer the logs to the baking sheets and pat down until about ¾ inch high and 2 inches wide.

4. **Bake the logs** until firm to the touch, 20–25 minutes. Transfer to a cutting board and let cool 5–7 minutes. With a serrated knife, cut into ¼-inch thick slices, making 72 biscotti. Lay the slices in a single layer on the baking sheets.

5. **Reduce the oven temperature** to 300°F. Bake the biscotti 10 minutes, then turn over and bake until very dry to the touch and slightly crisp, about 10 minutes longer. Transfer the biscotti to a rack and cool completely.

**PER SERVING (2 BISCOTTI): 69 CALORIES**
1g total fat, 0g saturated fat, 12mg cholesterol, 47mg sodium, 13g total carbohydrate, 1g dietary fiber, 2g protein, 21mg calcium

COOK'S HINT COOK'S HINT **storing biscotti** COOK'S HINT COOK'S HINT COOK'S HINT COOK'S

Store the biscotti in an airtight container at room temperature for up to 1 month, or place them in a large zip-close plastic bag and freeze them for up to 6 months.

# espresso biscotti

*1 POINT* PER SERVING | MAKES 36 SERVINGS

*A double coffee jolt makes these biscotti a java-lovers dream.*
*For an even greater coffee sensation, dunk them in a cup of espresso.*

1. **Preheat the oven** to 350°F. Spray 2 baking sheets with nonstick spray.

2. **Combine** the flour, ground coffee, baking powder, cinnamon, and salt in a large bowl. Whisk the sugar, eggs, brewed coffee, and vanilla in a medium bowl until frothy. Add the sugar mixture to the flour mixture; stir just until blended.

3. **Gather the dough** with lightly floured hands and transfer to a lightly floured surface. Divide the dough in two and work each into a 1¾ x 15-inch log about 1 inch high. Transfer the logs to the baking sheets and pat down until about ¾ inch high and 2 inches wide.

4. **Bake the logs** until firm to the touch, 20 to 25 minutes. Transfer to a cutting board and let cool 5 to 7 minutes. With a serrated knife, cut into ¼-inch thick slices, making 72 biscotti. Arrange the slices in a single layer on the baking sheets.

5. **Reduce the oven temperature to 300°F.** Bake the biscotti 10 minutes, then turn over and bake until very dry to the touch and slightly crisp, about 10 minutes longer. Transfer the biscotti to a rack and cool completely. They will crisp as they cool.

PER SERVING (2 BISCOTTI): 55 CALORIES
0g total fat, 0g saturated fat, 12mg cholesterol, 47mg sodium, 12g total carbohydrate, 0g dietary fiber, 1g protein, 18mg calcium

2¼ cups all-purpose flour

2 tablespoons
ground coffee

2 teaspoons
baking powder

½ teaspoon cinnamon

¼ teaspoon salt

1 cup sugar

2 large eggs

3 tablespoons strong
brewed coffee

1 teaspoon
vanilla extract

# dry and liquid measurement equivalents

If you are converting the recipes in this magazine to metric measurements, use the following chart as a guide.

| TEASPOONS | TABLESPOONS | CUPS | FLUID OUNCES |
|---|---|---|---|
| 3 teaspoons | 1 tablespoon | | ½ fluid ounce |
| 6 teaspoons | 2 tablespoons | ⅛ cup | 1 fluid ounce |
| 8 teaspoons | 2 tablespoons plus 2 teaspoons | ⅙ cup | |
| 12 teaspoons | 4 tablespoons | ¼ cup | 2 fluid ounces |
| 15 teaspoons | 5 tablespoons | ⅓ cup minus 1 teaspoon | 2 fluid ounces |
| 16 teaspoons | 5 tablespoons plus 1 teaspoon | ⅓ cup | |
| 18 teaspoons | 6 tablespoons | ¼ cup plus 2 tablespoons | 3 fluid ounces |
| 24 teaspoons | 8 tablespoons | ½ cup | 4 fluid ounces |
| 30 teaspoons | 10 tablespoons | ½ cup plus 2 tablespoons | 5 fluid ounces |
| 32 teaspoons | 10 tablespoons plus 2 teaspoons | ⅔ cup | |
| 36 teaspoons | 12 tablespoons | ¾ cup | 6 fluid ounces |
| 42 teaspoons | 14 tablespoons | 1 cup minus 1 tablespoon | 7 fluid ounces |
| 45 teaspoons | 15 tablespoons | 1 cup minus 1 tablespoon | |
| 48 teaspoons | 16 tablespoons | 1 cup | 8 fluid ounces |

Note: Measurement of less than ⅛ teaspoon is considered a dash or a pinch.

| VOLUME | |
|---|---|
| ¼ teaspoon | 1 milliliter |
| ½ teaspoon | 2 milliliters |
| 1 teaspoon | 5 milliliters |
| 1 tablespoon | 15 milliliters |
| 2 tablespoons | 20 milliliters |
| 3 tablespoons | 45 milliliters |
| ¼ cup | 60 milliliters |
| ⅓ cup | 75 milliliters |
| ½ cup | 125 milliliters |
| ⅔ cup | 150 milliliters |
| ¾ cup | 175 milliliters |
| ⅔ cup | 150 milliliters |
| 1 cup | 225 milliliters |
| 1 quart | 150 liters |

| WEIGHT | |
|---|---|
| 1 ounce | 30 grams |
| ¼ pound | 120 grams |
| ½ pound | 240 grams |
| ¾ pound | 360 grams |

| LENGTH | |
|---|---|
| 1 inch | 25 millimeters |
| 1 inch | 2.5 centimeters |

| OVEN TEMPERATURE | |
|---|---|
| 250°F | 120°C |
| 275°F | 140°C |
| 300°F | 150°C |
| 325°F | 160°C |
| 350°F | 180°C |
| 375°F | 190°C |
| 400°F | 200°C |
| 425°F | 220°C |
| 450°F | 230°C |
| 475°F | 250°C |
| 500°F | 260°C |
| 525°F | 270°C |